CHARACTERS

AND

CRITICISMS.

BY

W. ALFRED JONES, A. M.

In Two Volumes.

VOL. II.

NEW YORK:
I. Y. WESTERVELT, 371 BROADWAY.

1857.

LIST OF SUBSCRIBERS.

G. F. Allen, Esq.
William M. Allen, Esq. 3.
Abel T. Anderson, Esq.
Henry J. Anderson, LL. D.
William Austin, Esq.

Mrs. Banyer, 3.
E. T. Beadle, M. D.
J. P. Bellknap, Esq.
Rev. Beverley R. Betts.
William Betts, LL. D.
Samuel Blatchford, Esq.
G. B. Butler, Esq.

D. P. Campbell, Esq.
T. B. Coddington, Esq.
Charles Congdon, Esq.
Charles H. Contoit, Esq.
George H. Contoit, Esq.
Alexander J. Cotheal, Esq.
Prof. Alpheus Crosby.
John P. Crosby, Esq.

Edw. DeWitt, Esq. 2.
Rev. Morgan Dix.

W. Dodge, Esq.
E. G. Drake, jr., Esq.
Prof. Henry Drisler.

C. Arthur Ely, Esq.

R. M. Field, Esq.

Miss Gelston.
Thomas B. Gilford, Esq.
S. Hastings Grant, Esq.
J. Greenwood, Esq.

Rev. B. I. Haight, D. D.
John C. Hamilton, Esq.
William Heard, Esq.
Henry Wm. Herbert, Esq.
Edward Howland, Esq.
W. A. Hunter, M.D.

George Ireland, Jr., Esq.

Miss Jay.
John Jay, Esq. 5.
W. H. Johnson, Esq.
E. Jones, Esq.
Hon. D. R. Floyd Jones.
Gen. James I. Jones.
S. J. Jones, Esq.
W. W. Jones, M.D., 2.

Hon. William Kent.
Hon. John A. King.
Rev. John Knox, D. D.
John M. Knox, Esq.

John J. Latting, Esq.
W. H. Leggett, Esq. 3.
B. C. Leveridge, Esq.

John McAloney, Esq.
Prof. John McVickar, S.T.D.
Charles D. Mead, Esq.
W. B. Moffat, M.D.
C. B. Moore, Esq. 5.
W. Mulligan, Esq.

W. Curtis Noyes, Esq.

Daniel Oakey, Esq.
G. M. Ogden, Esq.
R. H. Ogden, Esq.
David Olyphant, Esq.
H. Onderdonk, Jr., Esq.

Alfred Pell, Esq.
Thomas Picton, Esq.
J. W. Platt, Esq.
G. W. Pratt, Esq.

John W. Quincy, Esq.

Robert Ray, Esq.
Charles B. Richards, Esq.
Thomas F. Richards, Esq.
John H. Riker, Esq.
Charles H. Rogers, Esq. 2.

A. T. Sackett, Esq.
W. A. Seely, Esq.
Daniel Seixas, Esq.
P. V. R. Stanton, Esq.

G. T. Strong, Esq.
Charles R. Swords, Esq.
R. S. Swords, Esq.

J. H. Titus, Esq.
R. H. Tucker, Esq.

G. G. Van Wagenen, Esq.
Hon. Elijah Ward.
S. L. H. Ward, Esq.
James H. Weeks, Esq.
John A. Weeks, Esq.
Thomas L. Wells, Esq.
H. C. Westervelt, Esq.
Rev. S. H. Weston.
J. C. White, Esq.
E. M. Willett, Esq.
G. H. Witthaus, Esq.
R. A. Witthaus, Esq.

Ch. Zabriskie, Jr., Esq.

Other names had unfortunately not been received in season to be included in the above list, the omission of which occurs for that reason, and is much regretted by the publisher.

CONTENTS OF VOL. II.

APPENDIX.

CHARACTERS AND CRITICISMS.

I.

ESSAY WRITING.—THE CHAMPION.

"Ten censure wrong for one who writes amiss," sang Pope, and a juster line he never wrote himself. We have daily evidence of its truth, especially in this era of multifarious and indiscriminate criticism. Every man is a reader, and a critic, of course; the corollary follows the proposition as closely as demonstration upon mathematical reasoning. To be a tolerable author requires some brains and tact in writing; but to become a regular critic, nothing is needed but the not uncommon union of arrogance, ignorance, insolence, and stupidity. To praise judiciously the rarest works (the verdict of love and knowledge combined) appears tame and insipid, to those who love the slashing style, who consider abuse, satire; and presumption, boldness; who vote ribaldry, wit; and give the palm of copious, manly eloquence to coarse, declamatory invective.

In a late notice of Chambers' Essays in the London Spectator, we find the writer, who gives the author his fair share of praise, speaking of the decline of the Essay, and of its gradual extinction, as if the shortest, the most direct, the most personal, the most natural, form of prose-writing could ever become extinct, any more than letters, or songs, or oratory. With all of these the essay has much in common, and especially in its personal character, implying a familiarity, a mutual confidence and an explicit directness, not to be attained in a higher or more ambitious form of composition. Since composition has become the business of men of the world and men of business—since it has found its way into other hands than those of the monks and scholastics of the Middle Ages, it has become more and more conversational, pithy, plain, and unpretending. Respectability in authorship is now nothing to be proud of, in intellectual circles and in the midst of a high civilization. No longer do we gaze with awe and admiring wonder at poet or philosopher. They have become commonplace people in the popular eye. They are as wise, as good, as imaginative as ever, but they do not seem to be so.

Essay-writing in prose is very much the same thing as song-writing in verse. A certain lyrical spirit is to be found in the best essayists, however homely and anti-poetical the essays may be; as in Franklin's, or the second-rate papers of Hazlitt (who is hardly a fair instance, for he was a poet as much as Burke or Jeremy Taylor.) Some of Lamb's are conceived in the highest poetic strain, as Bulwer has remarked of the Horatian Apostrophe to the Shade of Elliston, and numberless passages in the Essays of Elia. Hunt displays as much fancy in prose description often as in his poetry. Emerson's essays often *conceal* more poetic feeling than he developes in his poetry.

This kind of writing is as natural to a young prose writer to attempt as it is in a genuine poet to commence his career by songs, as natural as for the "feathered songster of the field" to pour forth his "unpremeditated lay." It is certainly a matter of impulse with most, and most naturally is with those who are destined to succeed in that way of writing. With the scholar, in one of the old comedies, the youthful aspirant may honestly confess, "I did essay to write essays." That a vast proportion of failures might be recorded, weighs no more against our views than the as frequent failures in lyric efforts. The essayist is thus an humbler sort of bard, a prose lyrist, a writer of the walk of poetry, which Horace includes under the designation "*musa pedestris.*" Under this class fall most of the essayists. Swift, in verse and in prose, is much the same; so we may say of Pope, and of the earlier English satirists.

Essays, too, are very similar to letters, in their variety of topics; in their familiarity of address, and in the "handling" or style. Most letter-writers address individuals only; the regular essayist addresses the public as well. There is only a wider circle of readers, and something by way of difference, in the feelings of professed authorship. Equal vanity, or egotism, or wise self-consideration, as you will, is to be allowed to either writer, equal room for portraits of character and sketches of manners, for humorous satire or generous compliment, for speculative or ethical discussion, for æsthetical analysis, or historical retrospect. Both are in the nature of confessions as well as homilies, though the latter are apt to predominate. The history of a man's mind, his only true autobiography, change of tastes and pursuits, favorite opinions held at different periods, why changed, and how often, these are to be studied in volumes of essays, with more confidence than in most volumes of biography. There are two remarks of Zimmerman that deserve to be noticed on this subject. Defending the practice of a man's writing memoirs of himself, he says, he thinks it wiser and more laudable, than for him to leave his body by will to a professor of anatomy; and, in another place, he tells an obvious truth, (not noticed perhaps for that reason,) that the great advantage of writing, is to give a man an opportunity to express that upon paper, which he could not with freedom or courtesy, in the ordinary intercourse with society. Now, essays give that freedom in its widest allowable limits, restrict the writer less in the development of his humors, whims, and agreeable prejudices upon paper than any other species of composition. It is indeed a mixed kind of writing, personal authorship, as free as possible from mere scholasticism or pedantry.

Neither is it any nearer extinction now than in the days of Montagne, who is commonly known as the father of the Essay. Its features may be somewhat changed, but there is the same outline, the same expresson. It may at one epoch handle different topics from those which engross it at another,—Fashion, manners, character, books and politics. The commonest leaders in the penny papers are strictly essays, no less than most of the Review articles. The best portion of the contemporary lectures and addresses is strictly of an essay character, and the passages in the greatest orations are of the same description, and can be taken from the text in which they appear as independent essays.

Trifling writers of insipid imitations of Byron and Moore speak contemptuously of essays, as dull or vapid. No more such, we venture to say than the same attempts of writers in verse of equal power. Dull essayists enough are to be found, but at least as many bad poets, and certainly a larger number of indifferent books of sermons. Indeed, a good essay is likely to be better than even a good sermon; we entirely exclude those of the great old divines, who rank with the poets and dramatists of their age. A sermon admits of many formal divisions, easily filled up in a mechanical manner; it allows a good deal of commonplace, in the way of logical discussion and incentives to devotion. Its exhortations and apostrophes are stereotyped. And only the fancy of Taylor, the wit of the South, the fullness of Barrow, the ingenuity of Clarke, can overcome the mass of arguments, illustrations and appeals, that encumber the path of the preacher. Even able men are often dull in the pulpit; while, at the bar, or in a contest of wit, they might become bright by the encounter. Sermons must be copiously written and illustrated, to suit the majority of congregations; essays must be close and compact; containing a page in a paragraph, an argument in an epigram, full of quick transitions, stating results and processes, which must be alluded to, and in a word giving in a few pages what a common writer might spread over a volume.

On this side of the water, notwithstanding its prevalence in the Review, the Magazine and the Newspaper, we find a clever critic in a Charleston paper, simultaneously uttering the heresy of the London Spectator. As for this last writer's general remarks upon the essay, the facts of literary history are against him, from Bacon to Leigh Hunt. English literature has always been rich in essayists, though in the reign of William III. and Anne they were most prominent. It is needless to make a long list, but we can promise this much: For every sterling writer of prose fiction in England, we will bring the name and works of a classic, among the essayists. This assertion may appear a little loose or careless, but we can support it with confidence.

Writers of this class have been quite too long huffed and bullied by the long-winded historical novelists and reviewers, who think the essay contemptible from its brevity, certainly not from its subjects, nor yet from its execution.

Our literature is pre-eminently a periodical one thus far, and slurs on the essay certainly do come with bad grace from those who know the reading community with us live almost altogether on journals of different classes. Our finest writers thus far have been essayists, Dana, Channing, Everett, &c., to say nothing of minor names.

It was once a common folly to depreciate a host of writers of short pieces, as minor poets, because the authors (thank heaven!) of no long poems; yet they have often flown higher, if they do not remain so long on the wing. A falcon is a nobler bird than the buzzard, who may be hovering over carrion all day, while the former towers in his pride of place, when there is fit occasion, and does not waste his energies on every petty one.

"The Phœnix Pindar is a vast species alone," yet that same Pindar came from a certain district of Greece where the owls predominated, who doubtless thought they could see far better and judge more wisely than he. *They* are not a *species alone*; we have critical birds of the same strain here also.

The political essay was that form first cultivated by the writers of consecutive papers, arranged in order, and under a leading caption. Thus the first *series* of essays in English (not the miscellanies of Temple and Cowley) formed a melange of politics, social satire, town sketches, personality, and criticism—of these Defoe's Journal—the Review, which preceded the Tatler and Spectator, is perhaps the first specimen of the kind we can point to. L'Estrange, who was the very first of the political pamphleteers, restricting his lucubrations chiefly to politics; but Defoe, in his Review, had his club, like that in the Spectator, who discussed similar questions, and to whom were allotted various duties. From Defoe to Hazlitt, there have been the admirable collections of Addison, Steele, Swift, Bolingbroke, Fielding, Burke, Junius, and Johnson, to mention only the most prominent writers.

In this list, Fielding, "the prose Homer of human nature," finds a place, on the ground of his Champion; a book little known, but worthy of being revived in company with the Freeholder.

In the Lord Mayor's grand annual procession, rides clad in complete steel, a doughty civic hero, who personates for the nonce the Champion of England. Now, alas! a mere burlesque on the original of chivalry. In transatlantic accounts of prize fights, we hear of the championship of England disputed or sustained by Caunt, or Bendigo, Burke, or the hero of Bristol. In a far better sense, we would nominate Fielding as one of the true champions of England, a genuine representative of the manly characteristics of the race of which he was a faithful advocate and zealous defender.

The title of his work, a collection of papers modelled on the early periodical essayists, more particularly on the Lover of Steele and the Freeholder of Addison, in its mixed character of a town journal and a political paper, in which the former very much predominates, is descriptive of its aim and character. It champions the right, and honest, and true, and simple, in politics and manners, in criticism and behavior. Not pretending a rivalry of the Tatler or Spectator, to which it is much inferior, it is a very pleasing, readable copy of those delightful originals. With more invention, force, and dramatic power than Steele or Addison, Fielding has little of the taste or delicacy of either. He has humor, but stronger and broader than Addison, without his charming elegance—he has wit, but not of the glancing, piquant style of Steele's best writing. He has manly sense, ingenious turns, and true feeling, with a style next to Steele. With rich abundance of character and description in his novels; in this collection of essays, Fielding is comparatively meagre in both, though superior to some writers much more talked about. The Champion is for instance a far better work of its class, than the Idler of Johnson, or Hawkesworth's Adventurer, or the World or Microcosm.

We are apt to suspect (we believe it is the fact) that this was merely one of a number of the jobs of the great novelist, and by which he should not in justice be measured. It is a work, upon which any living periodical writer might safely rest a good literary reputation, but which is not strong enough for the name of Fielding, had he not written Joseph Andrews and Tom Jones.

Still, there is hardly a paper in it, without sentences or paragraphs quotable for their acute sense or ingenius turn of expression; a talent Fielding inherited from Steele. And here we may stop to trace the parallel features, in which these two true wits and genuine good fellows resembled each other. Both gentlemen, men of the world, professed men of pleasure, living on the town, and by their wits, guilty of the greatest imprudences, but we believe of nothing more, according to the trite saying, their own worst enemies, although most friendly to all others beside; at one time living in affluence, and soon after in a spunging-house or a jail, or trammelled within the rules of the Fleet, cheerful, social, humane, and thoughtless, yet most acute and penetrating observers of life, and manners, and character, and as writers, matchless for an easy, natural, graceful style, that conveyed the justest and most sensible, if they were grave, or if gay, the most pleasing and subtile, agreeable sentiment: Sir Richard Steele, and

Henry Fielding, Esq., were intellectually and socially and morally brothers, in pens as well as they might have been in arms.

Fielding, as a metaphysician and painter of character, is as much above Steele, as he is above all other novelists, in his peculiar style. Yet as a mere essayist, Steele is the master, the original, whom his later disciple is content to follow with admiring steps.

II.

TRAITS OF AMERICAN AUTHORSHIP.

De Tocqueville, in one of the chapters of his work on America, thus characterizes the literature of a democratic state: "There will be more wit than erudition, more imagination than profundity; and literary performances will bear marks of an untutored and rude vigor of thought—frequently of great variety and singular fecundity. The object of authors will be to astonish rather than to please, and to stir the passions more than to charm the taste." Without entering into the question, at present, of what may be yet expected from America, or even of what has been produced honorable to the country, and there is much to exhibit on the positive side, it may be a matter of curiosity to test the peculiar requisitions of the distinguished French critic by a few of the results of actual experience. Our literature has, in fact, been the very opposite of the conditions claimed by De Tocqueville. He demands originality, force, passion, fruitfulness. What have been the accepted productions of American authorship? They disclose, for the most part, just the opposite qualities, of imitation, tameness, want of passion and poverty.

In place of dramatic power, we find almost altogether descriptive talent; for energy, elaborate elegance; for passion, sentimentality, not even (the very few instances, again excepted of the best character) sentiment, and so far from fruitfulness in the case of our best writers, they are uncommonly meagre, and easily exhausted. Fecundity is, with us, rather a badge of disgrace, considered a mark of our worst pretenders to authorship.

Imitation is natural, or rather, we should say, was formerly pardonable, from our social and political condition. For to the end of the last century, or even the first quarter (perhaps) of the present, there were good English writers in the country, with no pretence to an American spirit, except in their political speculations. The grave writing of that period, and the lighter efforts as well, were conceived and modelled on English originals. The dependence of the colonies had not yet ceased: our independence was civil only. This was especially the case in New England from the fact of its early settlement by Englishmen. There the English race was kept pure, without the admission of foreign elements. This made New England the stronghold of the English feeling of the country. This kept her, for a long while, the most provincial and colonial part of the Union. This made Boston a literary town for English wares, and gave to it its peculiar character and attitude, in respect to English writers, who found their haven there, when as voyagers they arrived, all prepared for idolatry and man-worship. How different from New York, which is cosmopolitan, and truly a metropolis, the city of the

Dutch, and of the English, and of the native American, crossed by the French, German, Welsh, Scottish and Irish races—a city of the world like London, not a country town of literateurs and blue-stockings. There can be no doubt of the incalculable moral value of England to us as a means of culture. Our past is hers, and let no man undervalue the sacred influences of ancient times, when rivalries are forgotten, jealousies have disappeared, when the drama of life appears to us simple and complete, when evil has perished and good alone remains. The tree of American Literature will be found to have its roots in English soil. But we can only show ourselves capable of receiving those blessed lessons by having in ourselves the virtue to live an independent life. "To him that hath shall be given."

Tameness, as general as imitation, and its co-relative, may be deduced from the same cause. Coldness of temperament, and the unnatural development of the faculty of taste, have "repressed the noble rage" of our writers; even in those whose early or most spontaneous writings are instinct with strength and self-reliance. Taught to look up to certain English names as unapproachable, and only to be copied with assiduous care, they have feared to give full scope to their natural genius, which they rather confined within the barriers of propriety and decorum. Hence our finest poets have been, save when their Muse would not be trammelled, but soared

"Aloft, incumbent on the dusky air,"

in the majority of cases, themselves, gladly and humbly,

"Content to dwell in decencies for ever."

Hence the frequent charge of plagiarism, upon which, as between authors of original merit, little account is always to be placed—for what may appear to be a theft to minds of coarse perceptions, might perhaps be held by the great originals as simply a proof of honorable allegiance to themselves. There is such a thing as this allegiance, and the thoughts of great authors may be worn by later ones as modern piety wears and hallows the relics of ancient religion. For our own part, we like to trace this communication between the writers of distant times. It is proof of common symphathies; the zeal which reverences may not be very far from the original spirit which creates. But it is quite another matter when the jackdaw struts about in borrowed plumes; when "memory and her syren daughters" are invoked in quite another than the Miltonic sense; when affectation and pretence take the place of reverence; and imbecility challenges the seat of power. The evil unrebuked increases with alarming rapidity. When our critics talk of our poets by hundreds, they make it a matter of fashion to set up for a poet, and the regiment of the Muses is speedily filled by a crowd of fops and pretenders without strength or valor. We see delicate and tasteful artists and adapters rather than original authors, and the plaudits of the one transferred to the other; the phenomenon of the disciple above his master; a democratic highway to Parnassus travelled by witlings; Sancho Panza receiving in earnest the honors of governorship.

The want of passion is a defect so prominent, that we must try to account for it still further. Not to repeat the standard criticism, that the bulk of American writing hitherto has been done in New England, and thence received its cold impress from the local character; it is also to be observed, that the majority of our writers, serious and gay, alike, have come out from the profession of the law, a school, undoubtedly, of ingenuity, perspicuity and intellectual force, but not equally a nursery for the imagination, or fancy, or sentiment. The temple of Themis is not built upon Parnassus' Hill, and although we are honestly told by one of the old masters, that there are poets which did never dream upon Parnassus, yet few poets, we suspect, have ever lived who have not seen it at least in visions of the night. The law has given us our great practical statesmen, and fervid orators, and acute critics, and logical heads, and wise moral teachers, and sharp satirists of vice and folly; but it has no fair pictures, or noble forms, or aerial harmonies. It is not the true calling of the poet, though many true poets have been lawyers.

Circumstances have had their effect; the necessity of leaving literary pursuits for more profitable labors,—the love of gain or reputation in some other line, overlaying the natural—weak, since so easily benumbed—impulses of the mind. Characters have changed; the ardent youth has become a cautious man; trade has taken the place of poetry, and a love of art has been supplanted by a total indifference to all early impressions.

How stands the point of productiveness? To confess the truth, the few good, and the very few admirable writers we have, have done comparatively little, from one or all of the causes above enumerated, and have done that at a very early age. This reminds us of as frequent a trait to be met with as any of the rest; the *early maturity* of our writers, which has as often been followed by as early a decay of power. The vein was shallow and soon worked. Certain sentiments or fancies had early possessed the mind and heart, and demanded immediate utterance. These were produced, and produced, and with freshness, vivacity, and genuine force. Afterwards, the author, if modest and a self-student, a man of culture, feels he cannot do better, or, perchance, equal his first effort.

He retires from the arena, and become a miniature classic. This is the truth with our best men, but a vast herd continue writing worse and worse, until at last the severest punishment for them would be to read their own works, under which they have buried the little spirit or the small faculty with which they set out. From these hasty remarks one may readily infer the following conclusions: that our writers have been in general men of talent, and rarely men of genius; relying too much upon artificial aids, and by far too little on the ever-fresh resources of nature. That their greatest intellectual defect, too often with the best, has been want of independence; and the leading moral defect occasionally with others, a want of honesty.

III.

HOME CRITICISM.

Criticism should flourish in this country, if no other form of prose writing meet with favor, for Americans are confessedly an acute and shrewd race. These faculties applied to the judgment of books and authors, by educated men, ought to be made the most of in the absence of original power and creative genius. Goldsmith has remarked in one of his Essays, that criticism is more highly cultivated in the decline of the higher productions of art and genius; which opinion with those who consider American to form a supplement of English Literature, itself in their view effete, and in its very weakest phase, should be allowed as an argument in favor of our position. In the judgment of some of the ablest writers,

American critics stand in the most favorable attitude for judging English authors, as perfectly free from bias of any kind, not blinded by patriotism or party, beyond the reach of rivalry, and uninfluenced by malevolence or friendship. Many portions of English Literature are to be re-criticised, and that from a new point of view, such as is afforded only to American writers. Especially the contemporary literature of England can be best estimated here, where distance and difference of government placet he American critic in the position which would naturally be filled up by an English writer of the succeeding generation. In this surely we are the posterity of the present race of English authors, and consequently can judge more dispassionately and clearly than might be expected of contemporaries.

But we do not intend to go further into this question at present. Our object now is, to point out the prevailing character of our home critics: to depict the general defects of our criticism, rather than to paint the portraits of the few fine critics we have: to show what ought to be avoided more than what we should seek to attain: this is our present endeavor.

What is the character of our criticism? Is it reliable, is it sincere or thoroughly just? We may safely and truly answer, no! It is not reliable because it is not sincere: it is unjust because deficient in thoroughness. Morally and intellectually, it is unsound. Much of it is paltry and shallow: more is spurious and mercenary. From personal or party reasons on some private ground of pique or partiality, from prejudice or from prepossession, almost all of our written criticism is either directly hostile or friendly towards and on account of the writer, not his book. It is the man, not the author or his book that conciliates or repels, makes friends or enemies, and keeps them through a literary career. This is manifestly wrong. Criticism absolutely just, we hardly have at all.

Puffing and abuse form the two extremes of criticism; the two strings upon which its professors love to play, and incited to either much more from impulse than any settled design; and so well is this understood, that most newspaper notices have just the influence and tendency of the advertisements for quack medicines, to deceive nobody but the ignorant and simple. "Mr. Orator Puff had two tones to his voice," and so with the newspaper critics, they have but two also, the one "up high," eulogium, and the other "down low," detraction.

It is not intelligent. Few of those who sit in the seat of judgment are fit for the office; they rather sit in the seat of the scornful. And they generally do both, which is the reason their judgments are unjust and ridiculous. Themselves wanting in true literary feeling, in honest enthusiasm, or as honest indignation, in independence, in knowledge, we should not wonder at the vile subterfuges and miserable apologies for criticism that pass under its name. How many professed literary critics, conductors of literary journals, are adapted to their duties? From laziness, or want of training, we have few educated critics; a class of writers requiring knowledge of books more than any other. The poet may rely upon his fancies, the historian on oral tradition, the philosopher may study only his own mind, but the critic must have learning to compare and contrast, to distinguish and divide, to apprehend a variety of talents and topics, authors and manners of writing, and forms of composition.

The want of knowledge has led to the most prominent defect in our criticism—*indiscrimination.* This is shamefully common. The good are all good alike: the bad no worse than the worst. Everything like nicety or refinement is lost in a wide and sweeping confusion of epithets. Wycherly has said, in his manly way, that it is wicked to speak well of those who don't deserve to be well spoken of, since the good men are thereby indirectly depreciated. A good man, or writer, can but be so called; while if a knave passes for a gentleman, the gentleman passes for no better than the knave himself.

The character of the critic is misunderstood. He is not to be carping at every petty fault, but must be able to praise with judgment. He must have a natural capacity for his office. The true critic is as much fitted, by nature and education, for his office, as the poet is for his. With him, too, he must have a cordial sympathy, and a heart open to all the impulses of goodness and beauty. Truth and justice should be his leading guides, not pleasure or fancy; yet, to express the noblest truth, he must be much more than an exact didactic writer: an able critic of Locke will prove but an indifferent judge of Milton. Locke himself made sad havoc when he attempted poetical criticism. To be truly fair, the critic must have an intimate sympathy with his authors; Lamb, only, could write cordially of Donne and Burton. Hazlitt is the best expounder of Abraham Tucker, and John Buncle, Rousseau, the novelists and essayists. Hunt is best in writing on Chaucer and Milton's minor poems.

American criticism should be principally directed to American writers and their contemporaries, as well as to living European authors. American criticism of an English book should be so far impartial, that no review or notice, of it should be read by the critic before he has finished his work, which should be entirely individual.

We have had as much imitation and plagiarism of foreign

criticism as of foreign original writing. The reviewers have shown, at least, as much deference as the poets to their English brethren, and we are not sure that they have not been still more servile and dependent.

The reader can readily enumerate, on his fingers, the good, the fine, the just critics we have, while to enumerate the trifling, the malignant, the shallow, the illiterate, almost transcends the power of numbers.

IV.

THE TWO EVERETTS.*

We have here three volumes of miscellanies by two accomplished brothers, American writers, whom in their sphere and with their individual talents, we should cherish as among the ablest of their class we can point to, albeit we may not rank that class very high, nor consider its prominent members as the astounding and immense (that's the favorite laudatory adjective of the day) prodigies of genius and scholarship certain hyperbolical eulogists claim them to be. We have unfeigned respect for the man who at an early age filled the chair of Greek Professor, which he resigned for the pulpit of

* 1. *Importance of Practical Education and Useful Knowledge: a selection from the Orations and other Discourses of Edward Everett.* New York: Harper & Brothers.

2. *Critical and Miscellaneous Essays—first and second Series.* By Alexander H. Everett. 2 vols. 12 mo. Boston: James Munroe & Co.

a most desirable parish of which he was the idol, and which he in turn resigned for the editorship of the North American Review—after which, entering into political life, we find Mr. Everett, successively Senator and Governor of his native State, Ambassador to England, and finally, at the present writing (1847), President of Harvard University, the oldest literary institution in the country.

Mr· Alexander Everett has gone through much the same course, and with almost equal eclat; we are not aware that he was a *popular* pulpit orator, nor that he went to Congress; but he has filled successively, the offices of Clergyman, Editor, President of a College, and Diplomatist.

The volume of Edward Everett is filled with essays, addresses, &c., addressed to the audiences at the Mechanics' Institute and similar societies of Boston: where, in his lectures, his aim always appears to have been the improvement of artisans, and of making labor intelligent, to stimulate the invention of workingmen, to give them an object above the supply of those common wants which render labor necessary, but which does not give it a character of refinement or elevation, such as science or philosophy imparts. The Miscellanies of Alexander Everett are truly such, being essays (articles in reviews) on topics of history, literature, manners, philosophy; sensible discussions couched in a clear, readable, and sometimes graceful style.

The leading trait in the addresses of Edward Everett is a *graceful didacticism*, somewhat trite and commonplace it must be confessed, both as to topics and the manner of presenting them; he is too fond of recurring to certain stereotyped instances of industry and perseverance; yet if superficial, he is always correct and pleasing, his matter tells far more effectually in a spoken address (most of the present essays first appeared in that form) than in an elaborate article. His personal presence, carriage, and action, make up for want of boldness of views, for an almost utter want of imagination and fancy, and power of thought. Force, Everett has next to none, nor has he any degree of fancy, beyond an occasional streak of ingenuity in illustration, the least possible satiric sting, a glimpse of pleasantry. These papers are chiefly made up of facts and illustrations, very neatly compiled with care,

> "All rang'd with order, and disposed with grace,"

to confirm some popular principle or to set off an obvious sentiment.—The ground-work of his addresses into which these facts are woven, is very plain sense and very thin sentiment elegantly dressed up. His muse is an ordinary, economical, neat-handed housewife, with a pleasant voice, clean, dressed like a lady, and with agreeable manners.

Everett appears in his works, purely as a teacher, dogmatic and direct, his dogmatism (never obtrusive) and his didacticism being covered and wrapped up in the folds of his insinuating style. He is an accomplished rhetorician.

As a polished gentleman, man of business, diplomatist, and classic scholar, Everett stands "*primus inter primos ;*" we speak only of the author and of the volume before us. We know little of Mr. Everett as the editor of the North American, but we presume he was at least the equal of the Sparkses and Palfreys who succeeded him.

Alexander Everett is generally considered a man of more varied acquirements, as to the languages, literature, and philosophy of the nations of Europe—equally a statesman and a man of business ; originally, too, both Unitarians, and clergymen, and New Englanders; of much the same cast of mind and talent with his distinguished brother, only perhaps less airy and graceful in point of style. The brothers may be fairly considered as representing a particular phase of American literature, thus far, and as confirming certain established strictures upon it.

They represent the *New Englandism* of American writers; they represent the intellectual Unitarian sect, and the large body of respectable prose writers of this country, the literary orators, lecturers, critics, scholars, translators. They have carried taste, in its lowest form (cold and cautious), to its point of perfection, and they have exhibited all the marks of colonial writers; good and sensible writers, they are yet no more American (albeit Alexander Everett has writen largely of American literature, and Edward Everett has dwelt on the physical features of the country), than if writing from Ireland or the Island of Jamaica, or any other portion of the British possessions.

We have a few words to say on both of these topics. *New Englandism* has certainly made our writers imitative, constrained, tasteful, and timid. That portion of our country, more English and as decidedly sectional, perhaps more so, than either the South or the West, is certainly far better educated, more intellectual and more desirous of literary fame than either. As a district, New England has (as a matter of fact) produced on a fair allowance two-thirds of the best writers we have yet to show. We say this, though native born New Yorkers, and proud of Irving and Cooper, still the foremost American classics; we say this with a full knowledge of our best men here. The cause for this superiority lies in their exclusiveness and the sober qualities of the Yankee character, inherited from a peculiar race of men, earnest and vigorous; the absence, formerly almost entire, of public amusements, then held there in disgrace, and now little more than barely allowed; the fact of the establishment, in that part of the country, first of all, of universities and schools. *We* had no Harvards, Yales, or Berkleys. Our Dutch ancestors were not generally lovers of literature, either here or in the mother country (for though Holland was full of learned men, it has rarely had popular cosmopolitan writers); commerce, thrift, comfortable living, quiet, chiefly occupied their attention, not the quarrels or the amenities of literature.

The looking constantly to England gave its provincial tone to the writers of New England, and encouraged imitation, a trait in our writers almost universal. We have had American counterfeits of every English writer of this century, from Scott down to the conductors of the most scurrilous English Sunday newspapers. Too often, an inferior writer has been the model, and from being surpassed perhaps by his American copyist, some have come to place American literature on a par with, or above English.

The Everetts may be regarded as representing the force of the Unitarians who have yet much stronger men to boast of, and who, as including the moss intellectual *class* of Americans, are entitled at least to respectful mention. They count among them now, Bryant, the Sedgwicks, Mrs. Kirkland, the Everetts, Dewey, Bancroft—and formerly Channing and the Wares, Emerson, Brownson, and a number of individuals less able and less well known, yet intelligent and accomplished characters. *Rationalism*, a love of dialectics and of speculative inquiry, together with much elegance of taste, variety of information and skill in writing, distinguish this sect, and these are qualities and tendencies that curb the fancy and check the flights of imagination. They have, hence, but *one* Poet (we think) of their communion; most of them are reasoners, critics, scholars, lecturers, essayists, speculative philosophers. They address the understanding or the moral sentiment; rarely appeal to the feelings; still less frequently to the imagination. Hence their writers are apt to be tame and cautious; they are accurate and neat, but cold and superficial. They have no passion, not much enthusiasm, nor any marked individuality. Channing's eloquence is noble declamatory sentiment, not the fire of native eloquence.

The style and reach of thought and rhetorical skill of the Everetts (in a lower degree) are much the same; and we think any judicious reader must confess, that we have told only the truth, without circumlocution or evasion respecting these gentlemen; who, both as writers, scholars, public characters, and private gentlemen, deserve well of their countrymen, though merely as writers we should place them lower than in their other characters; not overlooking, in recording their best qualities, in a literary point of view, of elegance of mind and style, general justness and propriety of sentiment, with much varied acquisition.

V.

POEMS BY CLEMENT C. MOORE, LL. D.

This is a pure volume of refined and classic poetry, in its genuine sense. Not to be sure in the highest sense, for these pages include none of the higher aspirations of the muse.

There is nothing dramatic nor epical; no Pindaric strains, no Miltonic fervor and sublimity, nor the grand sweep of Dryden's glorious verse, but there is still a great deal that is truly excellent, nay admirable, both positively and negatively.

To begin with the latter cold praise, (which we do not mean to be so considered, in these days of extravagance and crudity, in poetical attempts), there is not a particle of affectation, cant, false pretence, or straining after effect, in the whole collection. Artistically and morally, it is one of the most honest books we ever read. The author does not once feign a sentiment or court popular prejudice; he is utterly without duplicity or ostentation.

It is true, circumstances may have had something to do with this. Dr. Moore, the son of the excellent Bishop Moore, of New York, himself not only a pure and refined character, but superadding to the accomplishments of the gentleman the nobler character of a benevolent Christian philanthropist, has been most fortunately placed as well for the culture of refined taste as for the development of individual character.

The author of this volume (we add this for the benefit of those who are ignorant of his name and position) is at present a professor* of the General Theological Seminary of the Episcopal Church, giving his services for the benefit of the Institution (to which he presented the grounds on which the buildings stand, with the beautiful adjacent green) and the Church. The poems here collected, are the fruit of leisure hours, and form the expression of personal feelings. They are mostly *occasional* poems: a description of verse often styled fugitive, but not assuredly to be such in this instance.

* Author of a Hebrew Dictionary, and the Life of Castriot.

and we risk little in predicting a permanent reputation for them and their author.

Refinement is their characteristic; not weakness nor sentimentality, but fine sense, elegance, graceful turns of pleasantry, natural and pleasing sentiment, genuine pathos. Gifford's highly praised verses to his Anna are weak and puerile compared with the verses to the Poet's Children, to his late wife, and on the death of a favorite daughter.

The purest moral feeling and polished versification are also to be remarked as prominent traits of Dr. Moore's poetry. Neither Bryant nor Dana is more careful in the musical structure of his verse; neither of these finished poets is more deserving of being read, for elevation and high aims. Yet there is no assumption on the part of the poet. From his natural elevation, and from a religious tone of character, surrounded by admiring friends and devoted children, our author writes naturally either as a moralist or as a companion, when he writes for others: it is different when he pours out the full tide of his own feelings, in the purest elegiac verse, far more touching than the verses of Hammond, whom it was once the fashion to call the English Tibullus. In humor, too, our author has been quite successful. His visit of St. Nicholas, we believe, has been regularly reprinted for some years past in certain of our city journals; and together with the two exquisite poems of "Lines to my Children, with their Father's Portrait," and "Lines from a Husband to his Wife," are to be found in most of the collections of American poetry.

Dr. Moore's poetical talents incline him to domestic themes and incidents and characters; he is a disciple of Cowper and Goldsmith; yet by no means an imitator of either. His vein is original: his manner is his own—still, his admiration for classic models may guide his taste and control his pen.

2

Both of these fine poets might be proud of such a follower, each of them would have gloried in such a friend.

We can see nothing in this writer of the ordinary sins of American versifiers, no plagiarism, no imitation, no morbid feeling, no rhetorical flourishes, no transcendentalism.

The poems are *occasional;* and so far, instead of being worthy of rejection on that score, they are the natural effusions of the writer's heart and fancy. After the highest walks of song, the drama and the epic, (only worthy, when admirable), what forms of verse are so enduring and so popular, as the songs and ballads which make up the popular staple of every national poetic literature? These are truly occasional, spontaneous, individual. It is in such poems the poet writes his life, gives his experience: proclaims his joys and praises: embalms a friend or an enemy; deepens a sentiment or renders his description most vivid. The regular forms of poetry seem strained and elaborate compared with this. They want, apparently, the impulse which gives truth to these, and which infuses its life into them. Other verse is more reflective or philosophical: this gives the essence of the art; the true poetic afflatus.

Much of our American verse (the best portion) is lyrical Not always verses for music, nor drinking songs, nor effusions of gallantry, though we can point to a rich anthology of that class. But a lyrical spirit runs through much of the serious poetry of Bryant, all of Halleck's and Brainard's; and most of the productions of Dr. Moore's muse are essentially lyrical, although they often run into the more purely elegiac form—of this, the following poems are more especially to be remarked, in confirmation of our criticism.

The Organist, a spirited address in epistolary guise, the Wine Drinker and the Water Drinker, two capital poems, that would have delighted Green, (author of the Spleen,) and much after his manner; and that must gratify every rational man, as well as lover of fine verse; and the exquisite lines To my Daughter on her Marriage, the equally admirable address to Southey, which, with the fine poems to the Poet's Children and Wife, we have referred to before, emphatically stamp our poet's mastery of the pathetic, in domestic scenes. The parallel may seem strained, but we are apt to compare these rare gems with such a poem as Cowper's Address to his Mother's Picture; and we think our bard loses not a whit by the comparison. With Goldsmith, our poet is a model of simplicity and natural grace, which shine out in the lightest copy of verses. A few of the pieces in this volume of this kind and exactly suited to the occasion that produced them, may not be adequately appreciated by the common reader, but none can fail to be impressed (who have a heart to feel or a taste sufficiently cultivated to appreciate our author's delicacy) with the poems we have mentioned above. They are, truly, classical poems.

VI.

AMERICAN VERSE.—RALPH HOYT.

WHAT is true, generally, of the best poets, holds with regard to our own writers of verse: they are almost invariably the briefest. Brevity is the essence of wit in its widest acceptation; of passion and imagination no less than of epigrammatic smartness. The very highest flights of Fancy cannot be long sustained; the most brilliant flashes of genius are the most evanescent.

This has ever been the case, from the days of the Hebrew Bards to the present epoch. And where great poets have written long poems, how few of these are fairly endenizened in the national heart, and have taken a firm hold on the popular feeling. Few, very few, great, long poems survive a very limited period; and even the classic national epics, which can be counted on the fingers, are by no means perfect throughout. In the grandest of epics, Paradise Lost, how much there is one could willingly let die. Many fine poets of the second rank assume that position from their perfect short pieces, not from mediocre long ones.

But a short effort must be complete and finished, in itself, to be valuable. It is, as in statuary: the critic demands perfection; whereas, in architecture, one is necessarily more lenient. Or, as in painting, an historical picture may be deficient in parts, while a portrait ought to reflect the living features. Yet, one shall often find the poet priding himself on his elaborate and longer productions, and contemning, as slight and worthless, those fugitive, occasional effusions which alone stamp him with immortality.

The length of the performances of our poets is in an inverse ratio to their intrinsic merits. Thus far, the longest are superlatively meagre and valueless, and fill single volumes, any one of which would probably contain the Gems of American Verse.

We need an American anthology, which should bring together many delicate blossoms, mostly reared in hot-houses, and which can ill bear the rude air of common criticism or the chilling breezes of neglect. Our Parnassus is a garden of exotics chiefly; we have no forest trees yet growing upon it. The soil is not hardy and vigorous enough for the towering oak or majestic elm: it produces, instead, the ever-sweet rose, the graceful lily, the variegated tulip, and the exquisite mignionette.

We have no cedars of Lebanon, but beautiful japonicas. The cactus is a true type of our poetical flowers. It is a foreigner; it is raised and developed with care and pains; and its flower is delicately fair.

Critically, the American poets fall within the class of minor poets. They do not as a class—none of those whose verse will last—write at length, or in the highest walks of the epic and tragic muse. Yet, their efforts may be and often are excellent. And we have thus far at least a score, but surely not over two hundred, as one collector affirmed, of true poets, whose works will maintain a desirable place in all select collections of poetry.

Of this nature, and belonging to this class, are the charming effusions of Mr. Hoyt's genius, who is not a great poet, because he does not attempt the highest walks of poetry, but who is a pure and sweet one, with judgment to boot, in not venturing upon flights without his reach, or wasting his powers on unattainable objects.

He has happily opened an original vein in these sketches, which display true pathos, and a delicate talent for satiric irony; descriptive skill and a fine ear, attuned to the nice management of his peculiar measures. A pleasing pastoral tenderness—a pure tone of domestic feeling runs through the verses of Mr. Hoyt, whose landscape is enveloped in an atmosphere of sentiment.

We remember some years since having read one morning a delicate piece of criticism in one of the morning papers (the News, a democratic journal, since defunct,) on a poetical brochure, by the Rev. Ralph Hoyt, then a new name in the American Parnassus. Certain stanzas from Snow were extracted, containing one of the very finest pieces of rural painting we ever read. It was a genuine transcript from nature, seen through the poetic medium, and executed with the happiest skill. Since that time Mr. Hoyt has produced a few more poetic blossoms, to endure as a permanent literary wreath. He has, in plain English, gained his place, which we run little hazard in predicting will be firm and undisturbed.

His aim is not lofty, his views are not extravagant: he has no prejudices to combat nor taste to create. He is a disciple, with individuality and independence, of the pure school of Goldsmith, and Campbell, and Beattie. He is no copyist, yet his spirit, subjects, and diction are those of the "approved good masters" of sterling English verse. Description, faithful, original, fresh, and spirited; a pleasing, narrative style; fine touches of good humored satiric wit, with a true vein of mild and gentle pathos, just and delicate sentiment, all couched in a style of transparent clearness, of limpid beauty, constitute the poetic capital of our poet.

Mr. Hoyt is to be considered chiefly as a rural, descriptive poet, and a domestic painter. He is at home in the fields and by the fireside. No grand, no brilliant, no profound bard is he, but peculiarly sweet and agreeable. He might be ranked, perhaps, with Parnell, (their lives are different, to be sure, but the sum total, to speak mathematically of his poetical traits and talents, might be accounted as nearly equal to those of the Queen Anne's poet,) who stands among the lesser lights, the Dii Minores of the poetical firmament.

Altogether, Mr. Hoyt has published very little; two very thin pamphlets, previously to his last collection, which includes the best things in the earlier publications, as well as his more recent efforts. But they "are choicely good," as Walton says of Marlow and Raleigh, better than most of "the *strong lines in this critical age*." Lovers of simplicity, of meditative reflection, of polish, sentiment, and purity of style, will admire the verses of Mr. Hoyt; but the majority of poetical readers will think him wanting in passion and excitement. Indeed he eschews passion, dramatic effect, and "exciting" topics altogether. His favorite topics are domestic scenes of fireside happiness, the joys of innocence and home, the heaven of childhood, the beautiful serenity of virtuous age.

Nor is he deficient in touches of ironical humor, without bitterness, and instinct with wisdom. He has a manly vein of satire and eloquence, as in World Sale and New. Snow and Rain are universally admitted to be finished landscapes; and, indeed, we agree with Mr. Hoyt's critic in the American Review, (we believe the late Mr. Colton,) that these are the best specimens of idyllic verse, or rural painting, that American poetry can show. Other names may be mentioned more brilliant, of more varied resources, of more profound philosophy; we have had lyrists and moralists in verse of the first class; but, perhaps, no one, who, in his peculiar sphere, has surpassed Mr. Hoyt. His sphere is limited; it is the province of the domestic poet and pastoral bard; its range is narrow, yet in it he is a master.

The peculiar measure of Mr. Hoyt's poetical efforts strikes us most agreeably, though they have affected other critics differently. The returning strain, the recurrence of a harmonious line, add, to our ear, to the rhythmical beauty. Yet it is a mannerism, and might become monotonous. Most of these poems have passed through a number of editions and meet a ready sale. Their popularity affords proof that an uncontaminated poetical taste still remains.

Mr. Hoyt has in print some delightful poetical *jeux d'esprit:* we wish he could collect them with these pieces in a larger volume. In the Evening Mirror, he has had several; and we have lighted upon verses in the Sun, so much superior to the common run of newspaper verse, that we charged upon our author pieces he confessed to be his.

We have not quoted a line, as we wish our readers to find out the separate beauties for themselves. The critic is a literary taster, but the reader must mark and inwardly digest for himself.

Mr. Hoyt is a clergyman of the Episcopal Church, and may be fitly regarded as the best clerical poet, by far, of that church. A modest, though manly preacher, he is not by any means a fashionable preacher; most fortunately for us and for his own true interest, though not for his pecuniary interest.

Able controvertists arise, flourish, die, are forgotten. Brilliant declaimers flash and vanish more suddenly still; but genuine poetry outlasts controversies and fashions in oratory, though it gives no personal popularity or worldly honors, or worldly gear. Gold is not lasting, but glory is; so the Poet, too often, is poor and famous.

In the case of a professional man, this should not be; and we hope will not be with our author. Such as he, the Churh should especially cherish.

VII.

THE LITERARY CHARACTER OF R. H. DANA.

The review of American novelists in the Foreign Quarterly, just and fair in the main, was yet guilty of omissions that should have been noticed at the time, and the authors neglected fully discussed by a competent critic. It is not our purpose at present to occupy the whole ground, nor to attempt filling the wide and unseemly gap left by the reviewer —more, we apprehend, from ignorance or inadvertence, than from any desire to suppress excellence, or hide real merit. That duty we leave to the American critic, who can honestly appraise the peculiar talents and unique productions of several among our lighter writers, whose names we might mention, not one of whom is alluded to by the critic; while two serious writers—the one a great painter, and the other a true poet, of unquestioned excellence as writers of prose fiction. Allston in his Monaldi, and Dana in certain tales, among prose fictions holding a somewhat analogous rank to that the masterpieces of Heywood and Middleton would sustain in a comparison with the Shaksperian drama—have been passed over without attracting the most casual remark.

This extreme carelessness may furnish some excuse for the critical remarks we are about to make, and for attempting to sketch the features of one of the purest and noblest of our American men of genius.

An equally good reason for such a sketch may be found in the fact of the great injustice done our author by the present race of readers, to whom he is known only by name Genius and virtue like that of Mr. Dana's should be kept fresh and alive before his countrymen. Such men as he are not given to the world to be left in doubt as to whether they have lighted upon their appropriate sphere, or whether they have not wandered into some stranger orb. Though Mr. Dana has not been a voluminous writer, he has still written abundantly enough, and with adequate power to reveal to all who can understand him, the purity and nobleness of his aims, and to impress young and docile minds with the wisest lessons of life and duty.

It is now nearly a quarter of a century since we have seen anything in the way of prose fiction in print by the author of the Idle Man; during which period so many candidates for public honor, and claimants for a niche in the temple of fame, have been pouring in, that the public eye is well nigh clouded by the sparkling ephemerida, and the public ear confounded by loud clamors and noisy appeals. In the midst of this hubbub, the silent speculative genius of Dana, and the power, the purity, and the classic cast of Dana's writings have passed almost unregarded. Among the thousands who devour James, the tens who study Dana may be easily enumerated. The lovers of historical melodrama see nothing in simple, undisguised, unaffected, yet most real and vigorous true dramatic painting. Perhaps the American is too much of a philosopher for these readers, who are captivated by detailed narrative and circumstantial description; though, as a mere writer of tales full of striking characters, closely crowded with stirring incidents, set in a frame of poetic description, and enshrined within a halo of pure imagination, Dana is in the first rank of novelists. It is wrong to speak of him as a mere tale writer, for his tales are not only as long as certain short novels, (as long and longer than Rasselas, Zadig, Candide, or the admirable fictions of Richter, Zschokke, and other German novelists,) but they are so closely woven that they read sometimes like abstracts of longer works. There is nothing to be spared; the utmost economy is observed. Yet, as we said, the evident philosophic character of the author, the basis, indeed, of his poetical nature, as well as the love of speculating upon character, the motives to action, the principles of conduct, may deter the mere readers for amusement, since Dana is manifestly a teacher of men, and is to be estimated rightly only in that character. He has selected prose fiction, we imagine, only as a vehicle for conveying certain pictures of life, portraits of certain indivicuals, wholesome moral satire, an ideal of contented private enjoyments, and of a life of active enlightened duty.

Sentiment, we apprehend, forms the most prominent feature in the genius and writings of Mr. Dana. No mere sentimentalist, our author is emphatically a man of sentiment; no hypocritical Joseph Surface, full of cant and moral pretensions, but a genuine man of feeling, unlike, or rather superior to, Mackenzie's hero, in being besides a true philosophic observer of life and character, a stern self-student, and a powerful painter, according to the stereotyped phrase of men and manners.

This attribute of sentiment, in the instance of our author, is at one and the same time a moral and intellectual quality, religious, high-toned, upright, masculine, partaking of the pathetic sweetness of Mackenzie and the stern dignity of Wordsworth. Apart from this faculty, Mr. Dana is a writer of great purity and power, of much acuteness and elegance in other walks than in those of philosophic sentiment, or of sentimental description; but in those he is master and ranks first among his contemporaries and countrymen. He has vast power in depicting the struggles of the darker passions, jealousy, hatred, suspicion, and remorse. Paul Felton has touches of Byronic force, and discloses a similar vein to that so fully opened, and with such popular effect, in the works of Godwin and Charles Brockden Brown.

Sentiment furnishes the key also to the criticisms of Dana We noticed this in his lectures a few winters since, on the poets and dramatists. He finds this, his favorite faculty, beautifully expressed by the ballad writers and Shaksperian dramatists among the old writers; and by Wordsworth and Coleridge, among the new; and to them he has given his heart. The single critical paper in the volume of Dana's selected works on the acting of Kean is full of it, no less than of acuteness and deep insight into the mystery of art, and which are colored and defined by it, to a point and degree that may be honestly declared as not being very far distant from perfection. The paper is almost equal in its way to Elia's admirable sketches in the same vein of subtle criticism.

As a writer of sentiment, love in its forms both of sentiment and passion, (for it varies in different natures, and is the offspring of the affections and of the fancy, according to the individual constitution, mental, or moral, or sensitive, of the recipient and cherisher of it,) constitutes the staple of Dana's invention and speculation; of love, in all its degrees, he is a delicate limner or a vigorous painter, according as the subject is a delicate woman or manly man, a quiet, retired meditative nature or a stirring ambitious character. The female character has full justice done it by the writer of Edward and Mary. Judging from his writings, Mr. Dana has been a happy man. Yet he can paint a weak, credulous mother, or a dashing, heartless woman of fashion, (see Tom Thornton,) with as subtle skill as he can delineate the fond, confiding heart, the clear and nice judgment, the gentle and amiable tastes of a true woman, and a good wife.

With the single exception of the Buccaneer, his finest

poem, the entire body of his poetry is ethical and deeply imbued with the manner and cast of mind distinguishable in the great English Bards, the elder and later. This is no disparagement; moral verse (of all others) allows most of imitation, and is least marked by nationality: thus we think of Cowper, and Crabbe, and Wordsworth, in reading Dana; we think of them as fellow-workers in the same field. Dana is no copyist, if he does employ, to a certain degree, the manner of Cowper, which we think we perceive he does, in 'Factitious Life;' of Crabbe, in 'The Changes of Home,' and of Wordsworth in almost all the remaining pieces in the volume; except, perhaps, in 'Thoughts on the Soul,' which might have been written (all the speculative portion of it; indeed all but a few lines in the second page, in the more familiar vein of later writers) by Sir John Davies himself who furnishes a text for the poet. Dana's poem is like the verse of the Elizabethan writer, equally close, full of thought and austere. The characteristic sentiment of Dana these poems are full of: he imbues all nature with his peculiar feeling and purity, and solemn fancy, as with an atmosphere of meditation and religious musing. Wordsworth has not in England worthier disciples of his school than Dana and Bryant, and they have done some things that no other of the followers of the great English poet have ever attempted. Critically to speak of Mr. Dana, he is truly 'eldest apprentice in the school of art,' over which Coleridge and Crabbe and Wordsworth preside. With the soul and heart of a poet, Mr. Dana has more of the speculative intellect than mere imagination or fancy, not that he is deficient in either.

The critic's esthetical views are strongly tinged with his ethetical doctrines, and a turn for moralising, and vein of speculation runs through all of his critical papers, and forms the basis (as it were) of his critical opinions—with Plato and the highest spiritual philosophy, he seeks to unite invariably the good and the beautiful; he is not easy in their disunion, cannot properly admit their severance. Moral Beauty, the highest object of our love and admiration, is the sole beauty with him. Hence, our critic, like a true poet, includes in the scope of his admiration, the highest qualities both of writing and manliness; he would not take into his regard minor and lighter graces, unaccompanied by purity and religion.

Himself a poet, and skilled in the mysteries of versification, no less than in the subtle windings of the heart, and the affections, Mr Dana is admirably well qualified to judge of poetry, both as an artist and a thinker. To say nothing of his original capacity for the office of critic, with a judgment clear and refined, powerful imagination, depth and fineness of feeling, high, healthy and moral sentiment, purified by the practice of the manly virtues, and a life of single-hearted purpose, the poet has, besides the general cultivation of his qualities, mastered the old English literature, and the entire fruitful province of old English poetry, in particular. The structure and elaboration of the author's style prove this; his language and expression is uncommonly choice and select, full of meaning, perfectly simple and unaffected, and yet to a scholar's eye full of richness and discrimination; not the finest but the justest terms are used; nor is the manner above, but precisely equal to the matter, the latter is as abundant and copious as the former is refined and judicious. Much of Mr. Dana's prose (not in his Tales so much as in his Essays and Reviews) has all the sweetness and fluent rhetorical amplitude of Taylor and the old Divines, carried sometimes almost to redundance. In direct narrative, our author can be rigidly concise, and produce a powerful effect in description, also by a few touches.

VIII.

TALES OF THE SOUTH AND WEST.

ENGLISH critics have noticed, as a trait in American literature now becoming a veritable something, the facility of invention and power, with skill of execution, of our writers of fiction. American tales are at a premium at this present writing, in London and Edinburgh, and are employed to eke out the pages of some of the most flourishing of their magazines. From English critics of the present dynasty have come some of the most generous praises of American authors, as from Jerrold, Miss Barrett, and even Dickens, who at first copied Irving.

The article on American works of fiction, in the Foreign and Colonial Quarterly Review, some years since, was much the honestest and most liberal piece of criticism we have seen on American romance; but its excellence lies in its general judgment almost wholly; inasmuch as many capital writers are not even mentioned, while inferior scribes occupy their place, to their exclusion. Such sins of omission and commission can result only from ignorance of their works. Dr. Bird, Mr. Ware, and Mr. Carlton receive a just sentence; while we read not a word respecting Mr. Dana, Judge Hall, Mr. Poe, Mr. Simms, authors certainly entitled to honorable mention.

Not to speak of the finish, the humor, the delicate grace of Irving, in his Dutch and English tales; without referring to the fine invention, aerial fancy, and purely original vein of Hawthorne, in his admirable fancy sketches and admirable pictures of New England romance, that practical mingling of shrewdness and mysticism; entirely excluding the domestic histories of Mr. Dana, so earnest and true, instinct with genuine passion, and with its rare accompaniment, deep, rich, "marrowy" sentiment, the very breath of our intellectual and sensitive life; and leaving entirely out of question the powerful fictions of Brown and Cooper, we still can point to a large body of writers of fiction, tales, "minature novels," (which Schelegel thought the best form of the novel,) and narrative sketches, affording convincing proof, if any could be wanting, that imagination, at least adequate to the production of a prose fiction of the first class, and creative power, are not wanting here, and which, employed on American themes, whether of history, character or manners, legend or landscape, cannot fail to give to our literature a national character, which, indeed, it is every day acquiring.

Thus, besides the genuine originals we have mentioned, we have to fill out a good list of tale writers; Miss Leslie, a sort of modernized Miss Burney on a smaller scale, and like her, expert in strong satire of vulgarity; Miss Sedgwick, pleasing in her home pictures and tales for children; and pre-eminent among American female writers, Mrs. Kirkland, the cleverest sketcher of western manners we have, and the best western *raconteur*, at the same time; not in the same line with Judge Hall or any other western writer, but in a class unique and individual. Of the two Neals, John has tact and power; Joseph, humor, (of the broadest,) and copiousness. The Portland writer is expert in a love-history or life-assurance story; while the Philadelphian is best in city scenes of local and burlesque humor. Briggs is quite at home in a satirical tale, with his ingenuity, tact, keen observation and dry humor. Hoffman can throw off a better hunting or sporting story than any writer we have,. Mathews has both humor and pathetic skill, and in his Motley Book has done some excellent things.

Sands left some laughable pieces, verging on caricature. The critic in the Quarterly referred to, says, and says handsomely, though truly: "We rarely, if ever, take up an American Annual or Magazine, without finding some one contribution individually racy, and *without any peer or prototype on this side of the ocean.*" With the same critic we hardly agree, that though more unpretending in form than the regular novel, the list of tale writers, in their attempts, "contains more characteristic excellence than is to be found in the library of accredited novels." We have no one capital novel except the Pilot; all Cooper's fictions, admirable as they are in scenes and particular descriptions, being confessedly, even according to Mr. Simms, Cooper's heartiest critic, excellent only in those passages, and abounding in faults elsewhere.

Many of these tales have a sectional character and reputation. They are, professedly, so in their choice of subject and back-grounds. It is a history of love or hate, to be sure; but the locality is laid in Illinois, Michigan or South Carolina, with the scenery peculiar to those regions. It is a love-history, but of planter, Indian, negro, or early settler, and the interest varies accordingly. European readers cannot be supposed to read with sufficient knowledge, or with analogous feeling of patriotic interest, and hence these national and local narratives lose for them a striking and peculiar charm. To us, Americans, for this reason, they offer a very strong attraction, independent of the genius involved in the conception of them, or the artistic skill employed in their execution.

We have for the West, Judge Hall and Mrs. Kirkland; for the South, Mr. Simms; for New England, Mr. Hawthorne; Dutch New York has her Irving; for revolutionary historical novelist, Cooper; Philadelphia has her Brown; Virginia, Wirt.

Mary Clavers, the most agreeable and original of American female writers, the equal, not the imitator, of Miss Mitford, is perhaps the best writer of western sketches and manners we have seen; she pursues a course, and occupies a prominent place in her line of authorship, quite distinct from Judge Hall. The latter writer illustrates rather the historical romance of the West—especially that of Indian and French settlers' life, than the manners of the present race of emigrants. Her sprightliness, good sense, and keen penetration are inexhaustible, and her style is a clear and natural reflection of these fine qualities. Her circle is apparently confined to that region; but why it should be so, does not follow, necessarily, or by consequence. After the universal applause with which her Western tales have been received, what new tribute can we bring to her grace, humor and naturalness? Mrs. Kirkland is the Miss Burney of the new settlements, (not the Madame d'Arblay, for Evelina is the best of the fictions of that writer, as well as the earliest.) Her ordinary observation is not confined to the city or village, but flourishes in the back woods. The broad vulgarity, the rustic pedantry, the senseless pretensions of a certain class of vulgar minds the world over, is to be found wherever real coarseness but affected fastidiousness exists. Mrs. Clavers, with all her satire of such persons, has nothing of the same quality in her own writings, a criticism that cannot so justly be passed upon the authoress of Evelina, who cherished a certain artificial gentility, the reverse in appearance of vulgarity, but still its invariable accompaniment. The humor of Mrs. Kirkland is gay and sympathetic, as well as keen and satirical. She can jest as well as ridicule; she laughs with, as often as she laughs at, her characters.

We know nothing we can add to our previous judgment of Mr. Simms' Wigwam and Cabin, save in the way of parallel with the somewhat similar series of tales by Judge Hall, the Western historian, *par excellence.* Both are accomplished *raconteurs;* but Mr. Simms brings more of the novelist's art, and the concentrated force of the practised writer to his aid, than the Judge appears to us to possess, or to be able to control. In level passages, Hall is generally the neater writer, always correct and pleasing: yet Mr. Simms throws more power, passion and energy into his narratives. The Judge is something of a humorous satirist, and indulges in a playful vein of innocent raillery, which we are not apt to meet in the pages of the Southern novelist. Making a fair allowance for the difference between the Indian in the South or at the West, we still think Mr. Simms' Indian the more truly and graphically painted. Judge Hall seems to be most at home in his romantic legends and domestic history of the early French settlers, their manners, customs, character and disposition.

This writer holds a pleasing pencil, and with which he has sketched many a fair scene. His descriptions of the prairie, scattered through all of his tales, are peculiarly well done.

Judge Hall has been very justly classified by a judicious critic as a Western Irving, without his force of humor or fertility of resources; comparatively a feebler writer, yet still well worthy of a place among our first American standards. For Irving's rich humor and charming description, you find in him agreeable pleasantry. He has not equal fineness, yet as much truth of sentiment. In style, he is equally pure, though by no means as rich and musical.

If Judge Hall is justly styled a Western Irving, Mr.

Simms may be at least as appropriately called the Cooper of the South. For, with his favorite novelist, the Southern writer enjoys in common many of his best qualities; his directness, manliness, force and skill in painting details. Mr. Simms has produced no long work of the same sustained interest and power as the Pilot, but he has done many capital things which either his Northern rival cannot execute, or will not attempt.

In shorter tales, each of which embodies all the interest and concentrates the power of a fiction of higher pretensions of Indian and Planters' life, our Southerner is at the head of a very respectable class of writers. He is a faithful painter, also, of negro character, and perfectly at home with the average society and current manners of the South. He is admirable in his personal histories, as of Boone and Weems—in his local scenery, especially in Carolina and Georgia. His narrative is clear, racy, natural, constructed with practised art, (Mr. Simms has at least as much judgment as invention,) and thoroughly American. In these novelettes the interest is always well sustained—sometimes to a pitch of painful interest. Mr. Simms, besides, as critic and miscellaneous writer no less than as an imaginative writer, is the foremost writer of the South, and is naturally the idol of those generous critics whose blood runs warmer than in these Hyperborean regions. He has identified himself with their feelings and institutions, and labors manfully to earn an honorable place for his native State, not only in a political, but also in a literary point of view.

IX.

THE LECTURE.

THE lecture, as a form of composition, is a skilful union of the oration and the essay. The lecturer is, consequently, both writer and speaker, and enjoys the double advantage of an audience of hearers as well as of readers. Hence, the personal reputation of the able lecturer is much more captivating than the general reputation of even a popular author, and, consequently, the field is crowded with competitors. The lecture is to be tested, therefore, in two ways: as it reads, and as it sounds when delivered. In one of the two departments it must take, else it fails altogether. A skilful declaimer may palm off a worthless production on his hearers by the charms of voice and manner, but print is the final appeal; on the other hand, a careful thinker may be a tiresome reader or speaker; but in his case, too, print must decide his merits.

The lecture is the popular philosophical teaching of the day. It is essentially didactic, and here most popular lecturers err; they substitute the declamation, or literary address, for the lecture; they adorn and illustrate, instead of analysing and discussing, old or new truths. They appear to regard the lecture merely as an occasion for oratorical display. Now this, in the best instances, certainly forms a part of the true idea of a good lecture, though it is not its highest aim, nor its sole aim, but rather a quite inconsiderable incident in it. Such display, if in good taste, is very gratifying, and to most hearers, the most agreeable part of a lecture. But the better part of each audience go to learn something. Flourishes, and tricks of metaphor, and arts of elocution, can never effect this end. The first requisite of a lecture is perfect clearness, both of thought and style; the next is force and fertility of ideas and illustration; and the last, and the most important, is genuine sincerity, and a liberal cast of thought. The last gives a certain moral value to the lecture. We do not consider it necessary to add, that a complete knowledge and mastery of the subject is perfectly essential, nor that here, as in the other departments of oratory, an impressive manner and brilliant elocution cannot fail to carry very great weight with them.

We define the lecture as a skilful union of the oration and the essay. In our view, the essay should greatly predominate, inasmuch as the object is to teach. It is very well if amusement can be afforded; and to the right hearer, the most philosophical instruction affords the highest intellectual pleasure. All, however, occasionally require relaxation and amusement. A lively epigram, entertaining anecdotes, a quaint picture, or a story in point, may serve very agreeably to relieve the well-compacted chain of argument and deduction. An occasional golden ring of fancies may be soldered, as it were, into the delicate net-work of consecutive propositions. Breaks, and transitions, and episodes, will rest the mind, tired with a close discussion of abstract principles, as landing-places on the staircase of the palace of truth. But this by the way.—The principal design is to place in the most conspicuous light some one central truth, or idea, or fact in philosophy, criticism or history. In order to ascertain the proper position of this truth, the comparative history or anatomy of similar truths, ideas, or facts, must be gained. Thus, to fix one rule, to certify one fact, to arrive at a just notion of one doctrine, or the spirit of one system, the lecturer must be acquainted with, must allude to many. The lecture, then, is exhaustive, and in this resembles a philosophical essay, or a chapter in a history, or a review article, as the subject-matter may be. In addition to this, there should be similes and conceits. There must be expansion of one picture, or thought, and epigrammatic brevity. A tirade of declamation must serve as a *corps de reserve* to a battalion of arguments, and a fine fancy may sometimes occur as the *avant-courier* of a series of reflections.

The two most important talents in a lecturer are, the analytic power, and a brilliant fancy. Few possess both, and therefore, in general, the ablest lecturers either regard a lecture wholly as an essay, or a declamation, as their talent may be for analysis or rhetoric.

The lecture, in common with the essay, enjoys an universality of topics. It may be of very different kinds; it may be historical, or critical, or speculative. It may serve as a medium for the expression of political or religious opinion. It may offer a new view in natural or moral science. It may re-criticise a favorite poet, or introduce a new one to the public. It includes every subject, from æsthetical culture to steam navigation and lightning rods. It may be even an advertisement for the merchant, as it has often served for the itinerant quack and pill-vender.

The lecture, then, has become a most important means of popular instruction. As such, it should be carefully scrutinized; for it is capable both of great good, or considerable evil. It has its advantages as a means of instruction, and it also has correspondent defects. An able lecturer can impress, in the space of an hour's teaching, an important principle that may guide a man's conduct through life; he can dissipate a prejudice, and disabuse the mind of an ignorant man of some baleful error that blinded his eyes to the perception of the truth. He can give a picture of an epoch so vividly characterized, and so accurately painted, as to supersede the reading of a long history. He can expound in one lecture a moral or metaphysical system that months of hard reading might not so clearly elucidate and stamp on the memory. He can distinguish (for it is his business) between errors that were so contiguous as to seem to form a true whole. He can train the literary, as well as the moral, sense of the reader, and interpret for him the books of great minds. But in order to do all these things, he must be exactly informed, and perfectly trustworthy. He needs no originality, for he deals with the facts, or with the ideas of others. He is the expositor of the one, and the translator of the other. Pure originality might set him wrong where the path lay plain before him. Not a little modesty is therefore requisite to prevent the lecturer from relying too much on his own resources.

Instead of this, what do we generally find? Superficial information, a crude view of the subject, stale fancies—the thrown-off ornaments of greater intellects—stereotyped prejudice, a boastful arrogance, and a curious medley of styles. Instead of completeness, confused variety; in place of continuity, endless digressions. You ask for an argument, and you are helped to an allegory. You require a fact, and they give you a figure. Everywhere you see a constant attempt at display. A man of a barren imagination is at a forced-put to give birth to a simile, and no fancy aims at being very fanciful. There are some lecturers, who, like single-speech Hamilton, deliver but one lecture in the whole course of their lives. This is, generally, an outpouring of the contents of their common-place book—a curious composition—resembling in literature, as to variety, (though by no means in excellence,) what a mince-pie, or a plum-pudding, is in cookery. There are other abuses of the lecture that need a remedy. Men of wealth, who have the itch of authorship, or of oratory, must needs deliver lectures, as an opiate to their ill-regulated self-love. As men of a certain standing, capable of exerting considerable influence, committees always defer to them. These lecture gratuitously, though for our own parts, were we able, we would pay for their silence. These pretenders hurt the professed lecturer, by under-bidding him, and as the treasury is always first regarded, a gratuitous lecture, however inefficient, is generally preferred to a good one that must be well paid. Some who need pay, entertain a mawkish feeling in the matter, as most petty scribblers have a burlesque contempt for the profits of authorship. The truth should be felt, that lecturing, as authorship, is now become a profession; a profession, too, of scholars and gentlemen for the better part, though there are quacks enough in it, as in everything else. It is a profession to which such a man as Dewey is reported to have once thought of turning his attention, as a fixed pursuit—once honored in this country by Dana, Channing, Hawks, Longfellow, Emerson, Bancroft, and many other gentlemen of ability and high standing. It is very true that it has been taken up by inferior men, but how long have they suceeded? Unless they are happily gifted in the personal qualifications of a lecturer, which have enabled some mere quacks to get along, they sink very soon.

There is a common error that tends to distract the attention of audiences, and, consequently, to lower the proper value of lectures. This is, the jumble of lectures in a long course, on a variety of topics: of politics, morals, history, natural science, and literature. Now, the great body of lecture-goers

3

are supposed to go with but a moderate knowledge of the evening's topic; perhaps, ignorant altogether. The lecturer should assume the latter as probably true. Therefore, he should have time to produce a proper effect; instead of one lecture on morals, or one on the steam-engine, and one on the nerves, let him deliver three on one subject. Completeness and clearness aref ar more preferable to multiplicity of facts and experiments. We would suggest fewer topics, and more lectures on each. Three or four single courses, of at least two or three lectures, or a long course of six or eight by one lecturer, are much better than sixteen or twenty lecturers. This last produces too much the effect of modern education, which substitutes the encyclopædia for a few sound text-books.

This want of selection—of discrimination—springs from the incapacity, in most cases, of the lecture committee for their office of selecting lecturers; though, occasionally, it arises from the diversified tastes of the audience, and the endeavor to meet them. The chairman and his associates are either men of a respectable station in life, and wealthy, who know nothing of literature, authors, or the value of literary labor, or young clerks of a bookish turn, who wish to employ their critical propensities on their betters, in every sense of the word. Both of these classes of persons are utterly unfit to judge of the ability of a lecturer, or of the real merit of a lecture. They judge mostly from personal appearance, and general reputation. A dashing *bravura* sort of speaker takes them at once. They surrender to assurance. Modest merit never succeeds, as the lottery dealer confessed, when he found his newspaper puffs not sufficiently stimulant.

This requires the vigorous protest of scholars and liberal thinkers; that scholars should sit as the critics—that scholars should sit on the committee. It is an affair of scholarship, not of trade. An excellent man of business may be a very commonplace critic. The flour market has no connection with the fancy, and imagination and industry are not always found in company.

The lecture is a purely modern form of composition. The Greeks and Romans wrote dissertations, and published philosophical dialogues, but they have left nothing like our modern lecture. Probably Socrates talked lectures; but, like Ulysses, he was too wise to print.

England, France, Germany, and the United States have produced the most eminent public teachers. In Germany, the Schlegels, with a host of able men, equally distinguished for learning and eloquence; in France, Cousin, Guizot, Villemain, and the Professors of the Institute; in England, Hazlitt, Coleridge, and Mr. Fox, the Unitarian clergyman; in our own country, Channing, Dewey, Dana, Longfellow, Emerson. In the three leading divisions of the lecture, the literary, or critical, the speculative, and the historical, we would place Hazlitt at the head of the lecturers on poetry and the belles-lettres; Guizot, would stand the first of historical lecturers, and Dewey, the foremost of the speculative lecturers on practical subjects. Dewey does not lecture on abstract topics, but discusses practical themes in an abstract manner. Cousin is the most popular metaphysical teacher; but even here, a lecturer for students—not a popular lecturer. Dana is our most impressive lecturer on poetry. Longfellow, a picturesque scholar in his addresses, and Emerson, a modern mystic. The lecture is more sought after here, than perhaps anywhere else. As a people, we like to get knowledge by as short a course of study as possible. In lectures, the audience are passive students; they receive knowledge instead of working for its acquisition. It also finds favor among us from the love of mixing in public, which we, of all the people under the sun, most affect. It reminds the politician of caucuses, and the merchants of a meeting on 'Change. It jumps with our democratic humor of equalizing knowledge, and in this respect, resembles the popular periodical literature of the day.

What is the future influence of the lecture to be? Much greater, we apprehend, than it is now. When the class of lecturers shall comprise a majority of able men, scholars, gentlemen—we feel warranted in asserting, it will be the favorite method of public instruction. It will not, to be sure, take the place of really sound reviews and newspapers; but it will obliterate the inefficient organs of public opinion. Good lectures will kill off weak papers. Neither will it hurt the stage, but rather by refined criticism tend to elevate it. It will not interfere with the pulpit, since it will expressly enforce the precepts of moral duty, and speculate profoundly on the minor moralities. It will rather come in aid of the pulpit, giving audiences on week day evenings what an enlarged view of religion would give them at church on Sundays.

Perhaps we should have before discriminated popular lectures from lectures for students. There will always be both, as long as there is a distinct class of students in the world, and a large class of persons who are not professed students, but yet who continue learners all their lives. The use of lectures to students is rather for revision than the beginning of any study. They serve to revive or review old studies or doctrines, but they ought not to be heard at the beginning of their course. Lectures give results, not processes. Profound scholars must, however, go through certain processes to verify these results, whereas a mixed audience must build their knowledge on faith in the lecturer.

The present is allowed to be a critical age—an analytic age. We would rather speculate on principles than follow a long narrative of facts. We substitute, then, the historical lecture for the history. The same will apply to morals, and religion, and politics. For one who reads Locke, twenty read Cousin; for one who reads Cudworth, twenty study Macintosh. The Federalist is laid by when Daniel Webster is to speak; and the old divines are closed when a fashionable preacher mounts the pulpit.

We have spoken of lectures for students, and popular lectures. The last kind are infinite in variety, and as regards the class of audiences they address—from merchants to mechanics, from ladies to laborers. Every craft must have its lecture-room, and will have at some future day. The whole empire of knowledge will be ransacked for subjects of disquisition and amusement.

Many attend lectures now as they attend the opera, for the sake of the fashion. But good lectures require a capacity of attention, and a degree of thought, that are not always possessed, or bestowed. When placed on a right footing, none will attend except for instruction and partial entertainment. Few persons go to a lecture knowing what they have a right to expect. The subject is an abstract topic, and they expect an amusing narrative, or it is historical, and they look for sentimental passages. This is to be reformed.

On the whole, we are apt to consider the lecture a very important department of modern literature, and a most powerful instrument of popular instruction. As a corollary to this, it follows, the lecturer should occupy a dignified position. The public taste, to be sure, needs correction on many material points connected with this subject; nor are the best critics infallible in their judgments on lecturers. Like most evils in this world, these will mend themselves in good time. There must be no forced improvements; but gradual changes, and a wiser policy. Some of these errors, as the selection of committees, can be amended at once; but the taste of audiences is to be formed. The surest method to attain good ends is to employ noble means; and thus we hope lectures will continue to improve with the capacity in the public for appreciating them. We look for the time, with confidence, when the lecture shall occupy no neutral ground in the public esteem, and when the lecturer will be an established professional character.

X.

HUGH LATIMER.

This brave old Bishop, an apostolic prelate of the true stamp, a gallant chief in the Noble Army of Martyrs, is the earliest great name, now extant, in the long list of great English Divines. His humor and eloquence, rude and homely as they are, were in his day above rivalry; and to him was conceded the fame, not only of the simple minded and upright Christian, but also of the fervid, indignant, copious orator. He was, beyond dispute, the St. Paul of London, of the sixteenth century, who attracted the dainty ears of fastidious scholars, and high bred courtiers, equally with the unlettered, but not inattentive, audiences of a lower stamp. Admired by the gentry, except where he was feared for his honesty, he was the idol of the populace, who would crowd around him as he walked down the Strand, to preach at Whitehall, and endeavoring to catch but the hem of his cloak, would cry aloud, "Have at them, Father Latimer!" It is this paternal character, exhibited in his public discourses, as well as in his private conduct, that we would describe, in a portrait of the successor of the Apostles.

The life of Latimer is impressed with more than one important lesson. A great change occurred both in his doctrines and his preaching. He was, at one time, a zealous Romanist, and preached with severity against the reformers, reflecting bitterly against Melancthon, the gentlest of men: again, he renounced the Pope, and declared in favor of Henry, both as to his supremacy, as head of the Church, and in the matter of the divorce. Finally, he became a decided Protestant, and was a distinguished leader of the Reformation, under Edward VI., when he was at the zenith of his popularity. In the savage reign of Mary, he was burnt at the stake, with those other glorious Martyrs to Truth and Religious Liberty, Cranmer and Ridley. In his conversion, we may admit no question of his sincerity: and in his devoted adherence, first to Henry, and afterwards to Edward, (differing as the tiger and the lamb,) he was pursuing a single purpose. Always the sentinel of the Church, he was, besides, an effective champion. He attacked vice and crime, with all its pride of place, and pomp of pedigree, at the same time that he stood on the defensive; and, at last, lost his life in the same way that he had gained his just fame, by the exercise of a pure, undaunted, and holy zeal, that knew no obstacles to the propagation of truth and the extirpation of error, while the means of advancing the one, and destroying the other, remained.

The *paternal* character was the leading feature of Latimer's mind and moral constitution. He knew how, and when, to give wise and safe counsel, and feared not to administer it. He was indignant at the open vices of the clergy and nobles, and hesitated not to express his indignation, generally by way of strong humorous satire. He was the Patriarch of old, revived in modern days. Generally, the Priest has been said, and often truly, to defend the failings of his caste, in order to preserve an *esprit de corps*. This is, in a right sense, commendable. But Latimer sided with the people against the corruptions of the clergy. He openly and sharply rebuked them. He disclosed many an acknowledged evil, that the timidity of the good would have shielded from the vulgar eye, lest Religion herself, and the pure priestly character, might be indiscriminately attacked. But he feared nothing of the sort. It was he that so vigorously depicted 'idle ministers,' 'unpreaching prelates,' 'mock gospellers,' 'minting priests,' 'blanchers,' 'mingle manglers,' 'bells without clappers,' *i. e.*, unfurnished pulpits, from which lazy preachers drew regular salaries. In his comprehensive care of his people, Latimer was no less observant of the broad and undistinguishing corruption of the times, among the lawyers, and especially the judges, with whom bribery was considered a perquisite of their offices. He inveighed, with force and acuteness, against bribers, whom he also calls giffe-gaffes, against covetousness, against woodmongers (an odious class of monopolists), against flock-panders, against gratifiers of rich men. Latimer wisely joined religion with daily life, and moral censures to incentives to piety. So glaring were the corruptions above mentioned, in his time, that he devoted not a little space to a severe castigation of their abettors. Some of his sermons, in themselves, were true Juvenal strains: in all of them he has long passages of a similar kind. Many of his discourses might be collected under the same title, that Wither adopted for his satires, 'Abuses stript and whipt.' And the good Bishop's censures were far from unavailing. His keen rebukes cut many to the heart. In his second sermon, preached before King Edward, he refers to the common practice of giving and taking bribes, and also of restitution. He proceeds, in his plain, direct way: "I have now preached three Lents. The first time I preached Restitution. 'Restitution!' quoth some, 'what should he preach of Restitution? Let him preach of contrition, quoth they, and let restitution alone; we can never make restitution. Then, say I (what a whole-hearted Christian man!) if thou wilt not make restitution, thou shalt go to the devil for it. Now choose thee, either restitution or endless damnation. But now there be two manner of restitutions, secret restitution and open restitution; whether of both it be so that restitution is made, it is all good enough. At my first preaching of restitution, one good man took remorse of conscience, and acknowledged himself to me, that he had deceived the king, and willing he was to make restitution; and so, the first Lent came to my hands twenty pounds to be restored to the king's use. I was promised twenty pounds more the same Lent; but it could not be made, so that it came not. Well, the next Lent came three hundred and twenty pounds more. I received it myself, and paid it to the king's council. So I was asked what he was that made restitution? But should I have named him? *Nay, they should as soon have this weasand of mine.* Well, now this Lent came one hundred and fourscore pounds ten shillings, which I have paid and delivered this present day to the king's council. And so this man hath made a godly restitution. And so quoth I, to a certain nobleman that is one of the king's council, if every man that hath beguiled the king should make restitution after this sort, it would cough the king twenty thousand pounds, I think, quoth I. Yes, that it would, quoth the other, a whole hundred thousand pounds. Alack, alack! make restitution for God's sake, make restitution; ye will cough in hell else, that all the devils there will laugh at your coughing." In such a channel flowed the simple but vigorous rhetoric of the old master.

As adviser and defender of their rights, Latimer was the people's friend, no less than by his ripping open the abuses of the rich and powerful. He was, in one view, a democrat, more from disgust of the aristocracy, than from any individual tendencies. His true position was rather that of a conservative, or perhaps, if living, he would bear the same relation to the prevailing parties that the moderate whig sustains to the violent tory, or reckless radical. Robin Hood was a type of the perfect democrat, without many of the vices, and free from all the meanness of the modern demagogue: and to show Latimer's estimation of the generous freebooter, we read the following incident in one of his sermons, of which the burden is, the decay of religion, the necessity of preaching, and bells without clappers. On a holy day, Latimer stopped once at a village church, having sent word the night before that he would preach there the next morning. He found the door locked, and the key could not be found until more than half an hour's delay. He was then told, "Sir, this is a busy day with us, we cannot hear you—it is Robin Hood's day." Robin Hood carried the day away from the good Father. But ignominiously he styles the bold outlaw (in many features of his character, as, in his love for the poor, regard for female chastity, indignation at legalized corruption, strongly resembling himself,) "a traitor and a thief," forgetting what was really sound in the favorite ideal of the populace, and their generous defender.*

All Latimer's virtues partook of the same direct and inartificial character. He was honest, bold, simple, and pious. His honesty was enlightened by judgment and experience; his boldness was confirmed by truth and sincerity; his simplicity was the transparent veil of his free thoughts and manly actions, and his piety gave a tone to, and cast a lustre over, all of these. Instances of all these qualities are numerous. A single fact may prove his honest frankness, fearing no evil, as it had intended none, and utterly unsuspicious of malice, as he was free from guile. It was a current custom to present the king (Henry VIII.) every New Year's day with an annual offering: a purse of gold was the common oblation. Latimer sent, as his tribute, a New Testament, with the leaf doubled down in a very conspicuous manner at the passage, "Whoremongers and adulterers God will judge." Previously to this, and afterward, he had opposed Henry with a manly unconcern, and, by his fearlessness, gained the respect of that tyrannical despot.

The martyrdom of Latimer is one of the bloodiest spots even upon the reign of bloody Queen Mary. The familiarity of the relation in Fox's Book of Martyrs, renders it super-

* Robin Hood is rather to be regarded as a patriot, one of the last of the chieftains of the old Saxon race, who denied the Conquest, and persisted in living out of the law of the descendants of foreigners, than as a mere freebooter, the character commonly assigned to him. [Vide Thierry's History of the Norman Conquest.] Robin was canonized, and the holy day above referred to was his annual festival. The French historian, one of the ablest of the modern school, quotes this very passage out of Latimer, to show the strong hold the brave outlaw had on the popular affection.

fluous to re-state the details here: neither can any student of English history be supposed ignorant of the particulars of that disgraceful scene.

The style and eloquence of Latimer were characteristic of the man and of his age; homely almost to rudeness, yet vigorous, learned, manly, idiomatic, and practical in the highest degree. He was a humorous satirist, a sharp debater, a grave and ornate orator, and a keen student of human nature combined. His simplicity confirmed his honesty; and he was utterly free from any equivocation or duplicity. His understanding and talents, generally, were ot the true old English stamp, and which we see reproduced in the best modern writers of English. His age was a pedantic one, that had not left quoting Latin by the page; but in his case, the English mind was formed chiefly out of the best Saxon traits. The old Saxon formed the best parts of the moral character, as well as of the language, of the modern Englishman. Latimer has some of Hogarth's humor, and Morland's naturalness. He enjoys a talent in common with Cobbett, of calling names. He has not a little of honest John Bunyan's allegorical fancy. His style, like all of these, is completely English, and smacks of that sterling vein.

Inheriting the democratic tendencies of the Saxon, he feared not to rebuke nobles and prelates, though himself a priest; nor to recognise the god-like characteristics of humanity in the meanest individual; loved in life, honored in his death, though a suffering martyr, and venerated by all after ages. This comprises the history of good Father Latimer.

XI.

SIR PHILIP SIDNEY'S "DEFENSE OF POESY."

It may appear unseasonable and superfluous at this epoch of the literary history of the world, to re-write the defence of poesy, so much better done in the works of the best poets themselves; and such a defence would be no less ill-timed than impertinent, as if that divine art needed any advocates, and therefore we shall merely recur, for the purpose of analysis and criticism, to the earliest and perhaps the most elaborately eloquent argument in the English language, in behalf of the claims of the poet and his vocation.

The Defense of Poesy is the richest gem in the poetic crown of Sidney. It is a pure and lofty appeal to the god-like in human nature; it contains in itself the essence of an art of poetry; is full of generous sentiment, all clenched and compacted by the fine logic and finer declamation of the poet of the Arcadia. Indeed, so much at least to us critical readers is it to be preferred to the Romance of that name, that Warton recommended a separate publication of the essay, since, being generally printed at the end of the Arcadia, no one would be likely to read it.

Bad poets, unskilful critics, dull scholars, had united to make verse well nigh contemptible. Sidney was influenced by a loyal zeal to recover the lost purity and splendor of poetic triumphs, and therefore wrote the Defense of Poesy. A complete analysis of the essay would occupy almost as much space as the essay itself, so close and consecutive is the strain; we shall therefore be obliged to condense our notice much within the merits of the case, or the true value of the arguments.

The author commences by urging the great antiquity of poetry as a proof of its necessity and excellence. Verse was the earliest shape that language assumed: the first mould into which ideas fell. The first laws, the oldest moral and prudential maxims, religion, politics, were couched in metrical sentences. Oracle and prophecy were coeval with antiquity and fable. The poet was then priest and prophet: alas! that the characters have ever been disjoined.

The earliest Greek writers were poets; we read no author prior to the time of Homer and Hesiod and the Cylic bards. The greatest Italian writers were poets, and so of our noble literature. The noblest illustrations of the worth of poetry have occurred since the time of Sidney, for he numbered not among English poets, Shakspeare nor Spenser, Milton nor Wordsworth. Plato himself (vulgarly considered the vilifier of poetry, but in truth only of soft lascivious, enervating verses) was the most poetic of the philosophers. Herodotus entitled the several books of his history after the names of the muses. The northern nations preserve an original national poetry of the greatest antiquity. This is the first argument.

Next he compares the poet with the astronomer, mathematician, the natural and moral philosopher, the lawyer, the historian, grammarian, logician, physician—all of whom have a basis in nature or palpable reality to proceed upon, and therefore exercise not the higher faculty of poetical invention. "Only the poet, disdaining to be tied to any such subjection, lifted up with the vigor of his own invention, doth grow, in effect, into another nature; in making things either better than nature bringeth forth, or quite anew, forms such as never were in nature, as the heroes, demigods, cyclops, chymeras, fairies, and such like; so as he goeth hand in hand with nature, not inclosed within the narrow warrant of her gifts, but freely ranging within the zodiac of his own wit. Nature never sets forth the earth in so rich tapestry as divers poets have done; neither with so pleasant rivers, fruitful trees, sweet smelling flowers, nor whatever else may make the too much loved earth more lovely; her world is brazen, the poets only deliver a golden. But let those things alone, and go to man, for whom, as the other things are, it seemeth in him her uttermost cunning is employed, and know whether she have brought forth so true a lover as Theagenes—so constant a friend as Pylades—so valiant a man as Orlando—so right a prince as Xenophon's Cyrus, and so excellent a man every way as Virgil's Æneas?" He gives the derivation of the name, meaning, Maker or Creator, the highest of titles. He insists upon the philosophical doctrine now settled by Coleridge and Hazlitt, that the truth of poetic fiction is a wide and general verity, transcending the truth of common understandings—that feigned histories may contain more of philosophical probability than literal narratives; as Fielding used to say of the pompous writers of history, in comparison with his own inimitable pictures of real life, that in their works only the names and dates were true, whereas in his fictions all was true but the names and dates. All the purely didactic and critical portions of the Defense have now become trite from frequent repetition, such as that rhyme does not constitute the difference between poetry and prose, though an admirable adjunct; and the division of the several varieties of poetry, with a critical and enthusiastic commentary upon each.

We pass to his satirical picture of the moral philosopher, with his array of prejudice and pretension, and his comparison of the poet with him and the historian—the one giving precepts by the hour, and the other examples by the volume. Both pompous, proud, disputatious; neither of them reaching the heart nor moving the affections. Sidney rightly considers poetry to be the highest philosophy: he slights it not as a light, gay artifice of pleasure, but reverences it as the most spiritual art, the divinest form of letters. He urges the thesis of the poet as "the right popular philosopher," teaching not in a direct, set manner, but by implication and inference; investing life with the lessons of experience, animating the stage by scenes of deep tragic passion, or by keen satirical comic ridicule:—substituting Macbeth for an essay upon ambition, and Othello instead of a lecture upon jealousy. He regards poetry as involving the teachings of philosophy, as the greater includes the less, or as Campbell has elegantly expressed a similar doctrine:

"Oh deem not midst this worldly strife,
An idle art the poet brings,
Let high philosophy control,
And sages calm the stream of life,
'Tis he refines its fountain springs,
The nobler passions of the soul."

Our author quotes Aristotle, who, with all his devotion to method and science, determined poetry to be more philosophical, and more than history, as dealing with universal truth, and instinct with a living power. We agree entirely with Owen Felltham, who wrote, "I think a grave poem the deepest kind of writing!" Such poetry is beyond any philosophy, scientifically so named.

We now arrive at a summary of the character of the poet, by one who was himself of the craft:—

"Now, therein of all sciences, I speak still of human, and, according to the human concert, is our poet the monarch. For he doth not only shew the way, but giveth so sweet a prospect into the way, as will entice any man to enter into it. Nay, he doth, as if your journey should lie through a fair vineyard, at the very first, give you a cluster of grapes, that full of that taste, you may long to pass farther. He beginneth not with obscure definitions, which must blur the margent with interpretations, and load the memory with doubtfulness; but he cometh to you with words set in delightful proportion, either accompanied with, or prepared for the well-enchanting skill of musick, and with *with a tale, forsooth, he cometh unto you with a tale, which holdeth children from play, and old men from the chimney corner;* and pretending no more, doth intend the winning of the mind from wickedness to virtue; even as the child is often brought to take most wholesome things by hiding them in such other as have a pleasant taste; which if one should begin to tell them the name of the aloes or rheubarum they should receive, would sooner take their physic at their ears, than at their mouth; so is it in men, (most of which are childish in the best things till they be cradled in their graves,) glad they will be to hear the tales of Hercules, Achilles, Æneas, Cyrus, and hearing them, must needs hear the right description of wisdom, valor and justice; which, if they had been barely (that is to say, philosophically) set out, they would swear they be brought to school again. That imitation whereof poetry is, both the most convincing to nature of all other, insomuch that, as Aristotle saith, those things which in themselves are horrible, as cruel battles, unnatural monsters, are made in poetical imitation delightful. Truly I have known men, that even with reading Amadis de Gaul, which God knoweth, wanteth much of a perfect poesy, have found their hearts moved to the exercise of courtesy, liberality, and especially courage. Who readeth Æneas carrying old Anchisis on his back, that wished not it were his fortune to perform so excellent an act?"

And, of the influence of poetry upon himself, Sidney confesses in that oft-repeated sentence:—

"Certainly I must confess mine own barbarousness; I never heard the old song of Piercy and Douglass, that I found not my heart moved more than with a trumpet: and yet it is sung but by some blind crowder, with no rougher voice than rude stile."

A powerful argument of the noble, original and wonderful efficacy of true poetry, is to be found in the frequent use of fable and allegory in the Holy Scriptures, and especially by our Saviour himself. The beautiful parables of the New Testament contain the noblest moral lessons, and as narratives, are perfect in form and detail, full of a sweet pathetic sentiment, and of a friendly, expostulating eloquence. This brings us to a consideration we are prone to indulge in of the religious tone of all really fine poetry, whether it be dovotional, chivalric or moral. We have so frequently remarked upon this characteristic, as to believe it unnecessary to repeat the same reflections which must sooner or later be made by every diligent wooer of the muse.

We are now more than half way through the Essay. The remainder is chiefly occupied with replies to the various objections renewed from age to age, and by the weak, the malicious, the low and the ignorant, against the art of arts, the *prima philosophia*, the Harp of David, the Song of Solomon. The general, and the largest class of objectors are those who abuse everything that is good, and praised by others; those who hated Aristides for his justice, and Washington for his patriotism; those who could see nought but design in the most disinterested charity, and suspected self-interest in the wisest patriotism. In the same class he ranks railing wits, who delight to turn everything into ridicule,—(themselves too contemptible for less than the severest sarcasm.) The special objections to poetry he notices in turn;—that there are worthier walks of learning:—that it is the mother of lies:—by its softness enervates the soul, and by a copious lascivious fancy fills the mind with vicious phantasies; and, as a *fourth* objection, he repeats the old cry of Plato's banishing poets out of his republic. To these, he offers the following replies;—to the first, that it begs the question, and utterly denies that there is sprung out of the earth a more fruitful knowledge. The answer to the second, is contained in a defence of the *vraisemblance* of the poet's fable. The third objection, he admits, has some force; but then it is by the way; the incidental lapses of bad or wicked poets hurts not good poetry, any more than vice hurts the essential beauty of virtue. It may affect partially, and for a time, the character, but it does not affect the thing itself. As to the fourth objection, Plato did not depreciate fine poetry, but lascivous strains. He was himself a poet, and in his own person honored the muse. He was too religious to allow infidel rhymers (of which modern times is not wanting in parellels) to vent their impious blasphemies. He might have excluded Byron: but there is no question he would have received Wordsworth with open arms.

After an enumeration of patrons and favorers of poetry among the great and good, the wise and powerful, kings, nobles, senators, cardinals, philosophers, wits, orators, and statesmen, he proceeds to the discussion of some still mooted points;—*i. e.*, whether tragedy should be on the Grecian and modern French mode, free from any mixture of comedy, or whether like Shakspeare's dramas, it should partake of both? Such points as respect the unities are closely scrutinized, and even humorously satirized, wherein he appears to glance at Shakspeare, or at least, at his predecessors. There is a very nice and discriminating passage on laughter, which we would quote but for its length. The antithesis in this section may be regarded as a type of Johnson's style, in the use of this figure. Much sensible criticism is expended on diction, with lively raillery on the current euphuisms of the time. A liberal eulogy follows, on the English tongue, and the piece concludes with a page of rhetoric worthy of the subject and of the writer, clear, copious, insinuating and harmonious; a passage such as you often find the like of in the writers of the age of Elizabeth, and afterwards in the reigns of the first two Stuarts; but very rarely in the present day, or since that glorious era:

"So that since the ever praiseworthy poesy is full of virtue, breeding, delightfulness, and void of no gift that ought to be in the noble name of learning; since the blames laid against it are either false or feeble; since the cause why it is not esteemed in England, is the fault of poet-asses, not of poets; since, lastly, our tongue is most fit to be honored by poesy;—I conjure you all that have had the evil luck to read into this wasting toy of mine, even in the name of the nine muses, no more to scorn the sacred mysteries of poesy; no more to laugh at the name of poets as though they were next inheritors to fools; no more to jest at the reverend title of 'rhymer,' but to believe with Aristotle, that they were the ancient treasures of the Grecian's divinity; to believe with Bembus, that they were the first bringers in of all civility; to believe with Scaliger, that no philosopher's precepts can sooner make you an honest man than the reading of Virgil; to believe with Clauserus, the translator of Cornutu, that it pleased the heavenly Deity by Hesiod and Homer, under the veil of fables, to give us all knowledge, logic, rhetoric, philosophy natural and moral, and *quid non?* To believe with me, that there are many mysteries contained in poetry, which of purpose were written darkly, lest by profane wits it should be abused; to believe with Landui, that they are so beloved by the gods, that whatsoever they write proceeds of a divine fury; lastly, to believe themselves when they tell you they will make you immortal by their verses.

"Thus doing, your names shall flourish in the printers' shops: thus doing, you shall be of kin to many a poetical preface: thus doing, you shall be most fair, most rich, most wise, most all—you shall dwell upon superlatives: thus doing, though you be *libertino patronatus*, you shall suddenly grow *Herculea proles:*

'*Si quid mea carmine possunt.*'

Thus doing, your soul shall he placed with Dante's Beatrix, or Virgil's Anchisis. But if (fie for such a but!) you be born so near the dull-making Cataract of Nilus, that you cannot hear the planet-like music of poetry; if you have so earth-creeping a mind that it cannot lift itself up to look at the sky of poetry, or rather by a certain rustical disdain, will become such a mome, as to wish to be a momus of poetry, then, though I will not wish unto you the ass's ears of Midas, nor be driven by a poet's verses as Bubonax was, to hang himself; nor to be rhymed to death, as is said to be done in Ireland; yet thus much curse I must lend you in the behalf of all poets,—that while you live, you live in love, and never get favor, for lacking skill of a sonnet; and when you die, your memory die from the earth for want of an epitaph.

XII.

BURTON'S "ANATOMY OF MELANCHOLY."

The Anatomy of Melancholy is a book oftener mentioned than read, and upon the subject of which it is easier to write than upon the treatise itself. Connected criticism is out of the question, on account of the variety of the topics and the mosaic character of the text: to say nothing of the tedious diffuseness, (an extravagance in point of copiousness,) the harsh, crabbed accumulation of images and scholastic references, and the half medical, half metaphysical style of execution. Some stupid old physician placed this among the volumes "without which no medical man's library is complete." And it is so frequently entitled and ranked in booksellers' catalogues. Neither is it wholly a work of humor or the production of pure wit. It is not a burlesque, but a serious essay of rising seven hundred folio pages. But its chief character is a total want of decided character. It is a medley, a common-place book, a hodge-podge, a complete farrago. He touches, incidentally or purposely, upon almost every object under the sun and upon the face of the earth, things known and things unknown, dogmas and mere speculations, medicine and magic, anatomy and the arts, devils and diet, love and madness, religion and superstitious folly. Not a poet or historian, critic or commentator, naturalist or divine, of antiquity, of modern times, or of the middle age, but is called upon the stand as a witness, and requested to bear his testimony to the author's theories or counsel. A whole sentence of plain English occurs rarely. The usual style is a mixed manner, English cut on Latin, or an interlacing of the two. Half a passage in one language is balanced by the remaining portion in another, and one member nods to another, as Pope's groves and alleys. Never was a book so made up of quotation and reference. Montaigne used to say, if all his quotations were taken from him, nothing valuable would be left; a similar abstraction from Burton would leave him pretty bare, as his best passages are translations or imitations of rare old writers. This leads to an unnecessary fullness and repetition; and, indeed the whole matter might be reduced into one-third its present compass. From but a superficial knowledge of the works, we should suspect it to be tinged with the prevalent defects in two other celebrated treatises, the one political and the other metaphysical: we refer to "Grotius de Jure Belli et Pacis," and "Cudworth's Intellectual System," both of them works always alluded to with respect but very seldom familiarly read. And however it may astonish a vulgar reader, this fertility of quotation argues an innate deficiency of original power. A good cause or a sound judgment needs few witnesses and no propitiating patrons. A clear eye needs no spectacles to see through, and the unaided vision of good natural sight is blurred by the speckled glasses of prejudice and traditionary opinion. The learning, then, of this curious treatise, together with its length and perversely ingenious tautology; its jumble of phrases and ideas, realizing the witty strictures of Hudibras; the endless digresssions, and want of condensed, methodical argument, render it a work that will be sought after chiefly for its oddity and fantastic strangeness. It cannot ever reach popularity, and is indeed written only for antiquarian scholars. Lamb, himself the true lover and warm eulogist of the Anatomy, admitted this fact, nor can it be concealed that even liberal and philosophic students care for little else than a taste of it, a glimpse of its index and a few particular references—a mere sip at this Lethean stream.

We feel constrained to this confession at the risk of losing caste in the eyes of those who make no distinction among the writers of our elder literature. Yet we add, "Can these dry bones live?" Is a witty or eloquent description, buried under a long chapter of heterogeneous matter, to save that from decay? There is salt to preserve, but too little of it we apprehend. Ourselves, retrospective critics, we must admit we find not sufficient in Burton to reward a thorough perusal (if, indeed, any man but Lamb ever read it entirely through.) Johnson's criticism cannot be taken for a standard in this instance, since it proved so unequal and deficient in former cases. Sterne used the book well, but then for thievish purposes, which Dr. Ferriar has tracked with remorseless scrutiny.

And here lies its value, as a mine of thoughts—original, borrowed, imitated, and palpably exposed to view, in their crude state, and which a skilful plagiarist, one who can steal wisely, may work up to great advantage. For the systematic plagiarist, then, and the mere antiquary, Burton is a choice author, and for the reasons we have enumerated. Still, even to the most indifferent reader we can promise, that though discursive, Burton still possesses a method of his own and a plan ; that his matter is almost as copious as his style : both superabundant ; and that, unfinished, Latinized, and corrupt as is his ordinary composition, yet when especially in earnest, he is a writer of racy and idiomatic English. We love in him a true sympathy with the life, and pursuits, and character, of that strangely misconceived animal, the scholar. We admire his natural acuteness, visible through all his erudition, and a vein of caustic, homely, rustic humor. Above all, we respect in his case, as in that of all true scholars, that manly dignity of soul which is the most invaluable possession of humanity.

Little is known of the author of the Anatomy of Melancholy. He was a man of learning, and disposed to gloomy fits and desponding humors. To drive away these, he resorted to the writing of this work, which occupation, filling and occupying his mind, (the true cure for nervous diseases, hypochondria, and all affections by which the mind infects the body with aches and ills,) tended greatly to relieve him. He was accustomed, we learn, to frequent the docks and wharves about London, and would break jests with the watermen, enjoying highly their uncouth smartness. He had the wisdom to endeavor at counteracting his distemper by every occasion of jollity and laughter. When he adopted the name and title of Democritus, he assumed his proper designation of Merry Philosopher, whose creed was to laugh at the follies of mankind and jest at his own sufferings, feeling tenderly for those of others. Like the Italian jester, he made sport for others whilst tortured by nameless ills himself, and might now be condemned, as sufficient punishment for all the evil it is likely he was ever guilty of to read his book continuously through, word for word.

The Anatomy of Melancholy deserves this praise at least, that it is thorough and minute. The very heart of the matter is explored, and its *internal* system. The thousand causes and correspondent cures of hypochondria are enumerated and classified in three *partitions*. The first partition relates to the different *causes* of melancholy, physical and metaphysical; moral and religious; considered as diseases of the body, or diseases of the mind, or both, reacting on each other; induced by the operations of Nature, or inflicted by the hand of God, or consigned to the malicious employment of the devil and his spirits; the creature of temperament, the companion of sickness, the attendant upon age. It explains how it is begotten in infancy, (if not inherited,) through the careless treatment of nurses or the harsh behavior of parents; how it is caught from gloomy sights and infectious mourning. Its natural as well as moral history is investigated, whether it arise from scorn or calumny, servitude or want; whether produced by loss of friends, loss of health, loss of liberty, loss of reputation, or loss of property. It is more specifically derived from the indulgence of the passions of anger, fear, shame, rage, hatred, sorrow, discontent: or from excess in the gratification of laudable propensities, as the desire of glory, the accumulation of substance, manly pride, a temper disposed to enjoyment, the love of books and study, a disposition for repose and retirement. We may here introduce that fine passage on the poor scholar, which is one of the very best to be met with in the whole work. It is a sort of apologetic eulogium:

"Because they cannot ride an horse, which every clowne can doe; salute and court a gentlewoman, carve at a table, cringe and make congies, which every common swasher can doe, *hos populus ridet*, &c., they are laughed to scorne, and accompted silly fooles by our gallants. Yea, many times such is their misery they deserve it: a meere scholler, a meere asse.—They goe about commonly meditating unto themselves, thus they sit, such is their action and gesture. *Fulgosus*, lib. 8, chap. 7, makes mention how Th. Aquinas, supping with King Louis of France, upon a sudden knocked his fist upon the table and cryed, '*conclusum est contra Manichæos*,' his wits were a wool-gathering, as they say, and his head busied about other matters, when he perceived his error, he was much abashed. Such a story there is of Archimedes in Vitruvius, that having fouud how much gold was mingled with the silver in King Hieron's crown, ran naked forth of the bath and cryed, *Eureka*, I have found: and was commonly so inteut to his studies, that he never perceived what was done about him, when the city was taken, and the soldiers were ready to rifle his house, he took no notice of it. S. Bernard rode all day long by the Lemnian lake, and asked at last where he was. (*Marcullus*, lib. 2, chap. 4.) It was Democritus' carriage alone that made the Abderites suppose him to have been mad, and send for Hippocrates to cure him: if he had been in any solemne company, hee would upon all occasions fall a laughing. Theophrastus saith as much of Heraclitus, for that he continually wept, and Laertius of Menedemus Lampsacus, because he ran about like a madman, saying he came from hell as a spy, to tell the divells what mortal men did. Your greatest students are commonly no better, silly, soft fellowes in their outward behaviour, absurd, ridiculous to others, and no whit experienced in worldly business: they can measure the heavens, range over the world, teach others wisdome, and yet in bargains and contracts they are circumvented by every base tradesman. Are not these men fooles? And how should they be otherwise? But as so many sots in schooles, when, (as has been observed) they neither hear nor see such things as are practised abroad, how should they get experience, by what means? I knew in my time many schollers, saith Eneas Sylvius, (in an Epistle of his to Gaspar Sciticke Chancelour to the Emperour,) excellent well learned, but so rude, so silly, that they had no common civility, nor knew how to manage their domestique or publique affaires. Paglaresis was amazed, and said his farmer had surely cozened him, when hee heard him tell that his sow had eleven pigges, and his ass but one foal. To say the best of this profession, I can give no other testimony of them in generall, than that of Pliny of Isæus;—'*Hee is yet a scholler, than which kind of men, there is nothing so simple, so sincere, none better, they are for the most part harmless, honest, upright, innocent, plain-dealing men.*"

The second partition is occupied with the cures of melancholy. By magic, by company, by music:

"In sweet music is such Art;
Killing care and grief of heart."

Consolatory devices, the remedies of the Materia Medica and of surgical skill, air, and the numberless fantastic prescriptions Bacon and Sir Kenelm Digby advise, and all the old writers, traditional, fabulous and poetical. As might naturally be supposed, this head includes much good sense, with abundance of absurdity and nonsenses, set forth with no little pomp of reference and allusion.

The third partition is devoted entirely to the consideration of love melancholy, and religious melancholy. Here, our author ranges at will in the boundless field of quotation and theory. He is far more minute than Shakspeare, who has described but a few prominent characteristics of this disease:—"The scholar's melancholy, which is emulation; the musician's, which is fantastical; the courtier's, which is fraud; the soldier's, which is ambitious; the lawyer's, which is politic; the lady's, which is nice; the lover's, which is all of these." Every symptom of affection, or love-sickness, or frenzy, or jealousy, or disappointment; all the marks of superstition, remorse, hopelessness and despair are noted down with mathematical particularity.

Among a variety of topics, it is hard to select an example, but we have chanced upon this, of *artificial allurements*, and transcribe it:

"When you have all done, 'veniunt a veste sagittæ,—the greatest provocations of lust are from our apparell.' 'God makes, man shapes,' they say, and there is no motive like unto it; a filthy knave, a deformed queane, a crooked carcass, a maukin, a witch, a rotten post, an hedge stake, may be so set out and tricked up, that shall make as faire a show, as much enamour, as the rest: many a silly fellow is so taken. 'Primum luxuriæ aucupium' one calls it, 'the first snare of lust.' *Bossus* 'aucupium animarum; lethalem arundinem,—a fatell reede, the greatest bawde;' 'forte lenocinium, sanguienis lachyrmis deplorandum,' saith Matenesius, and with tears of blood to be deplored! Not that comeliness of clothes is therefore to be condemned, and those usual ornaments; there is a decency and decorum to be observed in this, as well as in other things, fit to be used, becoming severall persons, and befitting their estates; he is only fantastical, that is not in fashion, and like an old image in Arras hangings, where a manner of attire is generally received; but when they are so new-fangled, so unstaid, so prodigious in their attires beyond their means and fortunes, unbefitting their age, place, quality, condition, what should we otherwise think of them? Why do they adorne themselves with so many colours of hearbes, fictitious flowers, curious needle-works, quaint devices. sweet smelling odors, with those inestimable riches of pretious stones, pearles, rubies, diamonds, emeralds, &c. Why doe they crowne themselves with golde and silver, use coronets and ties of severall fashions, decke themselves with pendants, bracelets, eare-rings, chaines, girdles, rings, prunes, spangles, embroideries, shadows, rebatoes, versicolor ribands; why doe they make such glorious shows with their scarfs, feathers, fannes, maskes, furres, laces, tiffanies, ruffles, falls, calls, cuffs, damasks, velvets, tinsels, cloth of gold, silver, tissue? with colors of heavens, stars, planets, the strength of metalls, stones, odors, flowers, birds, beasts, fishes, and whatever Afrike, Asia, America, sea, land, art and industry can afford? Why doe they use and covet such novelty of inventions; such new-fangled types, and spend such inestimable sums on them? To what end are those crisped, false haires, painted faces, as the satyrist observes, such a composed gait, not a step awry? Why are they like so many Sybarites, or Neroe's Poppæa, Assuerus' concubines, so long a dressing, as Cæsar was marshalling his army, or an hawke in pruning? Dum moliuntur, dum comuntur annus est. A gardiner takes not so much paines in his garden, an horseman to dress his horse, scour his armor, a mariner about his ship, a merchant his shop and shop booke, as they doe about their faces, and those other parts; such setting up with corkes, streigthening with whalebone; why is it but as a day-net catcheth larkes to make young men stoupe unto them."

Burton concludes this complete map of the region Hypochondria, with his excursions into every quarter of it, by these words of mark and wisdom: "*Bee not solitary, bee not idle.*" To which Johnson pertinently added, clenching the point: *but if solitary, be not idle; and if idle, be not solitary.* Sagacious Quarles discriminates justly: "Let not the sweetness of contemplation be so esteemed, that action be despised; Rachel was more faire, Leah more fruitful; as contemplation is more delightful, so is it more dangerous. Lot was upright in the city, but wicked in the mountaine."

The portion of the volume with which we have been most gratified, is the Preface, or Democritus to the reader. It is personal and characteristic. The poetical abstract prefixed to the preface is very smooth and neatly turned. But the finest thing ever written upon melancholia, containing the romance and essence of the subject, is unquestionably that perfect poem, the Penseroso of Milton. Almost equally fine are the following beautiful lines from a play of Beaumont and Fletcher.

Hence, all you vain delights,
As short as are the nights,
Wherein you spend your folly!
There's nought in this life's sweete,
If man were wise to see't
But only melancholy;
Oh, sweetest melancholy!
Welcome folded arms, and fixed eyes,
A sigh that piercing mortifies,
A look that's fastened to the ground,
A tongue chained up, without a sound!

Fountain heads and pathless groves,
Places which pale passion loves!
Moonlight walks where all the fowls,
Are warmly housed, save bats and owls!
A midnight bell, a parting groan!
These are the sounds we feed upon;
Then stretch our bones in a still gloomy valley:
Nothing's so dainty sweet as lovely melancholy.

These dainty lines leave a sweet relish behind them: after reading which, the reader will acknowledge the prudence of an immediate conclusion.

XIII.

MEMOIRS OF LADY FANSHAW,

WRITTEN BY HERSELF.

As a true wife, a kind but judicious mother, as a woman of wit and spirit, no less than of feminine softness and modest beauty, the life and conduct of Lady Fanshaw, in a corrupt age and in troubled times, is one of the most pleasing and one of the most useful narratives of the olden time. The memoirs of Lady Fanshaw were written for the instruction and entertainment of her son; and, like the conversation of a wise old man, rich in experience and tempered by trials, it abounds with practical lessons of familiar morality, and inculcates everywhere a high tone of principle. Sir Richard Fanshaw, her husband, who was chiefly known as ambassador to the Court of Spain in the reign of Charles II., had also been a devoted public servant of the first Charles; and, during the protectorate of Cromwell, whilst in England, managed to obtain the respect of Cromwell, (who tried all means to buy him over to himself), and to preserve his loyalty to his sovereign, whom he constantly attended on the continent after retiring from England. Sir Richard was one of the very few honest courtiers and able men in the service of Charles II., whose court and government was encircled by a set of witty rascals and heartless flatterers. In such a sphere, Sir Richard was out of place; his honesty suited not the office, and he was, after all his genuine merit and undoubted services, politely dropped. To the evil influences of Clarendon, (another honest and great man), the lady attributed the misfortunes of her husband. She suspected a very probable jealousy on the part of the chancellor, who, with his great qualities, had that defect of disposition. The lives of this faithful pair were of the most chequered grain. At one time almost penniless, at another living like viceroys; now in want, proscribed, and under apprehension of death; again rich, flourishing, courted, and happy. But in all adversity, as in the brightest sunshine of fortune, ever constant, forbearing, and hopeful. The husband was a statesman of the best description, learned, (beyond the ordinary acquisitions of his equals in rank,) a great traveller, (who had gained much knowledge thereby), an accomplished gentlemen, down to the minutest formalities of the Spanish court, and yet no mere courtier; with a dash of the author, very expert and clever in diplomacy, and a practical Christian moralist in all his dealings and conversation.

The volume is, in almost equal parts, a biography of her husband, including the events of contemporary history, a description of her travels, an account of herself, and a miscellany of curious matters of fact. Under this last head would come the narrative of a singular trance, in which the mother of our heroine lay for two days; a good old-fashioned ghost story, the scene of which is laid in Ireland, and a fearful instance of the righteous providence of the Almighty in a case of incest and blasphemy. The relation of the principal events of the lives of Lady Fanshaw and Sir Richard, afford genuine materials for history. She describes a very affecting interview between her husband and Charles I., who loved him as a friend, and always addressed him familiarly as Dick Fanshaw. The plague in London and the horrors of the civil war are told with remarkable distinctness. Then a gayer scene, the Restoration, and the embassy to Spain.

Considered in part as a book of travels, the memoirs are full of pleasing sketches and descriptions, that might rank above that criticism. Among these are pictures of the chief places she saw in Spain and Portugal; of which the account of the Alhambra is circumstantial, and as picturesque as that building is magnificent. Washington Irving might have taken it for his motto to the delightful volumes he published under the same title.

But the charm of the book consists mainly in the engaging *naivete* and exhibition of personal character. Clevei as a writer, cleverer as a woman on the great stage of the world, it is as a faithful and affectionate wife and mother that Lady Fanshaw is best entitled to our regard, and even admiration. Instances are abundant and confirmatory of this character. At sea, with her husband, and the vessel attacked with pirates, she had been locked up by the captain, but bribed the cabin-boy to let her out and give her his coat and tarpaulin, dressed and disguised with which she "crept up softly to her husband's side, as free from sickness and fear as, I confess, from discretion; but it was the effect of that passion which I could never master."

When Sir Richard, as a "malignant," was imprisoned, his wife thus relates: "I failed not constantly to go, when the clock struck four in the morning, with a dark lantern in my hand, all alone and on foot, from my lodging in Chancery-lane, at my cousin Young's to Whitehall, in at the entry that went out of King street, into the bowling green. There I would go under his window and softly call him; he, after the first time excepted, never failed to put out his head at the first call. Thus we talked together; and sometimes I was so wet with rain, that it went in at my neck and out at my heels." The story of her procuring a pass to join her husband, when separated by the fortune of war, is a lively example of what a woman can by stratagem do at a pinch, but is too long to be inserted. Sir Richard knew the value of this admirable woman, who materially served him as a banker and agent, as well as in all the duties of a good wife. Often she went to raise money for him ; often played the diplomatist to serve his purposes. In both characters she was invariably successful, having wit, beauty, and accomplishments to set off her devotion, sense, and discretion.

Among the less remarkable traits of the memoirs are the genuine relish this fine woman took in two very opposite gratifications—in good living, and pomp and ceremony. She betrays an innate female love of dress and show, and occupies several pages with a minute detail of her appearance, and that of her husband, on public occasions. Court shows and ceremonies she recounts, with equal pleasure, and yet she is always remarking how much her husband and herself preferred a quiet retreat in the country, to the bustle, and crowd, and envy, and heartburning of a life passed at the court. As to her honest liking for the good things of this life, she never stops at a town or describes a country without a particular and minute inventory of its delicious products and artificial luxuries. These little exhibitions of an every-day sort let us into the real character, and are not to be neglected. Who does not love Dr. Johnson for his thousand-and-one peculiarities, especially for his partialities in eating. The anecdote of Milton praising his wife for the well-cooked dish, is grateful to us. Nor should we forget that Wordsworth was at one period, and is perhaps now, fond of cheese, and that Lamb has recorded his exquisite relish of roast pig. The man that would sneer at these trifling memoranda may be a very useful, but certainly not a very companiable, specimen of his species.

XIV.

THE SPIRITUAL QUIXOTE.

THIS is a very lively, and no less edifying, old-fashioned religious satire, directed against the extravagances of Methodism, just then coming into vogue, by the Rev. Richard Graves, a sensible divine of the last century, a man of wide and acute observation, and a humorous writer of no mean scope and abilities. The work is thrown into the form of a novel, in all probability to attract general readers ; and, apart from the palpable hits the author is continually making, it is full of adventure and reflection, a fair picture of the manners of the day, and the current fashionable follies of the time. It is interspersed with cleverly drawn characters, real and fictitious ; and altogether, to employ a common phrase, deserves to be much better known than it is.

It is modelled in a very distant manner, on the romance of Cervantes. The hero, Mr. Geoffrey Wildgoose, is the expectant heir of a genteel estate, and the only child of a widow lady residing in the country. After having gone through a regular university education, he comes home to represent the family in his own person. But soon after this, the young squire, conceiving a pique against the parson of his parish, who had got the better of him in a theological discussion, betakes himself to the systematic study of that swarm of sectaries and dissenting authors who flourished in England during the Protectorate, and which have not yet become extinct. Having pursued this line of study for some months, the operation of puritanical principles inclined his mind to the reception of Methodism, a lately published doctrine, and he forthwith embraced its doctrines with peculiar ardor. After trying his hand in discussions of a religious character with the lower class in his neighborhood, who were proud to be ranked among his disciples and followers, and by whom he was never once contradicted, (this silent flattery confirming his conceit,) and *giving the word*, on several occasions, to limited assemblies, he at last began to conceive the idea that he was called to the work of the ministry. Prepared (as he imagined he was) by personal experience of the power of faith and the working of grace in the soul. and still more, stimulated by a perusal of the journals of Wesley and Whitfield, our knight commenced itinerant, and for a summer footed it over the kingdom. What occurred during this period of time, occupies the major portion of this ingenious history.

Happily, his field preaching proved not so successful as his zeal had inspired him to expect, and he finally relinquishes his scheme and returns to the society of his family, re-embracing the doctrines and discipline of the Church into which he had been baptized.

His attendant, or squire, (a knight is nothing without a squire,) Jeremiah Tugwell, like Sancho Panza, is a shrewd fellow, and a great lover of good cheer. His idea of Heaven seems to have been, if we may judge from his literal interpretation of his master's spiritual allegories, that of a first rate ordinary, free to all comers. Not a chapter passes off without some mention of his hearty relish of creature comforts. He is a cobbler by trade, past middle life, and induced, by a strange mixture of motives, to follow Wildgoose; policy, perhaps, predominating. Yet he, too, has a vein of spiritual presumption, and expects to mend souls as he would patch shoes; one of that class, in a word, whom South has so admirably satirized in his sermon on the Christian Pentecost.

The Spanish Don was not more misguided by enthusiasm, made no more signal blunders, in his knight-errantry, than did our spiritual knight in his attempts to convert the world. Uniformly he is beaten off the ground, whether it be at the race-course or the fair. He is heard with applause, in the private conventicles of his own sect, but makes no proselytes out of it. He is heard with civil contempt in the drawing-room, which is suppressed in the servants' hall. A love adventure divides his attention with the concerns of the spiritual man, and he is continually engaged in a strife between the flesh and the spirit. The leading idea in the mind of Wildgoose, is the conversion of souls: that is his first object, in every company and under all circumstances. The leading idea in the mind, or rather stomach, of his follower is, a perpetual stuffing himself; and a thirstier soul never yet appeared as bottle-holder to any theological pugilist.

Many living characters of note are introduced in the course of this work; Wesley, and Whitfield; Beau Nash, and Shenstone the poet; Lady Lyttleton, etc. All of the portraits executed with spirit. Like the good old Novels, the history is full of episodes: there are the private histories of Mrs. Booby and Miss Townsend, Capt. Johnson and the poor tinker, and Mr. Rivers—capital pictures of an antiquary, a Welsh parson, a quack Doctor, and a hypochondriac. The two last are irresistibly comic. Not less humorous are the scenes where Wildgoose is consulted on several points of casuistry, and the scrapes he is continually involved in at taverns. There are two or three chapters of a rather warm description, and verging on coarseness. In general, notwithstanding, the humor is as pure as it is caustic, and the satire vigorous and well applied.

It is impossible to convey a fair impression of the book by

occasional extracts ; so we will advise, at once, a perusal of it, which will well reward a judicious reader. This novel, with Southey's life of Wesley, will give one a pretty accurate view of the two sides of Methodism ; in which sect there is much to praise, and a good deal to censure.

It is open to censure, among other reasons, for its sectarian spirit, to say nothing of its presumption in dissent. The distinguishing beauty of the Church, is its liberal tolerance of mere diversities of opinion, and in its including the elements of *all true* theological doctrine. Now, the Methodists, Baptists, etc., select some one or more dogmas of faith or practice, and pamper that, or them, out into an exclusive system, making the whole of Christianity to consist in but a portion of Christian doctrine. They slight other and more valuable truths, perhaps, to give prominence to one. The first Methodists were only stricter Episcopalians, endeavoring to revive a primitive simplicity of life, and corresponding purity of faith. But in the body of the Church they left, were to be found sincere, good, and wise men, seeking the same object, and only differing from them, in possessing greater prudential sagacity, and a truer, because less exacting and less arrogant piety. Pride and stubbornnesss led to a separation, most causeless reasons for dissent.

Even now, the Methodists can return to the bosom of the Church with a better grace than any other class of dissenters, for they have borrowed the Episcopal office, and we understand sometimes employ part of the Liturgy.

The leading doctrine of those who followed Whitfield in preference to Wesley ; of the party that held of faith, not only as superior to, but as independent of, outward actions, altogether ; which teaching, not only refrained from making a merit of works, but even did not sufficiently insist on the necessity of works as fruits of the Spirit, is often placed in a ridiculous light in the Spiritual Quixote. This division among the Methodists, (we know not to what extent it now exists,) affords of itself, a fact sufficient to warrant a prophecy of their final extinction. Dissenting sects, if not perfectly united among themselves, must fall to pieces, since they want a conservative principle of union. It is so with the Unitarians, every preacher of which denomination frames a creed of his own. It is so with the Quakers, and Presbyterians, and Baptists, who are divided into parties numberless. So, in all probability, it will be with the Methodists. And so, we trust, in time it may come to pass, that they too, may be gathered into the Church, and again united, one fold under one shepherd.

With all their extravagances, the absurdity of some members and the wickedness of others, Methodism may point to many brilliant exemplars of piety and talent united. But we have laid most stress on the corrupt parts of the system, as there is no fear that the really good portion will be overlooked by candid inquirers.

Apart from the soundness of the theological opinions advanced in the Spiritual Quixote, it is impressed with a deep, though simple moral lesson. The hero, after his extravagances and follies, finally settles down into a rational and sincere Christian, with an enlightened zeal and a spirit of liberal piety. The tendency of the work is most decidedly on the side of virtue and religion, though we fear occasional scenes may mar its real value, and lead an idle reader to regard it as a work of mere entertainment, without any idea of its admirable end, in point of religious instruction. For our own part, we can praise it highly for both qualities, neither of which is more inimical to the other, than a hearty laugh and cheerful spirit are adverse to the possession of the warmest heart, or the living up to the strictest principles.

XV.

SATIRE AND SENTIMENT.

Satire and sentiment represent the extreme opposite poles of conversation and authorship; the tendency of the first being to bitterness, and of the second, to affectation. The love of scandalous gossip is the offspring and bond of fashionable society, as weak sentimentality results from an unnatural refinement of the feelings. In their natural and healthy state, both of these faculties are of the utmost importance to society as well as to individuals; but we oftener find the instinctive appetite for both depraved, rather than indulged to a proper and satisfactory limit. As the virtue of censure may soon become debased into the vice of lampoon, and delicate generosity gradually descend into ephemeral sensibility, some line of distinction appears necessary to mark the province of each.

Honest satire, from a writer or speaker of worth, provoked by meanness or inflamed by dishonesty, serves as one of the strongest checks upon folly and crime. Without it, the world would run mad. Next to religion, it offers the surest moral restraint on the absurd conceits and wild passions of man. Nay, many who affect to despise religion dread the sharp pen of the satirist, when he has truth and justice on his side. Even the virtuous who are not endued with strength of will or intellectual courage, are too often deterred from praiseworthy actions by the dread of personal ridicule. Pope says of himself as a satirist—and the world has never seen a better—that they who feared not God, were still afraid of him; and this was written without presumption or hastiness. But is satire always honest? Is it so, generally?

We suspect the answer would be decidedly in the negative. Instead of correction of abuses, we meet abuse itself; in place of truth, we hear scandal; for general censure, we read personalities; we find bigotry where we should enlarged views.

The same holds true with regard to sentiment. By dwelling too much on the kind impulses that prompt to friendship and love among equals, and to compassion and assistance towards inferiors in fortune and station, the sensitive part of our natures overlays the practical. We write pathetically or talk like Howard, but refuse the aid common humanity expects us to bestow. Excessive indulgence of feeling paralyzes the active powers, and frequently unfits one, however charitably inclined, for the offices of charity. The moral influence of satire, pursued to more than an ordinary extent and without just intentions, is to embitter the heart. Few satirists have been kind-hearted men. The pen of the satirist is dipt in gall, and his fierce denunciations flow too often from a malicious diposition. Even light, airy ridicule, may come from the depths of a sore and wounded spirit, and of which it may serve as the cloak. Most writers of satire—those eminent chiefly for that peculiar talent—have been disappointed men, or somehow unfortunately placed in the world. A crooked back in Pope, a club-foot in Byron, and even slighter personal defects, have fretted many a noble spirit. Poverty, too, first animated the powers of Johnson, and sustained the keen rebukes of Churchill. Swift's ill success at court, and Walpole's luxurious leisure—the extremes of fortune—soured the one, and rendered the other flippant, cold, and unfeeling. And if we knew the exact personal history of the prominent satirists, we should learn how greatly their intellectual powers were modified by the mischances of life or the uncertainties of fortune. Scorn and scoffing, in turn, react upon the writer and produce ill effects in unhinging the whole harmony of the faculties and affections. The hard heart and the skeptical head, the unbelief in goodness and the triumph over the destruction of even the most criminal, are the natural fruits of this same satirical spirit.

A mere sentimentalist, again, is nearly as bad. His refinements as well as those of the satirist, serve to harden the heart, though in a different and more plausible way. His object is, to make a heart in the head; to change the sensitive into the intellectual part of our nature, and to make reflective ideas stand for genuine emotions. Authors have in this way been guilty to a great degree. How much false pity have not their books engendered! How thoroughly they have managed, by their soft tales of woe, to petrify the affections! Strange paradox, yet a truism. This whining sort of philosophy, in time grows into a levity of character and utter indifference. Objects of compassion are only regarded as objects of speculation, not as objects of charity. They are considered as topics for ingenious lectures, and the boast of analytic skill. A painter looks at a beggar for his picturesqueness, his rags, and colored skin, and forlorn air; the moral anatomist prefers to read an affecting description of him: the philanthropist alone offers him aid as a suffering fellow-creature. Practical benevolence is thus made the test of fine sentiment; all else is little better than an intellectual grace, and the cunning refinement of the elegant courtier.

In conversation, satire bears the palm, as the love of gossip is universal, and, indeed, forms the strongest bond of what is called fashionable society. Take away from that charmed circle its bitterness, its jealousies, its scandalous reports, its mean bickerings, its spirit of scorn, its self-sufficiency, its real emptiness, and what do you leave behind? Abuse well spiced, falsehoods well told, a want of charity handsomely set off, are they not the prime talents of the leaders of fashion? In books, too, nothing passes off so well, now-a-days, as a lively relation of personal history, and the domestic manners of the great vulgar. Sentiment is excluded from the very strictest circles of fashion, as too grave and serious. It cannot—such as it is, for the most part—withstand the attacks of ridicule and ironical eulogium. It takes refuge in the blue-stocking circles; not in the company of real scholars or authors of genius.

Satire is hence more generally appreciable than sentiment, as it appeals to a lower range of faculties, an inferior class of minds. Indignation is a commoner feeling than pity. We hate more heartily—taking the world in general—than we commiserate. Satire is more palpable than sentiment; applies oftener to personal than mental defects; is better gratified with ridicule of dress and manner than with contempt of character or abilities.

Sentiment, the simpler it is the better; satire must be fine to cut deep. A coarse and bitter satirist, who mangles while he "whips" abuses, is a mere butcher; a delicate censor is like a skilful surgeon, who probes the moral gangrene only to heal it the more completely. The finer satire is, the more lasting, though more indirect, its effects. The broader and rougher satire is, the more opposition it provokes, and the less benefit it affords. Elaborate sentiment is harsh and cold. The old ballad writers held this spirit in perfection; they were simple, because natural. The modern parlor poets, the sentimental song writers of the day, are full of frigid conceits and turgid ornaments. Compare Moore with Burns—the last of the old minstrels—and you may see the difference between true feeling and affected emotion. Moore endeavors to create a sensation among his audience; Burns, to touch the heart of the reader or singer. Of the sentimental talker of fashion, Joseph Surface is a fair specimen, eternally moralizing and making reflections upon trivialities. This is the true fashionable pedantry, more contracted than that of the scholar and antiquary.

True sentiment, the offspring of natural feeling and intelligent judgment, is the sure bond of friendship and love, for what is love but the purest and highest of all sentiments? which is only such in its essence, when wholly detached from all thoughts of a sensual description. The highest love is the noblest sentiment—self-denying, exalted, sincere. Next to that sublime emotion, and perhaps more lasting—where really constant at all—is generous friendship, of which, though the longer we live the more incredulous we become, yet which, when we do find it firm, we revere as the noblest passion that can fill the breast of humanity.

As to the requisites for writers in these departments: Satire requires intellectual acuteness; sentiment, refinement and nicety of thought. There is a sentiment of the head—already referred to—current among authors; there is a sentiment of the heart, native to philanthropists. There is a commoner sort still, the sentiment of conversation. To be a witty satirist, requires a keen understanding. To become a tolerable sentimental writer, a goodly quantity of interjections. In books, to be a strong satirist, demands greater force of intellect; to write delicate sentiment calls for ingenuity of perception and delicacy of taste. Sentiment requires an author with a certain effeminacy of thought and style, like Marmontel, who, in his memoirs, confesses the effect of female society and conversation on his writings. Satire, on the other hand, is masculine, and braces the powers of the intellect.

Sentiment is of three kinds: plain, honest, manly, simple —the outbursting of an uncorrupted heart—or, graceful and refined, cultivated by education, elevated by society, purified by religion; or else of that magnificent and swelling character, such as fills the breast of the patriot and the genuine philanthropist. The sentiment of old Izaak Walton—to take examples from books—answers to the first: the sentiment of Mackenzie and Sterne, to the second: the sentiment of Wordsworth, and Burke, and Shakspeare, to the third.

In the character of a complete gentleman, satire should occupy no position of consequence; it should be held subordinate to the higher principles and nobler sentiments. A desire to diminish and ridicule is meaner than the ambition "to elevate and surprise." It is even more agreeable to find eulogy in excess, than censure. A boaster ranks above a tattler, and a vain-glorious fellow is always better received than a carking, contemptible depreciator. Easy, pleasant raillery is not the thing we mean, but a cold, malicious, sneering humor, a turn for degrading and vitiating everything. Sentiment, in its purity, which continually leans to the ideal of perfection, is to be cherished—a remnant of Christian chivalry—as the fit ornament of the accomplished gentleman;—an ornament like that promised in the Book of Proverbs to the good son, "an ornament of grace unto thy head, and chains about thy neck."

XVII.

SUMMER READING.

Hazlitt, in one of his delightful Table Talks, speaks of certain of Hume's lighter miscellaneous Essays as mere "summer reading," in comparison with his Treatise on Human Nature, which he very judiciously calls "a metaphysical choke-pear." The distinction between the two classes of writing may afford a slight distinction between light reading and laborious study, or rather between winter studies and summer reading.

We are far from calling even the least labored and subtle of Hume's speculations, or those of any metaphysician, indeed, properly summer reading. They would rather rank among the studies of that season. By summer reading, we mean generally to express agreeable, pleasant, intellectual entertainment, to be derived from light, graceful, and interesting writers. It is true, that with most readers this summer reading extends over the whole year. That what should be kept for a season of lassitude and comparative indolence, is too often retained throughout the season of labor and study—the winter; the season, as Hunt sings,

> "To which the poet looks,
> For hiving his sweet thoughts and making honeyed books."

But we do not write to those who transpose the seasons, or rather make all seasons alike; like those birds of passage, who, at the close of autumn, leave the north for a more genial region; and unlike those wise and grateful (yet perhaps necessarily robust) natures, who delight in every variety of the seasons—who love the cordial heats of summer, and feel braced by the rough blasts of winter—who admire the fullness and freshness of life in spring, and are delighted with the rich glories and sombre tints of autumn. All pleasures are made equal: the summer morning "with song of earliest birds;" the winter evening by the cheerful fire side; the April showers, and the fine days of October; even the chill blasts of March, and the wintry sky of December.

Summer—"refulgent summer"—the period of repose, the season of early dinners and mid-day or afternoon siestas—of cool morning and evening walks—of iced drinks, and salt baths, and sea-shore breezes, and country visits; it is of this glowing period we write. And what are the books to be read now? Surely nothing difficult, or complex, or intricate, or dry, or subtle. No hard study for us, my masters; give us easy reading—not to be confounded with that which is easily written, whoever, by any means. On this sultry, close day, who would take up Locke, or Hobbes; Milton's prose, or even his poetry? No, we want something gossamer-light, the syllabub, not the *pièces de résistance* of literature. Even fine poetry of the more elevated desciiption is too high. No tragedy for hot weather, except the farce of that name: no epic strain, no ardent Pindarics, or flaming lyrics of love. Nothing that requires much thought or attention: nothing that deeply affects the heart. Banish sentiments, banish imagination; but not gay wit, nor ever-cheerful humor. Swift's saturnine humor is not the thing, nor the biting wit of the satirist; but the gay writers generally. Yet, as a class of books, none appear to me better fitted for this season than lively and sensible travels, especially in the South and East—the regions of the Tropics and the Orient. Eastern travels always read best in summer: the season is in consonance with the text. The sultry heat out o'doors gives a confirmation strong of the stifling air of the desert on the author's pages;

and the sweet spray of fountains is cooling, both to see and hear. Camels, dates, elephants, palm trees, the dusky Arab, the swart Moslem, all appear to be, and are, strictly in keeping with a burning sun and his ardent rays, in midsummer. By a slight exercise of imagination, we can easily transport ourselves over land and sea, by the aid of the warm weather, as well as on the wing of that sightless laborer, the wind. Sitting in a close room, of a hot day, how easy to think of cities in Spain or Morocco—of Stamboul and Grand Cairo—of the Nile and the desert. Fancy can travel faster than steam, and takes the willing voyager captive over the passages of leaded type, rendered heavy to give emphasis to light description.

It is difficult for a person of little imagination to reverse the matter; to think heartily, and realize the warmth and richness of oriental life, in winter. "Oh, who can hold a fire in his hands," etc. Some of the later books of travels, (Eothen, the Crescent and the Cross, and particularly Thackeray's Tour,) deserve to be especially remembered just now. They are to be read on a breezy eminence, or under a spreading tree, not as Midsummer Night's Dream, but as noon-day fancies.

We forget the name of the writer, (French, English or German, we are not certain,) who, some fifty years ago, made the remark, that in no department of modern literature had so great improvement been made as in the class of books of travel. Probably this was a fair judgment at the time, although (with regard to the mass of books of this kind, not the few we may select for praise,) if the case were to be reheard and tried over again on its merits, the decision might be reversed. For, to tell the truth, at this present writing, in no walk of authorship have there been greater failures, (tragedies and epic poems excepted,) than in that of travels.

The literature of travel is singularly rich in the article of copiousness, but it is almost equally meagre in real power, whether of thought or style. Among the hundred popular books on the East, perhaps ten will last a generation or so. And so of other countries. We are yet to have classic local geographies, that shall combine truth of detail and liveliness of style, with antiquarianism, philosophy, pictures of manners, and topographical accuracy.

The same places have been described, and the same adventures repeated *ad nauseam.* Hardly a town, a cathedral, a fall, mountain, or lake in Great Britain, or on the continent of Europe, that has not been abundantly prated about; while our own good country has been laid under contribution by every idle sea-captain, or petty official, on a holyday excursion of a couple of months—travelling divines, or wandering female Syntaxes, or (still preserving the sex) female reformers of church and state.

One who can write nothing else, can make up a book of travels. Many can write a volume abroad who have never written a page at home. This is true, both of literary amateurs and literary traders. The secret is *compilation.* At least two-thirds of the material of nine-tenths of these books is obtained from guide books, tourist companions, gazetteers, historical compends, newspapers, and an encyclopedia.

Such is travel-writing made easy for the tarry-at-home traveller, and by one who need not himself stir from his writing-desk. Even in two such lively works as the Cross and the Crescent and Hochelaga, there is a good deal of "cramming" for the task. Yet much of this work is done by actual *voyageurs:* dull fellows, who return from a year's Periplus with a couple of portfolios stuffed full of MSS.

In this way, apparently, shoals of travels are manufactured, especially travelling letters for the newspapers. Indeed, so common is the product, answering to a regular demand, that a writer of taste and spirit will not print his own admirable letters, because so many raw, stupid things have preceded his choice collection.

Among our writers, a considerable body have published Letters from Abroad, and Travels in Europe and Asia; yet how few live past their season! Almost every one rests his reputation on something else. Willis, perhaps, the best, as the most brilliant, on his tales and sketches; Cooper is dull and prolix, and must be read only in his admirable early novels; Carter is buried under his own newspapers, as well as Brooks. Slidell is elegant but feeble; (Irving's tales, and sketches, and histories, have done far more for Spain than all the American travellers;) Dewey is strongest in his pulpit and the lecture-room; Miss Sedgwick in fiction, &c. Two American writers are unique as painters of French manners and living—Sanderson and Appleton Jewett.

At home, far too little has been done to illustrate our scenery, habits, and customs, by native travellers; Irving, for Dutchland and the far west: Miss Fuller for the lakes; and Bryant in his fine letters on the South—are the best. Nor should we forget Charles Fenno Hoffman's Winter in the West, (his best book;) Judge Hall's Notes; Schoolcraft, for the Indian country; and Timothy Flint for the Valley of the Mississippi.

A good sized library might be made up of European travels; yet very few of the whole collection are worth reading. For France, Sterne's Sentimental Journey has not yet been, and we doubt if it ever will be, superseded; and, after the piles of volumes, perhaps the two best written on France, by English authors, and as books of travels, are Lady Morgan's and Hazlitt's Notes. Other books may be useful for other purposes; for scientific information, or contemporary historical evidence.

The soil of Italy is covered some feet thick with books of travels, by the nobility, antiquaries, artists, newspaper correspondents, and invalid tourists, (a part of whose disease is to scribble.) To know Italy tolerably well, one must read poet and novelist, historian and philosopher, native and foreign. The fourth canto of Childe Harold may serve for a guide. In Venice, one would, on the spot, try the effect of

> Radcliff's, Schiller's, Shakspeare's, Otway's art.

In Florence, we should read Machiavelli's and Roscoe's histories, corrected by Sismondi; the Decameron and Dante. And so throughout. Borrow and Irving have spoiled us for reading any other books on Spain, although within a year or two several sprightly works have been issued from the press.

England has sent two true humorists to Germany, as well as a horde of compilers,—Head and Hood. The Bubbles of the first writer are a happy hit, and Up the Rhine is a masterly copy of Humphrey Clinker.

At home, the English have sent a capital sketcher to Ireland, Mr. Thackery.

But to return to travels in the East.

Travels in the East had been heretofore pretty dull matters, given over chiefly to missionaries, (unlike Borrow,) to biblical critics, to topographical surveys and Bible statistics, sometimes a poet like Lamartine or Chateaubriand, or Milnes, but until the present day, no readable, picturesque prose accounts had appeared like those of Kinglake, Warburton, Thackeray and our own Stephens. We do not pretend to speak of the grave and learned works on the East—the labors of Niebuhr and Burkhart, and Professor Robinson; but of the sparkling pages of the various tourists we have referred to, and among whom there is much to choose.

Eothen is for instance, much superior to the Cross and Crescent—fresher, closer, more original. The volumes of Warburton smack too much of historical and geographical compilation, something in the manner of the voluminous medley of history, geography, and personal remarks, by Buckingham. Thackeray is a brilliant cockney everywhere, and cannot shake off the character. He is most of all so when he even plays at playing the character, more particularly his passages on Athens and the Pyramids. The writer is honest in despising affected raptures, and has a true hatred of cant; but there are certain objects which naturally inspire awe and a genuine feeling of reverence, which a man may be sincere in avowing himself deficient in; yet that defect (a real one) does not alter the character of the thing admired generally, in which he can see nothing. He is candid, who says with truth, that he has been disappointed in Niagara Falls; at the same time, he confesses himself without eye, ear, heart and soul, for one of the Wonders of Creation. Mr. Thackeray sees nothing to excite him on the ground sacred to enthusiasm; yet greater men have felt generous emotions there, and expressed their feeling nobly. In general, with all his admirable sense and picturesque eye, and tact for brilliant description, Mr. Titmarsh (a cockney name) sees the contemptible and absurd more readily, and paints it with stronger gust, than the beautiful or grand. The burlesque rather than the beautiful; fun more than fancy; and, generally, gaiety and not gravity, preponderates in his composition and in his writings. He lives in the present; the past appears to affect him very slightly, and he speculates with little enthusiasm about the future.

Mr. Stephens preceded these writers in point of time, and in this country in point of popularity. He has merits and qualities of the popular kind, effective in description, clear and sensible, with a knack of story-telling, and a readable style. He has been one of our few writers successful in a pecuniary sense.

Whatever relates to the East, is properly summer reading. History—Jewish, as told by Moses and Josephus; that of the Turks and Tartars, by Gibbon, and, indeed, all the oriental part of his admirable history. A delightful oriental library (as interesting, and perhaps as instructive, as the learned work of D'Herbelot) would include, besides the works just mentioned, the delightful fictions, Rasselas, Zadig, other Eastern tales of Voltaire, the Arabian Nights, Vathek, the Epicurean, Scott's Tales of the Crusaders, and Pillpay's Fables, and Keene's Persian Fables, the oriental poems of Lord Byron and Tom Moore, Sir Wm. Jones' tranlations, Life and Journals of Heber, Embassies to China, &c. In later English history, the splendid Orations of Burke, with Macaulay's articles on Clive and Warren Hastings.

Spain and Italy, South America and the West Indies, our own Southern States, Mexico and Central America, the islands in the Pacific Ocean and South Sea, are regions about which we read with more pleasure than even about the East. They are nearer to us; and the southern countries of Europe far more famous in story. The southern portion of our own hemisphere offers many rare attractions to the reader and student, as well as to the traveller. Just now, Mexico is a point of great interest to all of us. Why does not some enterprising man get up panoramas of the city of Mexico, and of the surrounding country? We have often thought it would prove a good speculation to exhibit here views of the cities of the South, Havana, New Orleans, Charleston, the prairies of the West and South West, plantations of rice, cotton, sugar and tobacco.

Those at the North, who cannot afford to visit the South, and yet wish to know something of their own country, remote from their own homes, could, in this way, get some idea of the scenery and localities of the South.

To say a good word for ourselves, and a true one, magazines especially form a favorite species of summer reading. Light, graceful, versatile and sprightly, they contain matter for all tastes and every disposition, "that the mind of desultory man, studious of change" may have no just reason for complaint on the score of want of attraction.

XVIII.

THE CULTURE OF THE IMAGINATION.

There is always danger in the pursuit of the immediate practical wants of life lest the fair claims of the imagination may be neglected. This tendency has invested the reasoning faculty, the intellectual understanding, with more than equitable attributes, and certainly granted it a more than reasonable sway. The culture of science is a culture of the reason, almost exclusively. Now, the culture of any one faculty in excess, or to the exclusion of a free culture of the others, is, of necessity, hurtful. More especially in the case of reason, which is but a co-worker with the imagination in the pursuit of truth, and its servant in the creation of beauty. The soul is the parent of them both, and an impartial mother.

The Americans, in a land comparatively destitute of those

historical landmarks that carry back the imagination to the past, are, more than the inhabitants of Europe, where the traveller is in a land of monuments and ancient temples, the devices of the early and middle age, forced to regard the present time as our peculiar age. Hence, we are almost destitute of antiquities and antiquari es, though our land be, perhaps, the ancient seat of creation and paradise. There are many projectors intó the misty vale of the future; but most of us live in and for the present. A very narrow horizon bounds that view. This would not be the case, had we formed a proper conception of that glorious faculty, which, more than any other, assimilates man to the Divinity, and which enables the creature to become a creator.

The imagination is commonly considered a faculty placed in man for the mere purposes of amusement and recreation. This was the old pedantic notion of poetry. Its province was, purely, 'to please.' But this is a very trifling and unjust view. The exercise of the imagination is not merely a matter of entertainment; it is the highest teaching. It charms, while it instructs; but truth delights in fairy fiction dressed; and even the naked truth, unadorned, simple, to an eye that can well survey its fair proportions, is more truly attractive than the most beautiful fiction.

It is not poetry, however, alone, that is affected by this depreciation of the imaginative faculty. The error tends to a low appreciation of the excellent in all art; tends to a material taste in speculative inquiries; to incredulity and coldness in matters of religion. It has an injurious effect upon all literature, which it materially degrades; preferring always science, business, and practical skill.

Poetry and religion—the highest fiction and the highest philosophy—both looking to a common principle, are based upon the imagination.—They both appeal to faith. Without this, neither could exist, for each would need a hold on man. In perfect sincerity, and firm trust alone, can they attach themselves to the soul. The poet must by illusion, the Christian by faith—a species of illusion—work and wait. Both must rely on this as their sheet anchor.

The imagination should, therefore, be cultivated, if only as an aid to the strengthening of virtuous resolves, and the heightening of religious aspirations. The effect of a pure imagination on the heart, is one of the most cheering evidences of the real nobility of man. The highest poetry, we repeat, is religious, and the greatest poets must be, necessarily, devout. The common opinion, sanctioned by great names, is against this position; yet the truer view, sanctioned by still higher authority, is directly in its favor. For who will place Dr. Johnson, Byron, and the sensual school, against Milton, Wordsworth, and Coleridge, to say nothing of the grandest poetry in the world—the poetry of the Hebrews? The old-fashioned critics thought or said, that dullness and insipidity were the genuine ingredients in religious verse. This is very true in its application to some religionists; but is very far from true when we come to the muses' hill—when we reach the enchanted city of poets. Their error could have arisen only from ignorance, or else from a minuteness of poetical and critical vision, that can see a world of poetry in Shelley and Moore, and nothing but prosaic baldness in Wordsworth and Milton. Milton is the most serious and impressive of uninspired lyrists. The whole cast of his mind was eminently religious. The Hebrew poets were his favorite reading, and after them the Greek tragedians and Shakspeare. His personal bearing is said to have been grave and austere. Even in youth, he was like his own archangel—

> Severe in youthful beauty.

He was religious in his tastes; he played anthems daily on the organ. What other instrument could have filled his mind with those magnificent ideas of space and sound of which his poetry is full!

The poet then, as priest and prophet in an early age; so, also as a Christian and as the world's teacher, must be a man of purity and holiness. He must have clean hands, and a pure heart, that would hymn the glories of the Almighty.

Besides the great poets we have mentioned, whose motto is 'Holiness before the Lord,' there is a galaxy of lesser lights, a poetic host, just before and after the restoration in England, professedly religious—Quarles and Crashaw, Herbert and Donne, and Vaughan and Wotton. It may be remarked, further, that the most irreligious poets discover, instinctively, at times, a vein of devotion, and even the lightest versifiers have their images of fear and terror. The gloomiest painters, occaionally, describe a fairer scene; and through the pitchy darkness are seen gleams of light, as from a heavenly country.

This arises out of a very natural cause. Religion, its hopes and fears; the grandeur and gentleness of the supreme intellect; the beauty of divine love; the hallowed influences of the spirit, form the noblest themes of the poet, painter, and musician. It is from interest, if no other reason, then, the poet should be religious. Not only is the grandest poetry religious, but also the finest music, and the immortal masterpieces of painting. The souls of Milton, Raphael, and Handel, could not be touched by common loves, or vexed by common cares. They required something vast and awful, or exquisitely tender and sweet, to fill their minds, and move their hearts. High fancies, rich colors, pealing harmonies—

Paradise Lost, the Holy Family, the Messiah. No themes have inspired such eloquence as religion. In fact, every art has laid its richest offerings at that shrine. The noblest cathedrals have been erected for the worship of the Most High; and in those temples, the choicest paintings are hung, the most solemn music is played, accompanied by voices almost cherubic, the most admirable verses have been written for its psalmody—what poem is finer than that Rembrandt strain of mingled golden and gloomy fancies, that rich monkish canticle, 'Dies iræ, dies illa?'—and the wisest powers of discriminative piety and judicious devotion have been exhausted in the preparation of a perfect liturgy. It must be confessed, then, the imagination is the most religious of our faculties, and conesquently, the grandest.

All imagination is either creative or sympathetic. The first brings man nearer to his Maker; the second, to his fellows. The one is invention, the other sympathy. By the first, we invent scenes of delight for others as well as for ourselves, and passages of pathetic wretchedness. By the latter, we feel, instinctively, for the happy and sad, the gay and the miserable. The latter makes us better philanthropists; the former, better poets. Is there any comparison between the two? None; except in the case of the highest poet, who is the greatest philanthropist. Most of the hardness of heart and coldness of feeling in the world, arises out of the want of imagination. We want sympathy to place ourselves in the condition of others. Our imagination is not strong enough to touch the heart; or rather, it does not act with reciprocal force, as it should.

With regard to the prominent position of the imagination in the mind, there is this suggestion to be offered; viz., that although it be the highest faculty in the human mind, it may not be the loftiest attribute of the Deity. The creative power of the All-Creator may be supposed to result from all wisdom, which instinctively perceives what is the only right, joined to an energy of will, such as we can have no conception of. The reason or intellect, properly so called, as distinct from the imagination, it may philosophically be inferred, is the ruling power in the Divine mind. For, compared with the realities ever present to Deity, our highest imaginings must be the merest commonplace. In God, the perfection of knowledge supersedes all room for probability and conjecture. All is clear to Him. There are no hidden mysteries, no inscrutable secrets, unrevealed to the Source of All. In us, imagination springs from ignorance; we never attempt to imagine what we can accurately learn. Therefore, as the Deity knows everything, he can, in the nature of things, imagine nothing.

We have now attempted to state the just position of the imagination. We proceed to the great question, how to cultivate it? After which, we shall consider the intellectual and moral uses this culture may subserve.

How, then, are we to educate the imaginative faculty? what aids are we to seek? whence the sources of its delight? Nature, the poets, art, the heart of man. These are at once both the instruments and sources of and for the culture of the imaginative faculty. It may be said, the poor cannot reach the delights of art, cannot procure access to them, and if they can, are not prepared by previous education to relish or enjoy them. The public taste, then, is to be cultivated.

A taste for natural scenery, to say nothing of the refinement of art, is, in its mere elements, inherent in man; but training and some study is needed to educe and perfect it. This educated taste is very rare. With what cold and insensible eyes do the majority of persons regard the fairest scenes of nature! They see with their eyes only. They never feel. There is no heart in their understanding; no sentiment in their perceptions. They are mere literal-minded observers. The earth is not to them a most cogent argument of the wisdom and benevolence of its Great Framer. They associate not matter with spirit—perceive no connection. They find no spiritual influences in themselves, hallowing the material objects around them. They see nothing but thick woods, and craggy rocks, and meadows spreading far.

The general study of the noble army of poets, and poetic philosophers, is, unquestionably, the best influence the brain of man has yet devised for the culture of the creative power. The numberless improvements in the art of engraving have brought the choicest works within the reach of even the laborer. People's editions, cheap libraries without end, furnish the means of mental culture to all. The poets have been oftener reprinted than any other class of writers, and this speaks well for the elevation of the public mind.

The time may not yet have arrived, but it must come some day, when the wealth of the state, joined to the munificent bequests of individuals, will unite to provide classic entertainments; not the mere dole of the Roman people in an early day—

Panem, circencesque,

but free lectures, free concerts, free admission to galleries of paintings and sculpture, to libraries and reading-rooms, to public walks and gardens of rare beauty; and lastly, to the 'well-trod stage,' which, it is hoped, will then have become what it once professed to be—a school of virtue and a discipline of the heart.

The rich may, indirectly, do much to improve the popular

taste, and fix a high standard. In many costly works, where the poor may not unite with them, they can display a richness, and yet a solidity of style and magnificence, that cannot fail to give a high tone to the character of even the lowest class, and impart a finer grace to the manners of all. The poor man's eye possesses a certain property in the elegancies of the man of wealth, who is also a man of taste, so that faculty will be improved in him, even if he cannot participate as an equal sharer in every luxury.

The rich can introduce a style of architecture, simple, yet solemn, in the public buildings of cities; in bridges, roads, and aqueducts, over the whole face of the country; and in the bosom of retired vales, or on the tops of high hills, erect temples of eternal stone, and rich with Gothic tracery and later skill. The imagination, and consequently the moral frame, is nobly affected by such monuments of immortality.

The rich can do more. They can maintain, if they please, a wise moderation in their private way of living, and not, by heedless profusion, give rise to envy, or by ostentatious display, to false pride. They can discard all tawdriness in dress and furniture, the frequent bad taste; and substitute Doric simplicity for Corinthian splendor. They can revive the art of landscape gardening; an art brought to comparative perfection in England, but almost unknown here. A great advantage resulting from these improvements would be the vast amount of refined labor thrown into the hands of the laboring class. This would have a more certain tendency to elevate and refine them, than all the declamations in the world on the Dignity of Man.

The intellectual benefits resulting from a liberal culture of the imaginative faculty, have been too much slighted. It is not sufficiently comprehended, that even the strictest logic must have a coloring of imagination. To conceive the clearest proposition, some invention is necessary; to frame an apt simile, demands some fancy.

The imagination is apparently lawless; yet it has its laws, and method and logic. But its associations are too nice and subtile to be distinguished by coarse or unreflecting minds. It proceeds in its inquiries on the higher instincts of the soul for its premises. It takes a wider sweep and a loftier flight than pure reason can. Hence, it sees more of a subject at once; takes in a broader field of relations and contingencies; more delicately distinguishes; more vividly contrasts. It is the argument by picture; a poetic analogy; a creative analysis.

The reason of so much severe censure of poetry and imagination, by logical men, is from the examples they have daily before them of men of weak imaginations, who are also weak reasoners. Generalizing, unfairly, from these, they conceive all imagination to be weak and puerile. In a strong man, however, the imagination is a robust and sturdy faculty, and can do its work manfully. Look at the imagination of Scott, when his whole sensitive being was almost overwhelmed, how it worked bravely on! Survey the ample expanse of Milton's mind; in poverty, in blindness, friendless, in trouble; his imagination never failed him, though all other of his human resources might.

And then the consolations of the imagination, a favorite topic of declamation, to the sick in mind, those suffering in physical pain, to the discontented, the ambitious, the unfortunate, the despairing, the miserable. What a balm to the spirit is the lay of the poet, then, or the moving tale of the artful romancer!

The phrase, moral use of the imagination, may strike

some strangely. What we mean to express is, the aid imagination may, by its pictures, its fair creations, its generous views, furnish to the perfection of man's moral nature. The moral value of the imagination refers to the influence of the imagination on the heart. This influence consists in the growth of a nobler sincerity than is commonly practised in the world; in a holier purity in act and intention; and in the expansion of private benevolence into philanthropy and patriotism. It assures faith, and confirms love. It assures faith by its inherent elevation and nobleness; it confirms love by its evidence of a single heart and a natural confidence of soul. The worldling may regard such a character as a simpleton; but he is, with all his boasted wisdom, a very fool himself!

In the case of the poor, for whose advantage we cannot suggest too much, the effects of a cultivated imagination would be readily perceived in a prevalence of temperance, cleanliness, and order; in a more cheerful aspect; a more decent and becoming appearance; in an intelligence that could resist the innovations of selfish ambition, and a calm strength that would dismay the attacks of overbearing power.

The general diffusion of the culture of the imagination would advance many objects with which it now appears to have but a slight connection. The oratory of the bar, and the eloquence of the pulpit, would become simpler, and more impressive. A more enlightened public taste would improve private and individual performances, and much would not be tolerated then, that is patiently endured now.

Religion and true poetry would then become co-workers with taste and fancy. The world would be purer and holier.

The artisan would be a Christian and enlightened; and equally a good man and a skilful craftsman.

The heart of man—that fountain of all that is good—or, if poisoned by the world's corruption, that sink of utter impurity—would be truer, and more affectionate; more earnest, and more confiding. Man would converse with his fellow-man as with a brother and a friend; and not, as is too often the case now, as with a rival or foe. The natural warfare of trade, the competition of business, would be merged in an universal harmony and brotherly love. The cordial grasp of the hand, the warm expression of friendship, would not be simulated for foreign purposes. The body social would then be in its most perfect state; for 'out of the heart cometh all the issue of life;' and then the heart would be the ruling principle of the world.

XIX.

POLITICAL SATIRE.

The most marked trait in the finest political writing is its personality. It is very plausible to reiterate the hackneyed maxim, "principles, not men," but it is next to impossible to separate the two. An intimate connection necessarily subsists between principles and those who hold them, as between a man and his dress, a book and its author. Certain abstract philosophers, (a very small class,) may be enabled by long practice and dint of study, to disabuse their minds of favorite prejudices, and set up a species of claim to impartiality and fairness; yet such thinkers are seldom actors on the great stage, but rather spectators of the stirring contests in the actual arena of politics. They may write philosophical treatises on Government, the Wealth of Nations, or the Spirit of Laws, but they make inefficient "*working* members." Even Burke was a partisan, and such have the ablest and honestest politicians of all ages been. There is unquestionably truth mingled with error in every party; yet a man of decided character will find more truth and less error on one side, than on the other. Many partisans have been hypocrites, but by no manner of means all. It is rather (unless there exist natural suspicions of interested motives or palpable deficiency) an argument in a man's favor that he is a zealous partisan; for in its integrity, such a character supposes vigor, earnestness, and fidelity, the three manly qualities by pre-eminence. Among the many reasons that incline a man to join this party or that, may be enumerated—hereditary tendencies, peculiarities of mental or moral constitution, personal gratitude, the influence of a superior mind, chance, or prejudice. We are apt to consider that this last cause is much more defensible than is generally supposed. Viewed in a certain light, some of the noblest virtues are no more than prejudices. Compared with the universal spirit of philanthropy, patriotism shrinks into a narrow passion; the worthy father makes by no means so distinguished a figure as the humane citizen of the world. Religion, too, in its most important article, impresses a refined selfishness at the same time that it teaches charity and general benevolence. For we must be most solicitous for our own souls; no man can stand in our place, nor can we become the substitute for another. So in the field of politics: a nobler contest than that of the "tented field," a man must take his side, and stand or fall with it. Middle men become indifferent, if originally honest and well-meaning, or mere trimmers, if the reverse; and it is difficult to determine which is the more despicable character. Imperceptibly, too, a man's principles become identified with himself, and by a natural consequence, if we have faith in the one, we learn to love the other. In the wisest men, we see every day the force of political attachments, which sometimes exhibit a devotion almost heroical. And this is right. One who hazards all for a great principle, a master-doctrine, should be strongly supported. A politician needs his backers as well as a pugilist, to give him heart and constancy. We never could understand the separation, upon which many insist, between the characters of the statesman and the private individual. We cannot distinguish the two different characters of the same person. A single mind impresses an unity of design upon all its performances, and an upright man should be governed by the same law of right and sense of duty, in his official position, that control his domestic and familiar actions. If we admire ability and trust to the unbiassed exercise of it, if we believe in the same creed and favor the same principles, how can we refrain from embracing the possessor of such talents, and the advocate of such doctrines as a personal friend?

To come back to our text. *Personality* we affirm to be the most striking trait of the most brilliant political writing. Party spirit begets political satire. Along with its evident advantages, partisanship includes a spirit of bigotry that displays its worst features. "Party spirit incites people to attack with rashness, and to defend without sincerity. Violent partisans are apt to treat a political opponent in such a manner, when they argue with him, as to make the question quite personal, as if he had been present, as it were, and a chief agent in all the crimes which they attribute to his party.

Nor does the accused hesitate to take the matter upon himself, and in fancied self-defence, to justify things which otherwise he would not hesitate, for one moment, to condemn."* Exact statements and precise deductions can hardly be expected when a man is making the most of his materials, and defending what he believes to be the true view, though it may have weak spots.

In politics, as in most things, the most striking arguments are those *ad hominem* and *ad absurdum*. Ridicule serves too often for a test of truth; and though this delicate instrument may be perverted to great injury, yet we all know very well how many people can be laughed out of notions which could not be removed by the fairest and most conclusive argumentation. A laugh is the best logic for these. How many subjects, too, of no little detriment to a cause, though in themselves of diminutive importance, cannot be appropriately treated except in the way of jesting and raillery. The littleness of some men is far beneath aught but the levity of a squib or a pun; whereas the specific gravity, (or, in plain terms, stolid presumption,) of others, requires merely a superficial exposition to make them ridiculous for ever.

There are other considerations that tend to confirm the usefulness of political satire. Much may be done indirectly that we cannot openly face and attack. An allegorical narrative may include real characters, which it might be imprudent to depict in express language. Bold, bad men, in power, may be scourged with impunity and poetic justice, by the dramatist and novel writer, when a faithful picture of them by a chronicler of the times would, in other days and lands than our own, send him into duress. Existing public abuses,

* From an admirable Essay on Party Spirit,—vide "Essays written in the intervals of business."—*Pickering, London.*

which, from their intangible and irresponsible character, cannot always be publicly met, may still be so described in a work of fiction, as in time to effect a thorough popular reformation of them.

The argument *ad hominem* affects a man's interest, and appeals to his pride, or excites his indignation, and moves his feelings. It is the most effective argument to be used with the majority of men, and when enlivened by comic ridicule, or exaggerated into something like vituperative eloquence by the presençe of a Juvenal tone of sarcastic rebuke, it displays the perfection of political satire, and such as we find it in the most eminent instances.

The finest and most permanent satire, whether religious or political, has been conveyed in works of imagination, which, falling into the hands of the greatest number of readers, have, consequently, at the same time obtained universal reputation, and exercised the widest influence. Of this nature, especially, are the immortal works of Swift, "Gulliver's Travels," and "The Tale of a Tub." the most admirable union of exquisite satire and allegory. The extravagance of unmitigated burlesque, however, does not in all respects become the true character of able political writing, which, when it does admit of satire, invariably demands that the wit be based on vigorous sense and logic, and that it appear rather in the form of great intellectual acuteness, sharpened by exercise, than in the guise of pure pleasantry, or jesting without an aim. And here we may remark, that not a single political writer is to be mentioned, of any eminence, and who has a reputation for wit or humor, whose wit and humor is not founded upon great strength of understanding, shrewdness, and knowledge of mankind. Political wit admits of little play of fancy, and few or no imaginative excursions. In fact, it is only a livelier mode of stating an argument. It is reasoning by pointed analogies, or happy illustrations, a species of epigrammatic logic. This is the wit of Junius, of Horne Tooke, of Tom Paine, and of William Hazlitt. They sought to reach the *reductio ad absurdum* by the argument *ad hominem.* The accumulation of ridiculous traits of character made up a comic picture, and demonstrated practical absurdities in conduct at the same time. On the other hand, by a process of exhaustive analysis, they *precipitated* (as a chemist would say) the ludicrous points of a subject. Cobbett's wit consisted in calling nicknames with an original air. Satire is a prosaical talent, yet it has been exercised by some of the first poets in the second class of great poets, as Dryden, Swift, Pope, Churchill, Cowper, and Young. It handles topics essentially unpoetical, and in a way that would deprive them of what poetical qualities they might possess. For satire tends to diminish and degrade, whereas true poetry aims to exalt and refine. Satire deals with the vices, the crimes of the worst part of mankind, or the levities and follies of the most insignificant. Much political satire exaggerates both, but that is the original sin and inherent defect of all satire. The value of satire in a practical point of view is great: it is the only curb upon many, and no ineffectual check upon the best. Next to religion, it exerts a happier and a wider influence than anything else, whether law, custom or policy. Such is forcible and well-directed satire in the worthiest hands. It is a true, manly style of writing, but it admits of wide aberrations from this standard, and may become hurtful and dangerous. It exposes hypocrisy, and encourages an open, frank, fearless spirit; yet this very openness, (in base natures,) will run into recklessness and a contempt of authority, a neglect of propriety, and a rash avowal of lawless and foul doctrines. It may convert liberty into licentiousness. Then again, satire is often unfair, morally unjust, or historically false. The acute perception of Butler, which, aided by his learned wit and matchless versification, saw with exactness, and has transmitted to us with picturesque fidelity, the mere canting, controversial, corrupt Presbyterians of his day, failed to recognise the sturdy vigor of the Independent, and the sublime fanaticism of even the wildest of the Fifth Monarchy men. Even Scott, though he came much closer to the truth in his pictures, unconsciously distorted and caricatured some of the noblest features of the Puritans. That stern race of robust men has hardly yet met with its true historian.

A too frequent consequence of successful satire, we have left for our last objection to its usefulness. It tends to beget a spirit of indifference. Men, looking on the excesses of either side with an eye of philosophic temperance, are too apt to conclude that there is nothing worth contending for; they become disgusted with what they (in their short-sightedness) esteem fruitless struggles, and give over all desire of victory. They become indifferent spectators of a stirring scene, and might as well, for all good purposes, be altogether removed from it.

XX.

FARRAGO.

—— nostri *farrago* libelli.—JUVENAL.
Farrago; a Medley.—JOHNSON.

WE have selected the above title for this miscellaneous assemblage of thoughts upon different subjects; for bringing together which, since they are, for the most part, dug up from comparatively unknown mines, we claim nothing but the praise of judicious research. The characters of Labruyère are full of good things, and the vein will bear working, but we shall not do more than indicate where some of the rich ore lies. It has always struck us that occasional lucubrations of this description are not unpleasing, especially in the varied pages of a monthly journal, "studious of change," and intended to hit the diversity of tastes of the best classes of readers. In the first and second topics, we have drawn from Labruyère, an author who is singularly little known. He is a prose Pope, writing before him, and as we are induced to think, giving him some capital hints, which the poet worked up with his accustomed skill. Labruyère has as much wit and judgment combined as Horace, after whom he too sometimes copies. He has something of Bishop Earle's humor, and a knowledge of artificial life and manners, equal to Pope, and Horace, and Earle.

Pope, in a few passages we have subjoined, appears to have drawn directly from his master; but the resemblance may be accidental, and the imitation unconscious. We will not call it plagiarism, but a singular coincidence of thought and expression; such as we often see in common life and in ordinary conversation. Yet we are somewhat staggered by these points. Rowe, the poet, Pope's friend, made or purports to have made (he possibly sold his name) the translation, a capital version, equal, in its way, to Cotton's Translation of Montaigne's Essays. Curll, one of Pope's publishers, brought out the work. But the hardest thing to get over is, the surprising resemblance of the verse to the prose, which certainly preceded it some years. This problem, however, we shall not attempt to solve.

SURPRISING COINCIDENCES.

"Affectation attends her even in sickness and pain; she dies in a high head and colored ribbons." Who can forget Pope's lines in the Universal Passion?

"Odious in woollens, 'twould a saint provoke,
(Were the last words that poor Narcissa spoke).
No, let a charming chintz, and Brussels lace,
Wrap my cold limbs, and shade my lifeless face;
One would not, sure, be frightful when one's dead,
And—Betty—give this cheek a little red."

Said to be actually true of Mrs. Oldfield, the celebrated actress. Labruyère has nicely hit off the ignorant book-collectors, not the "*doctor sine libris*," but "*libri sine doctore.*" "I visit this gentleman; he receives me at his house, where, at the foot of the stairs, I am struck down with the scent of Russia leather, which all his books are bound with. In vain he encourages me, by telling me they are gilt on the backs and leaves, of the best editions; ..... except *a few shelves painted so like books*, that the fallacy is not to be discerned." Pope sings:

"His study—with what authors is it stor'd?
In books, not authors, studious is my lord;
To all their dated backs he turns you round,
These Aldus printed; those De Seuil has bound.
Lo, some are vellum, and the rest as good,
For all his lordship knows, *but they are wood!*"

Here is a thought in Labruyère (of the fashion) which may be found expressed in almost the same language, in the poet's prose miscellanies. "A certain blue flower, which grows spontaneously in ploughed ground; it checks the corn, spoils the crop, and takes up the room of something better." Labruyère compares a fashionable man to this flower: Pope illustrates more judiciously, by this simile, the injurious use of conceits in a logical discussion.

But here is a remarkable parallelism, if not plagiarism.

"The colors are all prepared, and cloth stained, but how shall I fix this restless, light and inconstant man, who changes himself into a thousand figures?"

> "Come then, the colors and the ground prepare!
> Dip in the rainbow, trick her off in air;
> Choose a fine cloud, before it fall, and in it
> Catch, ere she change, the Cynthia of this minute."

Here, too, are the original of several trite remarks: "When a man is excellent in his art, and gives it all the perfection of which it is capable, he is then in some sort above it, and is equal to whatever is most exalted and noble." Sir Joshua Reynolds has the credit of having made this observation. Of the opera, thus writes Labruyère, anticipating Hazlitt (in his rich essay on the same subject.) "I wonder how 'tis possible the opera, with all its exquisite music and almost regal magnificence, should yet so successfully tire me."

Is it not Bolingbroke who has the following idea, very prominently brought out, in his Historical Dissertations on Sir Robert Walpole? "When the fury and division of parties cease, they are forgotten like *almanacs out of date*."

One more parallelism between Labruyère and Pope: the wit describes an angry man as "in an agony, for a china dish broke in pieces." Pope, who disdained help from no source, praises the female, blessed with fine temper, as "mistress of herself, *though china fall*."

6

Labruyère's Coquette forms the original of Cibber's picture of a "Grandmother without Gray Hairs," and Burke's "Beautiful Vision of the Queen of France." "*Years with her have not twelve months*, nor add to her age."

These passages struck us, at once, in the reading: doubtless, a careful comparison might reveal still more and closer resemblances, if that be possible. Meantime, we pass to another subject.

CHESS.

Labruyère asks pertinently enough: "Is there no occasion of forecast, cunning or skill, to play at ombre or chess? And if there is, how comes it we see men of weak parts excel in it, and others of great ingenuity who can't reach to a moderate ability; whom, a man to be moved, or card in their hand, perplexes and puts out of countenance." Hazlitt has remarked the same fact, and we have known and are acquainted with men of unquestioned ability, who can't play tolerably well; while we could point to many more of very ordinary intellectual powers, even dull and weak men in other things, who at whist and chest are invariably victorious; displaying skill, resources, judgment, and temper. This was the case with Napoleon, among the great men of this century, who was readily vanquished by the ladies and triflers at his court, in almost every game.

But we do not apply this term to chess; it is a study, a labor, a discipline: taxing and not relaxing the faculties, bracing and not unbending the mind; in a word, a matter of vexatious trifling, and a piece of studious impertinence. Lest the reader think we are hasty in our judgment, we quote the advice of one of the wisest wits of the old English time, Thomas Fuller, the divine and Church historian: the jester, full of sense and feeling. In his Holy State, he advises, (chapter of Recreations,) "Take heed of straining thy mind in setting it to a double task, under pretence of giving it a play-day, as in the labyrinth of chess, and other tedious and studious games." And Montaigne, too, speaks of chess as "this idle and foolish game." From a long passage, we extract the following sentences: "I hate and avoid it, because it is *not play enough*, that it is too grave and serious a diversion, and I am ashamed to lay out as much thought and study upon that as would serve to much better uses." Dr. Franklin, in his Morals of Chess, has taken and confirmed the popular view of its utility. If, indeed, skill in this game begets and perfects the good habits of mind he ascribes to it, then, indeed, (and such we believe is often the case,) it may serve the same ends as the study of mathematics or logic, with this great difference in favor of the latter, that the subject matter they are employed upon is of far greater intrinsic importance, in the world of matter and of spirit. Chess is commonly made a test of intellectual power and ingenuity; but we think, after the testimony of Labruyère, Fuller, Montaigne, and Hazlitt, we may conclude, without disrespect to those idle, weak men who succeed in it, that the victory may be as often gained by some instinctive knack, (like Zerah Colburn's computations and arithmetical prodigies,) as by the exercise of the faculties that are supposed to be employed. Some of the very stupidest men we have ever met, were miracles of patience and prolixity, in playing chess or in holding a discussion, which was either not worth the words wasted, as having been settled long since, or as impossible to be determined to the satisfaction of all parties, if indeed of any one person. In both cases "*the game was not worth the candle!*" to use Sir William Temple's familiar illustration, and which might be literally true.

Forbes tells us, in his Life of Beattie, the poet and Scotch Professor, that "To chess he had a real aversion, as occasioning, in his opinion, a great waste of time, and requiring a useless application of thought."

Another poet, romancer, and still more famous Scotchman, held similar language. Scott, as a boy, we are told by Lockhart, "engaged easily in the game, which had found favor with so many of his paladins, but did not pursue the *science* of chess after his boyhood. He used to say it was a shame to throw away upon mastering a mere game, however ingenious, the time which would suffice for the acquisition of a new language. 'Surely,' he said, 'chess-playing is a sad waste of brains.'"

AUTHORS IN PRISON.

Some of the cosmopolitan classics have been composed in a dreary dungeon: as Tasso's Jerusalem, Don Quixote, Pilgrim's Progress. During the civil wars in England, some of the finest writers of the day were imprisoned for their loyalty, as Howell, who laments his confinement in his Letters, while Wither sent out from his cell the sweetest strains of his muse, in the well-known passage Lamb and Hazlitt have quoted. At the same epoch, the sagacious and manly Quarles, the first devotional poet in point of time, and second only to Herbert in point of genius, of the English Church; the mild and gentle Hammond; the gallant and poetic knight Lovelace; L'Estrange, the virulent pamphleteer, and many more of a similar stamp. Earlier, there are more notable instances, as of Chaucer, in the reign of Edward III.; Sir Thomas More, and Latimer, and the noble army of martyrs in the reigns of Henry VIII., and Bloody Queen Mary. In the reign of James I., his pre-eminent names were state prisoners, Bacon and Raleigh. Later, there is Minshull, of whose curious book we have written in Literary Studies; and Defoe, who also was placed in the pillory to which he dedicated a burlesque ode; Wycherly, confined seven years for debt; poor Savage; accomplished Sir Richard Steele; we believe also, admirable Henry Fielding, though he afterwards became a police justice; and a number of the wits and men of letters about town of that time, down to Dr. Dodd, executed for forgery; and Leigh Hunt, incarcerated for a harmless piece of political pleasantry, miscalled a libel, upon the Prince Regent.

Pictures of prison life abound in the pages of the old novelists, Fielding, Smollett, Goldsmith, &c., down to Dickens, their true successor. The spunging-house was, alas! the refuge of some of the finest writers and most accomplished men, from the reign of Anne, and her predecessor, William, down to the commencement of the reign of George IV.

We have thought a sermon might be written for prisoners, who are scholars—the best may get within those gloomy walls—entitled St. Peter in Prison, (the title of a sermon of Donne's, we believe, which we have never read,) which, besides giving a fuller account of the authors we have mentioned, and many more, might recount the story of the sufferings of the apotles, Peter and Paul in particular, and the early Christians. Crowned heads, too, might be included, as Richard of England, Elizabeth, and Charles I.

James of Scotland, the Royal Poet of Irving, and Mary, the beautiful and unfortunate, and Louis of France. Among philosophers, the wise Boetius, and the great Galileo. Among the latter instances, the Italian poet Pellico, with his friend Maroncelli.

Celebrated exiles should be referred to: Ovid and Clarendon, his sovereign, Charles II., Bolingbroke, and James II. The French writers, Voltaire and De Staël, are, we believe, the most celebrated of that nation who have suffered exile within a century.

CELEBRATION OF AUTHORS' BIRTH-DAYS.

Why should not the anniversary of the birth-day of a great author be kept as a festival, as well as that of a successful general, or able statesman! Would it not be admirable to celebrate such annual returns, bringing the most delicious memories with them, as well as the days on which a battle was fought or gained, which must have given pain to a multitude of persons, who could not blame the author of genius for a single pang, but rather bless his name as the creator of more fictitious delight than could be easily gained from the real world under the happiest circumstances? It seems to us that (to keep themselves in countenance, to preserve a cordial *esprit du corps*, and to perpetuate the memory of great authors too easily disturbed by novelty and the distractions of care and sorrow) writers should have annual dinners or suppers, or convivial meetings of some sort, held in honor of the acknowledged master, in their particular departments from dramatic poetry to the humblest prose essayists. The novelists might select their

Fielding; one class might choose Marivaux, a third Le Sage, a fourth Scott, a fifth Cervantes, &c. And so of all the rest.

DISTINGUISHED VISITORS.

Among those who have crossed the Atlantic to see for themselves the working of our institutions, are many great names; more have come for the sake of travel and pleasure; but most, for some profitable end. Not to include the generous and gallant Frenchmen and Poles who fought for and with us during the revolutionary contest, Lafayette and his brave compeers, Pulaski and Kosciusko, nor ambassadors or official persons; we find, in the list, Volney, Chateaubriand, who wrote his charming Atala and Natchez here in a hut; Tallyrand; the late King of France, one of the Murats, Augereau, (if we do not mistake,) and two of Napoleon's nephews. Two English poets only, of repute, (and they Irishmen,) Moore and Lover; among celebrated writers of fiction, Captain Maryatt, Dickens and Seatsfield, and one well-known critic and Edinburgh reviewer, Jeffrey, who married here. Dr. Priestley and Cobbett both lived here for some time. Tom Paine became endenizened, and did more, as a pamphleteer, for the Revolution, than any American writer. We came near having the three great poets of England for our citizens: Southey, Wordsworth, and Coleridge, proposed in early life, to settle on the banks of the Susquehannah. Howard, the philanthropist, visited the United States in his "circumnavigation of charity." De Tocqueville and Chevalier were truly philosophical travellers. The mere travellers have been generally an unworthy importation—the Halls, Fidlers,

Trollopes, &c. Miss Martineau is the most sensible and Mrs. Jamieson the most pleasing writer of this class.

We have had the English stage fairly represented by Cooke, Kean, and Macready, the greatest tragedians since Garrick; by Mathews, elder and younger, Dowton, Jack Reeve, Power, the Kembles, Ellen Tree, Madame Vestris, the Keeleys, Buckstone; the ballet, by the fascinating Ellsler; Italian and German music by Malibran, (then Signorina Garcia,) Jenny Lind, Madame Sontag, Grisi and Mario, Jullien, and the best English singers from Phillips, Incledon and Braham, and Mrs. Wood to the present day.

Founders of sects have established many religious societies and communities all over the country. Wesley and Whitfield, the leaders of the Methodists; Wm. Penn and Barclay, George Fox, and his first disciples among the Quakers; Zinzendorf and his followers, the Moravians; Rapp and Owen, with the Socialists and Fourierites. If we do not mistake, Mother Ann Lee, the Shaker prophet, came over to this country. Religious missionaries had almost colonized this continent from the beginning. First the Catholic Jusuits, and then, almost contemporaneously, the Pilgrim (Puritan) Fathers, at Plymouth, and the Church of England settlers at Jamestown.

OF BOOKS AND LIBRARIES.

After all that has been written upon this interminable theme, a vast deal yet remains behind. From Montaigne's charming essay to the delightful papers of Charles Lamb, there have been exquisite morceaux of sentiment, gossip, and the best, the truest, the finest genial criticism. In common with all critical lovers, and readers, and collectors of books, we have a whim or two of our own with regard to such matters —a fancy, a taste, or what you please.

A scholar's collection should be select rather than full; or it may and ought to be both; large libraries are for public institutions, even the smallest of which contains very much ordinary matter; professional and scientific libraries may be more comprehensive and less choice; for facts, statistics, etc., are more requisite with those who use them—they are filled chiefly with elementary works and books of reference.

I dislike complete sets of voluminous authors. Give me rather the choicest works of the best writers. I entertain an equal aversion for encyclopedæic collections of travels, poetry, fiction, and criticism. I do not care to own every one of Sir Walter Scott's historical novels; (the only readable works of that class) neither do I like serial (a current phrase) editions of the poets and old dramatists. I prefer to select for myself a volume of poetry, or a poem, one play or more; a few dramas of Jonson are admirable, and Marlowe, and Webster, and Dekker; but heaven forfend my having all their works thrust down my throat! This applies also to Massinger, and Beaumont and Fletcher, and still more to the later writers of comedy. I may exclude what another might relish; but I speak for myself. Shelves full of reviews and magazines we like no better. Singly, the last magazine always has an interest. But when they get to be as long lived as the Edinburgh or London, one wants a selection.

Many books, as well as many faces, require constant perusal before you have their true value, or catch their spirit or meaning.

To think of the old heroical romances, for which we have substituted the truer novels! Two or three served for a summer's reading for the ladies, in their visits to the country.

We read of even Johnson, and we think of Chesterfield, wading through these gigantic efforts of absurdity, extravagance and prolixity.

A few words of the size of books :—It was a pleasant and shrewd saying of Horace Walpole, that arch epicure in all intellectual luxuries, that " he preferred books *in fructu* rather than *in folio*." We heartily agree with him, save in the case of journals and maps. Poets and essayists should always be in neat pocket form, if they are to be read; if merely to be looked at, they may as well be in folio or quarto. Histories, philosophical dissertations, sermons, &c., read best in octavo; novels and travels in duodecimo. We assent to Johnson's judgment, that " books that can be held in the hand, and carried to the fire, are the best after all !"

Fine bindings are fit only for centre-table books.

Hazlitt, in his modern Pygmalion, has painted the poet and the scholar in a line. All he seeks is " Books, Venus, Books ;"—Learning and Love.

XXI.

THE LITERATURE OF QUAKERISM.

The Society of Friends has been so useful a body of reformers and citizens—practical philanthropists and worthy neighbors, after the fashion of the good Samaritan, despite all the satiric sneers from Hudibras downwards, that their literary character has not been much regarded. Indeed, up to quite a late period, Literature and Quakerism were considered by the public as quite incompatible, and, we doubt not, within the penetralia of the sect, the sister arts are still considered vain, worldly, and almost heathenish. We will not recount the great benefit society has received from the zealous labors of some of these true friends of humanity. It were sufficient merely to mention the names of a few; of Clarkson and Mrs. Fry, and Jonas Hanway. The abolition of the slave trade; the apostolic love and charity manifested in the reform of prison discipline; the abolition of capital punishment—these three glorious reforms are sufficient to cast a halo around any sect or society out of which the advocates for them have come; advocates indeed, practically acting upon their doctrines; men not afraid to promulgate truth, and to execute their own convictions in living up to them.

Peace—the atmosphere of heaven—the gift of that Holy Spirit, one of whose noblest attributes it is—is the mission (so to speak) of the sect of Quakers; one which they have unfalteringly upheld and never once swerved from. These are some of the noble features of this sect—the most zealous, yet temperate—the most reasonable, and yet sincerely Christian (as it appears to us) of any of the numerous sects that have sprung from the Church of England, their common mother.

It is unnecessary, and apart from our present subject, to enter into any disquisition of the philosophy of the Quaker doctrine—its spirituality and metaphysical character—the serious and the ridiculous sides of the subject. All this, and more, has been done by Bancroft, in his admirable chapter on the Quakers, in the settlement of Pennsylvania, for which reason we shall restrict ourselves to the topics which naturally fall within the province of the present paper.

The Quakers are indebted to Charles Lamb for his exquisite sketches of them, which must be familiar to the readers of Elia. Lamb's correspondence, too, with Bernard Barton is equally an honorable bequest to the society, and shows him the kindly friend he was no less than the delightful humorist.

Hazlitt (in one of his essays, in the Round Table,) says, "A Quaker poet would be an anomaly." He must have forgotten the Spleen, whose author, Green, was a Quaker, though he discarded his early faith. The critic, too, probably, knew nothing of Bernard Barton, and had lost sight of Milton's Quaker friend, Ellwood, who, though he has left (we believe) no verses, was yet "the proximate cause" of Milton's writing Paradise Regained. The anecdote is told in all the Lives of Milton, and as we are not endeavoring to swell out this sketch by superfluous quotations, (a common method of making long magazine papers,) we shall merely refer to it. The Howitts had not then commenced their literary partnership, and Whittier had not probably penned a line of verse. The philosophy of Hazlitt's remarks is doubtless correct; yet there have been exceptions to their general application.

The first of these, we believe to have been Green, of whom Hunt has given a pleasant sketch, in his Wit and Humor. The Spleen of this author is a perfect *jeu d'esprit*, and the sole effort, after Butler's manner, worthy of comparison with Hudibras, in regard to fertility of ideas, wit, facility of rhymes, and sterling sense. The author was troubled with lowness of spirits, and wrote his poem for the same reason that Burton compiled his Anatomy. Like Lamb, he was a clerk in one of the public offices in London, a pleasant companion and a worthy man. This poem is in

Aikins' Selections, and, if we are not mistaken, in the Elegant Extracts. Hazlitt has strangely omitted it. Hunt has selected but a small portion of the rare beauties of this admirable poem. Almost every couplet is as good as the following lines, we write from memory, not having the book by us:

> And, in whose gay, *red letter'd* face,
> We read good living more than grace.

Here are a few of his innumerable felicities of language:

> "——A coquet *April-weather* face."
> "——News, the *manna* of a day."
> "—— *Tarantulated* by a tune."
> "——Adjust, and *set the soul to rights.*"

His remarks on the various remedies for the spleen; the mode of passing a rainy day agreeably; and his persuasions to cheerfulness and good humor, are as delightful as they are full of true wisdom.

Melmoth, the translator and author of Fitzosborne's letters, used to say, he could not easily find anywhere so many ideas in the same number of lines as in the Spleen.

Dr. Aikin has edited a delightful edition of Green's poems, illustrated by Stothard, a gem for the reader and hypochondriac.

How happens it this capital poem is so little known? A lively writer, but by no means a master of his native literature, on Green's poem being highly praised, sneeringly exclaimed: "Oh, yes! he is quoted by Rush!" as if the sensible Philadelphia physician gave fame to a sterling English wit.

Barton is a pleasing, religious versifier, with little or no force or character as a poet. Lamb's correspondence with him will probably preserve his name long after his verses are forgotten.

The poems of the Howitts fall under the same category as those of Barton, with more of variety, and perhaps more of poetic spirit. It is not probable that they will be long read.

But Whittier's is a name that will last, if only for a single poem he has written on a print of Raphael, which is now hanging, or did hang last summer, in a quiet parlor in Newburyport. The verses are in the Estray. If the very finest of our Quaker poet's poetic efforts were selected from the mass of his writings, he would rank much higher than he does at present. This poem and the fine ballad of the New Wife and the Old, Hampton Beach, Randolph of Roanoke, etc., would, with some score of spirited lyrics, fill a volume of American poetry to last. Like the leaders of his sect, (we do not know if Mr. Whittier still remains within its pale,) our poet has taken a warm interest in the great moral questions of the day, especially abolition of slavery and of capital punishment. He is (judging from his writings) an earnest, strong-souled man, and a genuine patriot; the poet of reform rather than of romance.

Yet much of his verse we think cannot live. His early imitations of Scott in narrative, and his latest songs of labor, which appear mechanical and cold, compared with Barry Cornwall's Weaver's Song, (the palpable model of Whittier's attempts,) or the songs of Burns. Gallagher's Laborer, in this department of poetry for the people, (where Elliott is the foremost bard of the present day,) strikes us as superior to anything of Whittier's in the same way.

The list of Quaker writers is short. Besides those we have mentioned, whose writings made a part of the current popular literature, we may add John Neal, a Quaker born and bred, though, doubtless, long since read out of meeting; Hannah Adams, the worthy spinster; and Mrs. Opie, if we are not mistaken, excellent in her tales for the young: Wiffen, the translator of Tasso, and Scott of Anwell.

We do not comprehend under our caption much the largest proportion of Quaker writings, by members of the Society of Friends—the piles of controversy and sectarian history. The early writers and founders of Quakerism, Fox and his ablest disciple Penn, and Barclay the Apologist, were voluminous pamphleteers and ready disputants The historian, Sewall, (a classic among the Friends, as Neal among the Puritans,) is preferred by Lamb to Southey in his Life of Wesley, an epitome of the History of Methodism. The author of Elia speaks highly of the life of Woolman. But Bancroft is abundantly sufficient for the general reader, in whose single chapter is condensed the marrow of a shelf full of Quaker histories, by men who have not yet learned the art of historical narrative and philosophical criticism.

In the elder literature, the Quakers meet with but scurvy treatment. The scholar will recollect Tom Brown's famous sermon, and the pungent epigrams of Butler. Dr. South, in his admirable sermon on the Christian Pentecost, has expended some of the finest prose satire in the language on the Puritans, which might apply with equal force to the Quakers, particularly of that day.

The character of the Quaker has often been caricatured on the stage, where he is generally made out a quack or a hypocrite or both. As the Quakers neither see nor write plays, this is hardly fair. Among the classic comedies, the Bold

Stroke for a Wife contains the liveliest and best drawn character, Simon Pure. The songs and music of Dibdin, with the rich tenor and fine acting of Incledon, has given the opera of the Quaker, in which he performed the part of Steady, a permanent reputation.

Seriously, however, Americans should cherish the Quaker. He has founded one of our finest states, and given it a peculiar character. His spirit is seen and kept alive in our wisest reforms, and his own character is such, that if it may not always be refined into that of the polite gentleman or agreeable companion, it is, nevertheless, made of the same material, and shares, as well and as constantly, in the characters of a true patriot, a zealous friend, an honest philanthropist, and a virtuous citizen.

XXII.

POETRY FOR THE PEOPLE.

The predominant fact in the history of the nineteenth century thus far—and there is slight probability of the fact becoming a fiction—is unquestionably the importance and elevation of the mass—the People, by distinction—the *tiers-etat* of France, the Commons of England. This fact is no less encouraging than novel. Before the era of the French Revolution, and our own antecedent to it, the People, as such, were considered with indifference, if not contempt. They had been regarded much in the same light as the Helots of Sparta, or the servile castes of Russia and Poland. Their rights were never mooted, for they had never been declared; they were supposed to exist only through the sufferance of the superior nobility and the will of the sovereign, and their lot was to toil, to suffer, and to pay taxes. This comprised their history, which might have been written in a very concise epitome. But modern science and modern philosophy—and, let us add, the silent influence of the true republican spirit of the Gospel—gave rise to a new state of things. Respect for the claims of human nature in the abstract, and of the individual in the concrete, begat sympathy for the former and reverence for the latter. Man, as such, was admitted by his brother as a brother, and his name and title allowed to rank higher (as our admirable Channing wrote) than King or President. Humanity, in her naked magnificence, asserted her inherent privileges, which were as openly acknowledged. Rank, riches, and royal power, lost their hold on the popular imagination, and Europe saw, at that late date, the sovereign of an ancient house treated as an usurper and punished more ignominiously than even a usurper merited. Force of character, moral energy, intellectual resources—these became wealth in that trying hour, and the weak, the bigoted and wavering, naturally fell the necessary victims of the conqueror. Yet as evil generally precedes good, so out of this chaos of tumult and crime emerged a benefit, the bow of promise, as from an atmosphere of storms and physical convulsion. This benefit we have already mentioned and it is this peculiar feature in the character of the age, the present position and claims of the people, that has given birth to a new and striking application of poetry to life, which may be expressed in the phrase, Poetry for the People.

In its most comprehensive sense, we might call all poetry political; for all truly inspired verse is the outpouring of the Spirit of Freedom, and the Spirit of Humanity. A similar love of freedom animates both the Poet and the Patriot, and the latter acts out what the other in song exhorts all men to act. Music, declamation, and all the refinements, both of art and learning, flourish in the most servile communities, and under the reign of despots; only true poetry and vigorous eloquence, (worth all the rest,) decay and wilt away, uncongenial plants in such a soil. All the master-bards, and the vast majority of lesser lights, (so they burn with original lustre,) of necessity are eulogists of freedom in the abstract, as of the Law of Right, the Law of Truth, and the reverence of the Beautiful; for, without these, what were poetry but a mere heap of fables and false devices. But that generous code of criticism which followed the trained system of the French classicality, has taught us the infinite worth of Poetry, as a mine of the highest truth and the deepest wisdom, apart from its beneficial moral tendency, and quite separate from its claims upon us as the sweetest of charmers, "most musical," though by no means "most melancholy." Of all writers, the Poets are the most moral, the most metaphysical, and we may add, the most political.

As philosophers, (for the Poet is the right popular philosopher,) they cannot avoid the propagation of free principles and liberal ideas; if only on the shallow grounds of diplomatic expediency; and this applies with greater force in a free country and an enlightened epoch. As humanitarians, (since the poet by his vocation is a philanthropist,) the poets feel as no other class of men can feel; for the whole circle of human necessities, from the lowest animal desires, up to the most elevated spiritual impulses, is included in their sympathies; and those, too, of the most delicate and intelligent description. The poet is the brother of his fellow-men and "Creation's heir," with the same fortunes and a similar destiny.

The genuine poet, then, is a patriot; sometimes, he is a bigot, a satirist, a partizan. Personal gratitude has inclined many a man of political genius to embrace a particular side; the prospect of future fame, or a desire to secure present patronage, has been the motive with many for enlisting under the banners and swearing by the shibboleth of party. The Muse is, sometimes, seen in a political livery; though Freedom has been, not inappropriately, styled "the Mountain Nymph." Yet there have been, and still are, authors who unite the poet and the partizan of admirable genius in the former capacity, and of unquestioned integrity in the last. These have been the noblest defenders of true independence, "Lords of the lion heart and eagle eye," as Smollett, a writer of this rare stamp, styles them.

Poetry always conveys the truest and most striking features in the countenance of the time. The most accurate painter of men cannot fail so to portray their master passions, reacting upon contemporary opinions and current modes of thought and action, but that he must needs also depict the contemporary influences by which these, too, are moulded; and these influences combine what we popularly describe as the Spirit of the Age. The patriarchal period, the splendid hierarchies of the ancient and modern world, chivalry, classic heroism, popular mythology, national traditions, legendary superstitions, the maxims even of the court and the mart, all point to peculiar tendencies in the times wherein they flourished. The present epoch of literature and popular sentiment must have its mouth-piece also, and this it finds in Poetry for the People.

At this phrase, let not your fine scholar nor your fastidious gentleman smile; the people have their political theories and representations; they have their magazines, encyclopedias, lectures and science; they have their theologians and newspapers, and the active brain of the wise legislator. Universal in its native region, Poetry is restricted within the boundaries of no caste or condition of society, but ranges at will through every department of life, and every grade of rank, till (as at present) it finds its sweet home in the breast of the simple-hearted though humble, and the true lovers of the divine art, among the popular body. For them, too, the modern historian ransacks the archives of the past to ascertain the starting-point of modern liberty. For them, he turns over the fascinating pages of cowled friars, or the lively chronicles of the courtly historiographer, illuminated no less by the pictures of genius than the colors of the artist, to be enabled to put his finger on precedents of priceless value and concessions of royal bounty, or to paint a Saxon freedman, a Norman knight, a German count, a Romish cardinal, a French king, a Spanish emperor; to note the democracy of the Romish Church, the republican character of commercial cities, the origin of parliaments and congresses, and to infer, from historical deductions, the dawnings of an intellectual and religious revolution long prior to the appearance of Luther.

The writer of prose fiction, (the most popular form of contemporary literature,) addresses himself to the people. Let him address scholars, like Lamb or Landor, and he is read by few else, even if he possess a degree of mental power that bursts beyond any confined limits of coventionalism or taste. Let him, however, write of the past with revereutial retrospection, or of the future with gladness and joyful hope; let him present a faithful mirror of the present time, in his pages, and he is read by all. The substance of his work may happen to be grounded on history or real life, or land or sea, in the walks of busy, or the picturesque variety of common life; impressed with this spirit, it must be popular, for it is, in effect, a history of the people.

Still further to exemplify this universal prevalent popular tendency in all our literature, at the present day, take the most abstract and (as vulgarly conceived) the least entertaining department of it, speculative philosophy, ethical or metaphysical. Here we find the appetite as keen as in the regions of fiction. Not only in the lecture-rooms and in the pulpit, but also in books * and even periodicals. Our leading magazines contain essays on these subjects, that would have been seen, in the last age, nowhere but in the volumes of professed writers on philosophy, and these too of the first class. We will not be so invidious as to attempt a comparison in the case of other periodicals, though we might point to papers in this Journal, to which no parallel can be offered in the monthly critical periodicals of the last century. An inquisitive tone of critical speculation is to be seen in the most ephemeral productions of the day, and we need no other test than the growing intelligence of the people than the character of newspaper literature, the excellence of which must continue to advance in proportion to the demand for it. But it is in poetry especially that we must look for the purest expression of the popular feeling. It is in poetry that (anti-poetical as we are thought to be) the national spirit is most faithfully evolved. Poetry, forsaking the knight in his bower, the baron

* We learn from one of the largest publishing houses in this city, that more copies of Abercrombie's Philosophical Compends have been disposed of by them, than of any other work, whether of reality or fiction.

in his castle, has taken up her abode, "for better for worse," with the artificer and the husbandman, not restricting herself, to be sure, to such society, but including them in her wide province, and watching over them with affectionate care. The poor man, upright, sincere, earnest, with deep enthusiasm and vigorous self-reliance, he is the hero of our time. The old-fashioned heroes of war and slaughter, one foot on land and one on sea, we are apt to consider with pity for their Quixotism and contempt for their absurd pretensions, at the same time that we are captivated by their brilliant accomplishments, and charmed by their humanity and knighlty grace. The struggle of life, the war with circumstances, that is the great battle to be fought, and one in which different qualities are required from those that bear away the palm in the warfare of blood and the contest for dominion and power. For hypocrititical professions of gallantry, the modern poet sings the real happiness of domestic love. The wife has supplanted the mistress, as a social tie; and marriage has put an end to the frivolities of idle gallantry, in the so-called age of chivalry. We say *so called*, because we conceive true chivalry repudiates most of the current vices which were cloaked beneath the broad mantle of its name; and because we apprehend a true and accomplished knight to be the ideal of glorious manhood, and far beyond what that character was supposed to represent in the persons of the Templar and the knights of the Hospital. Tournaments are long gone by, the duel is fast becoming extinct, and the contest of rivalry is, now-a-days, limited to a contest of worth and spirit, not a trial of martial skill or physical prowess. A single illustration will express our meaning, and mark distinctly the characteristics of the past and the present; then they had the trial by battle, now we have the trial by jury.

The necessity and dignity of labor, of endurance; the native nobility of an honest and brave heart; the futility of all conventional distinctions of rank and wealth, when opposed to the innate claims of genius and virtue; the brotherhood and equality of men,—not necessarily a social uniformity, independent of character and education, but the equality of civil rights and political advantages, for even actual blood brethren are not necessary equals, in aught beside the accident of their birth; the cultivation of manly liberality, of charity, in all its forms; of generosity, in not trenching upon the exactions of intelligent prudence and clear justice; an honorable poverty and a contented spirit, the richest of gifts these are the favorite topics of the Poet of the People. To attain this title, the poet must be master of his age, its wants and privileges, the traits of his countrymen, and the general aspect of society. Possessed of this knowledge, with a full heart, a firm hand, the "vision and the faculty divine," the rich resources of his art, and the aims and aspirations of humanity for his theme, what lessons can the poet not read the world—in what stirring tones will he not plead for his fellow-men! How indignantly may he not repel the scorn cast upon them, how vehemently upbraid their oppressors, how manfully exhort and how wisely persuade! Of all men, he is their dearest friend and strongest champion. No statesman, no patron, no general can effect a tithe of what he may accomplish; for give a man heart, and true counsel, and warm sympathy, and you give him what kings have never been able to purchase or capitalists to monopolize.

The vocation of such a writer is almost on an equality with the highest office that can be imposed on humanity, and his labors should be met by gratitude and love. The greatest bards of all time would not frown upon the humble attempts of the homeliest rhymer, so his verses had a life of their own, and an independent origin. It is not essential that the Poet for the People should be one of themselves; but that fact would certainly add weight to his teaching, and lend an energy to his appeals. The personal character and private life of such a man should be stainless; his life one of labor and honorable exertion; his benevolence bounded only by his means, which would be something more than merely pecuniary donatives, not neglecting those. With a pen informed by experience, and exercised on the immortal themes of the poet and the philanthropist, with hope in his heart and love on his tongue, with the fire, the fervor, the frankness of genius, such we would gladly hail, the Poet of the People and the Poet of the Poor.

XXIII.

ÆSTHETICAL FRAGMENTS.

MODELS.

I CAN recollect scarcely a single instance, in which great authors have written after models—where they have not imitated writers much inferior to themselves. In the history, also, of almost every man of genius, some inferior person is to be found, to whom the great man once looked up, and from whom he gained something. Thus, Burns imitated Ferguson; and Cowper, Vincent Bourne. Hudibras was modelled on a very trivial production of the same class, and Coleridge, at one period, almost adored Hartley. Burke expressed great indebtedness to an obscure clergyman, of the name (I think,) of Mudge; and Johnson has left an affecting retrospect of his gratitude for Gilbert Walmsley.

The greatest minds disdain not help from any source, and the most original writers are the greatest borrowers.

Some of our finest writers, among others, Pope and Goldsmith, openly professed imitation, and prided themselves on their skill in copying.

All of Washington's eulogists have been equally successful with all of his painters. None have failed to hit the marked traits of his character, as well as of his countenance. This, of itself, proves the harmonious beauty of his character.

To misrepresent a man's story, or repeat a tale differently from the way in which it was related, is the next crime to forgery, and may be still more injurious.

Belsham has neatly defined character to be 'the sum total of affections and habits.'

WIT AND HUMOR.

The distinctions between wit and humor are, that wit is intellectual; humor, sensuous; wit is artificial; humor, natural; that is, wit is employed on artificial objects—the follies of fashion; humor represents real farcical objects, and the traits of less refined society than the world of fashion.

A humorist is not, necessarily, a *man of humor*, but of *humors.* He cannot describe, or point out humorous peculiarities in others; but affords, in himself, a subject for the comic painter.

Wit is the scholar's quality, and partly acquired; humor is the quality of genius, and cannot be derived.

Wit is perceptive; humor, reflective. Learning assists wit; but rather impedes humor. The best instances of learned wit are, Rabelais, Butler, Swift; of learned humor, Sterne and Lamb. The finest humorous writers are Cervantes, Sterne, Smollett, Goldsmith, and Washington Irving.

Humor is, in part, constitutional--a matter of temperament; wit, rarely so. There is saturnine, gay, delicate, and powerful humor. It ranges from a subtle association to broad burlesque. Wit is exceedingly 'versatile and multiform' in its modes, but of one texture—always intellectual. A satiric poet is a wit; a humorist writes mock-heroic. Wit is bitter; humor, good-natured. Saturnine humor and sarcastic wit are very opposite. The first is melancholy, concealing tenderness; the last is brilliancy, pointing malice.

In description, humor appeals to the eye; wit, to the mind. The finest humorous writers have generally been poor talkers, because humor requires a fulness of development and detail too complicated and extended for conversation.

Wit, merely glancing at a topic, is, for that reason, admirably adapted to animated colloquy. There is a marked difference between the styles of humorous and witty writers. Humorous writers are more fluent and melodious; witty authors are generally short and pointed.

Humorous thoughts glide into the mind, are sympathetic; witty ideas, like cold abstractions, dazzle, but never charm. Wit and fancy, humor and imagination, are correlative.

A humorous satirist sympathizes with the object of his ridicule, as Cervantes with his hero; but a witty satirist always despises the subject of his satire.

Humor paints directly: wit illustrates indirectly. Wit is never descriptive at length; it paints miniatures, or sharpens an epigram. Humor is vividly graphic: wit is occupied with analysing character; humor rather paints manners.

Dialogue is the *forte* of a man of wit; *monologue* the property of the humorous writer.

IMAGINATION AND FANCY.

Imagination is the leading faculty of the mind; fancy, an accessory quality. The one has a general fusing power, the other is distinct from it and does not assimilate. Imagination is shown in conception: fancy, in particular illustration. The first looks to general effect: the last, to special ornament.

Imagination may be said to bear the same relation to fancy, as the firmament above us to a bright star. The first is grand and general: the second is fine and minute. The description of Death in Milton is an effort of imagination: the picture of Queen Mab in Romeo and Juliet is an instance of sparkling fancy.

Milton had a sublime imagination, vast and powerful: Shakspeare was almost, if not entirely, his equal in this respect, and was far more inventive and copious. Milton had not much fancy in his Paradise Lost: but his Comus and earlier poems are full of a fantastic, quaint fancy, enriched by and based upon, a fund of brilliant erudition. His fancy afterwards became more a matter of learning and elaboration.

Shakspeare, universally gifted, was blessed with a most luxuriant fancy, rich, romantic, and picturesque. Among contemporary poets, Coleridge had most imagination, and Keats the freest fancy.

A scholastic fancy is the result of subtle association.

TASTE AND JUDGMENT.

Taste is finer quality than judgment, but by no means so exact or clear. It has less penetration, and wants the spirit of forecast and prediction.

Taste is an instinct. Judgment, an intellectual act. The one is partly a matter of organization; the other refers itself solely to the intellect.

A man of refined judgment is the better critic on men and characters; a man of delicate taste excels him in criticising books, particularly poets and works of art. Taste depends on sensibility: judgment on principle. The first distinguishes the man of genius: the second, the man of talent. Taste is an impulse and a sentiment: judgment, the deduction of reason, and the fruit of experience. Judgment is sure. Taste is uncertain. The first is a fixed star: the second, a wandering comet. Judgment is the quality of a strong taste of a fine intellect. A nice judgment is the effect of harmony existing between all the faculties of the mind, is a state of calm and collectedness. Repose and quiet alone can give the judgment fair play. Fire and heat bring out other qualities. Passion alone can sometimes arouse the muse:

Indignatio facit versos.

Taste is much more susceptible of culture than judgment, since it depends so much on natural and organic sensibility. Judgment once fixed, retains an impassive character.

Taste is a positive; judgment, a negative quality. Taste loves to find beauties; judgment, rather to detect imperfections.

We often apply gusto to taste; never to judgment. Taste is an assimilating faculty. Judgment is solitary. Taste is governed by prepossession. Judgment should be entirely free from any foreign influence. Our choicest tastes may be only delightful prejudices; our soundest judgments must be determinate conclusions of the reason. The one is affected by its own perceptions; the other judges without emotion.

CONVERSATION.

Conversation is an art. It is neither a lecture, nor a comedy, entirely; but partakes of the nature of both. It is for instruction; it is for amusement. But it differs from other instruction, in being the readiest—the most familiar. It teaches indirectly; it amuses agreeably.

The satirist and the sentimentalist, the professed censor and the professed moralist, are the pests of conversation.

There are two classes of satirists among talkers; the first, "bitter bad judges of men:" the second, elegant wits, who can trifle with grace, and ridicule without ill-nature.

Conversation may be a war, or a treaty; a negotiation for peace, or a manifesto of hostilities.

Conversation is more dramatic than composition. It is an acted dialogue.

There are those who succeed best in argument, or exposition; some in new speculation, more in trite disputations; one tells a story in a lively manner, or describes with life and spirit.

Few excel in retort; fewer in repartee.

Most reasoners, in general conversation, have a few cant phrases and set expressions; beyond which, they grope in the dark.

A judicious jest is the rarest thing in the world,—as rare as an honest man. Most jesting is rudeness, or impertinence, or coarseness, or frivolity.

A jest in which the wit ministers to the wisdom, is a prose epigram and a proverb combined.

Many truths may be told in a light jest, that politeness would not allow one to speak out in serious earnest.

Satire is almost always ill-humor well expressed. Satiric wit breaks up free open conversation. People fear and hate it. A certain respect is due to every man's opinion and character, if respectable, and even to his weaknesses.

A bitter satirist, (as religionists generally are), can never claim to be either a gentleman, or a Christian.

"We ought never," says Labruyère, "to venture on the most innocent and offensive raillery, or pleasantry, unless it be amongst polite men, or men of wit."

Some persons are above jest; some, below it. It is irreverence to jest with some; it is cruelty to jest with others.

It is the least part of wisdom to speculate on the petty defects of every-day people.

I never knew a man entirely destitute of a love of music, and an eye for natural scenery, who was not at bottom hypocritical and insincere. No man can be strongly or tenderly affected by music who wants generosity of sentiment. It is certain there is something in music which goes quicker to the heart than anything in poetry or painting. It was the voice of nature before language was formed. Some feelings can only be expressed by certain indistinctness of sound, since all language is conventional. That ancient displayed fine imagination in his conceptions, who taught the voice is the soul.

I never enter a watchmaker's shop without being sensibly reminded of all the topics enforced by the moralist and preacher. In the midst of these memorials we seem to run an even race with father Time. That tall clock clicking in the corner so orderly, is no more a chronicler of time than myself with my pulse beating its vibrations equally with the pendulum. It seems a catacomb of dead men's pulses reanimated, since nothing but that part of man is represented by them. Their faces are blank surfaces, with figures marking the hours; our faces are something more than blank surfaces, although in the countenances of some there is no vast difference between the two.

XXIV.

CORRESPONDENCE OF RICHARDSON.

The Letters of Richardson present a fair reflection of his life. From them it is easy to imagine his daily habits and moral dispositions. The prominent virtues he possessed, unconsciously disclose themselves on his pages, as well as his no less prominent foibles. The tastes of the man, and his selection of companions, mark his own peculiarities as strongly as any limner could draw them. Thus his hospitality and kindness are shown to one in trouble and distress; his love of discussion and moralizing, with a polemical friend; his vanity is apparent in an egotism, badly concealed by a mask of assumed modesty; his knowledge of the female heart may be gathered from his artful manner of composing letters addressed to ladies.

The early life of Richardson, as of every man of genius, determined the character of his later years. Born in very humble circumstances, with little opportunity of liberal instruction, bound to a trade, he passed through his seven years of apprenticeship with fidelity and zeal. In these years, he laid the foundation of sober, upright, exact principles, and frugal, diligent, methodical habits—fairly realizing Hogarth's Industrious Apprentice—upon which to rear an after fortune. He obtained, by these means, the sincere respect of his master, of whose interest he was so careful as even to buy the candles by the light of which he read at night. When a mere boy, he was noted for invention, and was often called upon to exert his peculiar talent for the gratification of his favorite school-mates; and in later life he always used to boast that he never forgot to add a good moral. Shortly after this period, he began to exhibit his strongest propensities; a love for letter writing, and for the company of women. The letter was the vehicle by means of which he conducted his narratives to the conclusion, aud which,doubtless, became the easiest syle for him, from long practice and natural inclination. Being a modest, and perhaps rather timid, young fellow, he was encouraged, it seems, by the young women of the neighborhood, to read to them some entertaining volume, when they met together for sewing. From the reader, he became the principal confidant of their love adventures, and finally, their devoted scribe in all cases of emergency, requiring epistolary skill and the habit of the pen. The little secrets disclosed to him, the varying conflict of duty and desire, the hopes and fears of bashful love, the tenderness and liberal charity of the passion in its most engaging state, these pages of the book of human nature, the author conned with a careful eye, and thence secured his richest stores. This was the best part of Richardson's education as an author. From one step to another, making the best honest use of opportunities, Richardsonson gradually became a settled tradesman, of wealth and respectability. His first published efforts were prefaces, indexes, and what he called honest dedications, for the printers. Himself a printer and publisher, he became acquainted with some of the first men of the day, though with more of a much inferior grade; with Johnson, Young, Warburton, Cibber, of the first class; and such men as Aaron Hill, who stood on a sort of middle ground, between the best and worst. He was very liberal and hospitable to authors and scholars. He assisted Aaron Hill; he had the honor to bail Doctor Johnson. He was a kind master, laying pieces of money for the first man in the office of a morning. Accident led him to a proper appreciation of his powers. At the request of a number of "the trade," he undertook to write a volume of familiar letters for the youth of the lower classes, in which he would not only aim at giving them words for composition, but also infuse his own ethical code of practical duties; thus he meditated directions to young women going out to service; he intended to give his views of the parental and filial relations, and similar mutual obligations. From a letter of the first sort—a mere acorn to the oak, into which it expands—sprang the History of Pamela. The way once found, and success attending the novel attempt, he was induced, once and again, to appear in the same character of a fictitious writer, embodying, in his second work of Clarissa Harlowe, his idea of a "perfect woman, nobly planned;" and in Sir Charles Grandison—a sort of male Clarissa—the abstraction of a perfect man. We may hereafter consider the second work of Richardson with more attention. At present, we give the brief outline oi his literary history, as illustrative of his personal character. How came an illiterate tradesman, who acknowledged that he wrote more than he read—who, in a letter to Cave, the bookseller, confesses to having never read all the Spectator, and yet writing a paper for Johnson, which the gross flattery of his admirers set above the Spectators—to attain an insight, and reveal powers, yet unseen, in fiction, and to gain the applause and acquire the admiration of the wise, the great, the happy, and the gay? The answer is, by a deep study of the human heart, and especially of the female breast, and a consequent power to move it. To look through his correspondence, selecting merely the chief names, with what a variety of characters was he not connected!—the sensible and grateful, but vain and unfortunate Aaron Hill; with the sturdy Warburton, who condescended to compliment him—and that in an elaborate letter; with the metaphysical Harris, the author of Hermes; with his companions in business, Cave and Strahan; with the fastidious Lord Orrery; with the Poet Young; with Miss Sally Fielding, a relation of the author of Tom Jones, and who wrote the engaging tale of David Simple; with the vivacious veteran, Colley Cibber; with Miss Highmore, sister to one of the fashionable painters of that day;

with Meeta, the wife of Klopstock; with Miss Mulso, afterwards the didactic Mrs. Chapone; with Dr. Delaney, the old name so familiar in the verses of Swift; with Mrs. Sheridan, the mother of Richard Brindsley—authoress of Sidney Biddulph—and wife of Thomas Sheridan, the actor and elocutionist; with ladies of quality, of whom Ladies Erskine and Bradshaigh were the most unfortunate; and with a number of the clerical body, numbering one bishop and several clergymen; one of whom, a Mr. Skelton, is a hero, after the pattern of Amory's heroes.

The characteristic traits of Richardson, was a certain prudence, which was yet warmed by generosity, and a tenderness of feeling, that, nevertheless, was subdued by an austere manner. His character was a good deal formed by circumstances, and undoubtedly much affected by the circle of which he was the centre. "He lived in a kind of flowergarden of ladies," who were at once his models and critics. He drew the character of his heroines from the characters he saw around him, and subjected his writings to the judgments of that body of his readers, whom he thought best fitted to appreciate them. Women, he thought—not always correctly—the best judges of female character. Dr. Johnson gives another reason for his being surrounded with women, that he loved superiority, and hated contradiction; but he has left out another point, that our author really loved their society for its own sake, and for sympathy. His own nature was somewhat feminine, and like Marmontel, and Hume, and Cowper, he found the society of virtuous women most congenial to his mind. Wordsworth is a rare instance of a man, living for years chiefly in the society of his sister and wife, whose writings exhibit few or no traces of the influence of female conversation. Authors who have honestly enjoyed the delights of a home, and the affections of wife and children, have, in most cases, been apt to express their sincere gratification in lively colors, and to modify their views of life and human nature by the influences a fortunate home can alone exercise. Such passages are read with pleasure in Hunt, and Lamb, and Jean Paul, and Goethe. A variety of slight anecdotes gives us sufficient clues to the true character of Richardson: he was fond of children—always a good trait—and carried sugar-plums and candies about with him for them, as Burchell carried ginger-bread. In proof of his vanity, so much and so severely, as we think, charged against him, there is the story of his giving Speaker Onslow's servants larger veils than ordinary, in order to command their respectful deportment. This tells, at least, as much against their master as against Richardson; and, after all, may be only an envious exaggeration. He was always a liberal man, and may have been profuse to the servants from no other feelings that those of generosity. It is true, Richardson liked attention, as who does not, who deserves it? It is true his correspondents indulge freely in compliments, and sometimes in extravagant praises. His works generally formed the subject of conversation, when he was present. But then we are to consider the novelty of the form of writing he originated, its unprecedented success, that it was to woman he devoted his talent, and from women expected his praises; that his great and general reputation threw a lustre over his private life; that he was, moreover, a man of acute sensibility, and such men are generally vain and generous, the two passions appearing to take their rise in a complexional temperament, and peculiar intellectual constitution, and finally running very much into each other.

Richardson always had about him a number of young women, whom he treated as daughters, and whom he appears to have been more attached to than to his children. His girls, he called them. They were at one period Miss Mulso, afterwards Mrs. Chapone; Miss Highmore, sister to the painter, and afterwards Mrs. Duncomb, marrying a gentleman she met at Richardson's; a niece to Secker, the Bishop, to whom Pope gave "a heart;" Miss Prescott; Miss Fielding; Miss Collier. These ladies constituted a sort of virtuous harem, where the main business done, was listening to the letters fresh from the pen of Richardson, and proceeding in their criticisms as he read. When we consider the way of life of Richardson, in the midst of his admiring coterie, and contrast it with a Turk's seraglio, we are at once reminded of the lines of Congreve's two lovers, one of whom thus addresses the other:

> You take her body, I her mind—
> Which has the better bargain?

Richardson seems to have resolved this question for himself, by choosing the latter.

An odious feature, we had almost forgotten to remark, in Richardson, and which we will dismiss now very briefly, is his mean jealousies of his rivals, Fielding and Sterne; of both he speaks with great, and we hope, ignorant contempt. He speaks of that "brat," Tom Jones; of its run being over "with us;" of its not being tolerated in France; of almost every character in it, with scornful disdain. Amelia comes off little better. He can read only the first volume. It is all so *low*. Parson Adams he appears to regard as a pure burlesque. He allows Fielding low humor, but nothing else. He can see nothing but indecencies and irreligion in Sterne: to his finest strokes he is wholly indifferent.

The correspondence of Richardson forms a voluminous collection, to the entire perusal of which we would, by no means, invite the reader, but would particularly urge a reading of the very interesting biographical account of Mrs. Barbauld; a discriminating production. The fullest portion is the correspondence of Mrs. Bradshaigh, the history of which contains a strange mixture of absurdity and romance. She wrote, for a long time, under the assumed name of Mrs. Belfour, entirely a stranger to Richardson, and after revealing her name, and making an appointment to meet our author in the Park; to enable her to recognise him, he sent her a minute description of his gait, and personal appearance, and manner in the street. She several times disappointed him. He, an old man, with a large family, patrolled the public walks daily to see her, with all the ardour of a youthful lover; which anxiety, she, with a coquetry natural to her sex, kept in suspense for some time. Her letters, and his answers, turn either almost wholly on a discussion of the characters of his novels, or of topics incidentally touched upon. The very best and most attractive, correspondence, to our minds, in the whole collection, is that of Klopstock's wife, of which the least praise we can give it is, that it is worthy of a wife of a poet. It seems she was first attracted to Richardson by his novels, then, and we believe still, very popular with the Germans. She gives him a history of her engagement with Klopstock, how she first became attached to him, how he won upon her by his noble aspirations and purity, how she venerated him—then a mere youth,—how she lived so happily; her thoughts of him during his absence, and her continued joy in his presence. All this is told in a charming style, a vein of simple tenderness, which a crude critic will be sure to call lackadaisical, but which a genuine critic will read with pleasure. She calls upon Richardson, in what certainly reads a little extravagantly, to paint an Angel, since he has done all that can be done for humanity. From the characters of the writers, generally, we may gather the tenor of their letters. Those of Richardson himself, have a very unpleasant formality about them. He is somewhat, it must be confessed, of a proser, and if not writing to those who solicited his correspondence, would have been regarded as no great accession to a list of letter-writing friends. He has sense, but no vivacity: his lively attempts are very awkward. He is a clumsy humorist, and by no means a refined sentimental writer. The sources and occasions of his sympathy are always palpable, and meagerly expressed. His style is loose and bald, and nowhere shows the close thinker, nor accurate author.

Thus much of Richardson, the familiar correspondent; we hope to be able to say more of the author of Clarissa Harlowe.

XXV.

THOMAS MOORE.

THE present century has produced many able writers, some brilliant critics and essayists, careful and scrutinizing authors in history and philosophy, a few men of real wit, one or two true humorists, many sweet, lively versifiers, and, fewest of all, a band of genuine poets. But in the list which includes Byron, Wordsworth, Coleridge, Keats, and Shelley, posterity will not place the name of Moore, who, at the present moment enjoys, perhaps, a more varied and general, not to say enviable and exalted reputation, than any of the poets just mentioned. In the end, the permanence and character of an author's reputation must solely rest on the character and merit of his works. The epic seldom read, if a really great work, is sure of immortality; the collection of songs, however popular, unless equally admirable in their way, must give place to the next new fashion of the hour.

It must not be thought we underrate the song because it is brief, and offers less pretensions. It was the earliest form of poetry, and is consecrated by the numberless gems, the bright thoughts, the dark fancies, the glittering conceits of poets of every age and country.

Of songs the earliest are the best, for the above reason, they were fresher, had the advantage of coming first, were unhackneyed. We, therefore, greatly prefer the early song-writers, and agree sincerely with Izaak Walton, who is speaking of a similar kind of poetry, such as Raleigh, Marlowe, and Walton wrote: "They wrote old-fashioned poetry, but choicely good; *I think much better than the strong lines now in fashion, in this critical age.*"

Moore is essentially a song writer. It affords the best scope for his genius, which flags beyond a limited distance, yet a song writer of a different stamp from the old masters of the lyric art, as we shall have occasion to show.

Mr. Moore is a parlor-poet. We have all known parlor-orators: old gentlemen, who would descant with all the flourishes of rhetoric, on some topic of business, or politics, or family history. Yet here we have a bard, whose best audience is a fashionable company, whose best position is sitting at the piano and whispering one of his own melodies into the charmed ears of school-girls and the titled dames of English society. You would never have caught Milton exhibiting himself in this fashion. He knew how to preserve the dignity of the poetic character, which was the ruling character in him. Moore is rather a man of fashion; writing verses for his own amusement, and singing them for the entertainment of others. His fancy is of proper dimensions to suit a drawing-room; he may flutter amongst china ornaments, gilded vases, and ormolu clocks; rustling behind the curtains, or burying himself, with Rabelais, in his easy chair of luxurious construction. In the open air of the world, on the broad stage of society at large, he is lost. He wants ballast to support him, so light and volatile is his genius. He has no energy to propel him onward. He has no weight of sentiment; no force of thought.

What, then, has he? A lively wit, a vein of glittering conceits, cold and hard, in proportion to their polish, great power of language, running into mere verbosity, and a fatal facility of turning off any given quantity of rhyme, at the shortest possible notice. His muse is always on the alert, "coming," "coming," like the tapster at a popular inn. He has not the slightest pretensions to the three great requisites of a great poet. He has no lofty imagination, no deep sentiment, no curious felicity of expression. His fancy is a tricksy sprite, smart and epigrammatic, capable of doing justice to a political satire, or well-bred courtly scandal. It conducts him easily and pleasantly through the mazes of a comic song, and even enlightens the honest heartiness of his patriotic effusions. But in sentimental pieces, it becomes mere affectation. His serious notes are mere grimacings of sensibility. The feeling of his songs is such as his fashionable readers can appreciate, but so hollow and superficial, with a very few exceptions, as to be appreciable by no other class. One reason of the popularity of the Melodies, is the sweet music to which many of them have been married, and the sweet voices we have heard sing them. Mrs. Wood gave a new lustre to the treble part of "Love's Young Dream." "Oft in the stilly night," has called forth the sweetest tones of the finest tenor; "The Soldier's Farewell" has been answered by many a heart. Peculiar circumstances have given reputation to some of the songs: as the history of the song, "She is far from the land where her young lover sleeps." There are, perhaps, ten really natural expressions of feeling in the collection of Melodies, but we doubt if more. The rest of the sentimental songs are sad stuff. The Orator Puff's are much better, and the "Two-penny Post Bag," a separate satirical poem, the best of all Moore's attempts.

Moore's Lalla Rookh is an instance of palpable failure. We know, nowhere, more elaborate, voluptuous description, and complicated, fanciful illustrations, so entirely thrown away as here, except in the versified form of the Epicurean, properly a rich, oriental prose poem, but, as translated into verse, a meaningless desert of poetical commonplaces.

The Anacreon of this author is not so good as Cowley's version; which proves that the very airiest poetry must have a basis of powerful sense, as the hardest marble takes the finest polish, and the loftiest pillars are crowned with the lightest chaplets of Corinthian grace. Ben Jonson, whose finest lyric, "Drink to me only with thine eyes," is continually ascribed to Moore, affords one instance among many others, of stern, rugged, vigorous sense, lightened and relieved by delicate and graceful fancy. The majestic old tragedians, Marlowe, Webster, and Shakspeare, and the rest, exhibited this refinement. But mere fancy, without vigor of understanding, fails to give momentum and passion to poetic flights. An excess of levity is visible in such poetry, which, on grave themes, is converted into as intolerable dullness.

The imitations of Moore are among the best tests of the real want of excellence in his poetry. His copyists are mawkish ballad-mongers, or else libertine philosophers, as they may affect real feeling, or a perfect indifference to it. These gentlemen substitute the French wines for Byron's gin, and if not as furious and terrible as the followers of Don Juan, are more light-hearted and skeptical.

There is an unhandsome notion lurking in the community, that the quantity of wine a poet can drink, and its effects upon him, exhibit the measure of his powers. Willis, himself, has lately fallen in with this absurdity, by which proof he attempts to make out Wordsworth to be a dull fellow, but Barry Cornwall a "glorious" poet. Proctor has certainly written some spirited songs, but the general tone of his poetry is feeble elegance, with occasional delicacy. The sentimental songs of this school may be generally classed with Pope's Song by a Person of Quality, and are filled with an equal number of senseless epithets, and inexpressive expressions.

The next generation will probably hear of Moore as a lively political wit, an accomplished diner-out, an agreeable companion at the summer *fêtes* of the great, in the country, and the admired of all admirers at the crowded routes of wealth and fashion in town. His songs will be sung—most of the good ones are now threadbare—until a new Haynes Bayly springs up, when he will be forgotten. His scholarship, being kept to himself, will be matter of tradition.

Lalla Rookh is now a dead letter; the History of Ireland is a dull book, though it may run an even race with Mr. Grattan's History of the Netherlands, which is another dull book. In a word, Moore's reputation is mostly personal, and will die with him, like that of the Sedleys and Killegrews of a past age. Having written no such songs as Burns, like him he cannot live, nor emulate the fame of the truly great poets of this period, since his most elaborate attempt is a failure.

XXVI.

LITERARY PORTRAITS.

MACAULAY.

MACAULAY the Edinburgh reviewer, is, probably, the most brilliant writer of English prose now living, the last remaining member of that glorious band of wits, critics, and fine thinkers, who constituted the force of the Edinburgh in its prime — Jeffrey, Macintosh, Hazlitt, Brougham, Carlyle, Stephens, and himself; uniting also the fame of a successful politician to that of a splendid periodical writer, he has obtained an accumulation of honors rarely to be met in the person of a single individual. Review writing has now become an art, and one, too, in which very few succeed even respectably and in which innumerable failures occur quarterly. It is methodized into a system. It has its rules, and canons, and peculiar style. It must be exhaustive and thorough in its analysis; the writing must be neat and clean; the wit, bright and "palpable;" the logic, close and ingenious; the rhetoric, elaborate and dazzling. The style must never lag behind the story. There must be animation, at all events, even with error, (for the sake of piquancy,) rather than dullness, however just and sincere. A flat review, however accurate and true, must fail; a true story does not answer the purpose of a lively reviewer, while a clever conjecture passes for more than an acknowledged truth, which wants the stimulus of novelty. This, surely, is not as it ought to be. Is it as we represent? You have only to read Macaulay to become satisfied as to the correctness of the criticism. Macaulay's reviews are the very Iliad and Odyssey of criticism—models of that kind of writing. Abler men and deeper scholars have written review articles yet without that mastery of the art. Hazlitt had a more copious fancy, a richer vein, and was altogether a more copious thinker and critic, yet his reviews lie buried under a mass of duller matter. We doubt whether Macaulay could have written the Surrey Lectures, but that is *travelling out of the record.* Macaulay's articles are not to be mistaken. It is like love at first sight, you may always know his hand. He wants, to be sure, the solidity of Burke, the rich philosophy of that poetic thinker; yet even Burke could not have hit the mark with greater nicety. He would have carried too much metal. Macaulay is essentially a critical essayist; not a mere critic, not an original judge, not a lecturer, but that rare union of critic and miscellaneous writer—a critical essayist. Probably, in no other form of composition could he have succeeded to such a degree of excellence. He could not compress himself into a monthly or weekly essayist. He wants, moreover, fineness and delicacy, for purely elegant writing. He paints on too broad a canvas, and aims too much at striking colors and at effects, to elaborate ingenious beauties, and perfect the almost perfect beauties of nature, in his style. Then, again, in a long work he would soon tire: his genius would droop when he got beyond his hundred pages. Pamphleteering would, perhaps, better suit Macaulay's genius than review writing, for he is a partizan in everything he writes. In his capacity of critic, he too often allows his political bias to influence his judgment — the cabinet minister is sometimes a mere smart, ingenious paragraphist, by no means so intent on the truth as he should be. We remarked this particularly in two consecutive papers, the one on Southey's Colloquies, the other on Moore's Byron. The first writer is treated as a tory; the second as a whig. Contrast, also, the papers on Milton and on Boswell. Once understood, this partiality does no harm, but rather gives an edge to his style. History, no less than Letters, has been vividly illustrated by Macaulay, and many of his articles, in themselves, preserve the essence of books of great size but not equal value. Portrait painting and finished declamation have been carried to perfection in his articles, in which we find, besides, a treasury of fine and ingenious thoughts, richly illustrated and admirably employed. He is so much, in a word, the opposite of Carlyle, that a characteristic sketch of the latter will not fail to include all the qualities opposed to his own, that we have omited in the above notice.

CARLYLE.

Thomas Carlyle is a name to be treated with respect, for, notwithstanding all his absurdity and pretension, he is undeniably so vigorous, and even sometimes so profound a writer, so sincere and genial a critic, and when warmed and in earnest, so powerful, that it would argue a deficiency, both of acuteness and candor, to deny his very great merits; at the same time, there is so much in the writer to excite a quite contrary feeling, that we hope to be pardoned for indulging in a free censure that may not seem warranted by the idolaters of his genius Carlyle has distinguished himself in several lines of excellence; let us glance at his proficiency in each. As the biographer of Schiller, his first attempt at criticism and narrative, he has surpassed all his future efforts, except in his translations, his admirable Sartor Resartus, and his later endeavors in behalf of sincere and intelligent Reform. In the light in which he is most frequently considered, that of a mere speculative reformer, we do not rate him so highly by any means as we do regard him in certain other characters. He insists, in a right manly strain, on the nobleness, the necessity, of those great virtues—truth, sincerity, perseverance. He preaches many an old text with new life and vigor, but we cannot think that he is eminently original, if, indeed, he has any pretensions that way at all. We do not ask for novelty; it is something to make the most of what we have, a truth very few, either moralists or legislators, seem to consider. But when a great outcry of discovery is made, we do certainly expect something more than Carlyle furnishes by way of substitute. With Rob Roy, our author may unite in declaring that,

> "Of old things, all are over old,
> Of good things, none are good enough."

And, in effect, he makes the same vaunt:

> "We'll show that we can help to frame
> A world of other stuff."

Yet, after all, we stand where we stood before; the world has not moved a jot, we mean as to practical, perceptible benefits. It is undeniable that Carlyle's writings have done great good, if only by making men think, and suggesting an appreciation of the terrible evils that hang, like a thunder-cloud, (ready to burst on our heads;) over the mass of society. The political atmosphere, charged (as in England and France) with the groans of the oppressed, the sighs of suffering, and the curses of outraged humanity, must needs be furnished with some safe conductor to protect the miscreants in power and place, who thus goad on their fellows, by misery to crime. An awful doom awaits the merciless legislators of England, if they cease not to obstruct the path of freedom, nor lay heavy burthens on the back of the much wronged poor and working-classes of that country. Carlyle's practical suggestions of education, emigration, and the like, are not sufficient. They are highly useful, but much more is needed, and which ought to come from the landholders and manufacturers themselves, else others may work in vain. To regard the writer, however, purely as such. He is a singular mixture of Scotch shrewdness with German scholarship and fancies. The races in him are mixed. He is best as critic and of German authors, whom he has translated with equal force, fidelity, and spirit. The German romances, in his hands, are very different things from the common translations of the Sorrows of Werter, or Kotzebue's tragedies, or Klopstock's Messiah. His papers, too, on Novalis, &c., are excellent; that on Richter, (his favorite and model) is a masterpiece. Some of his papers on English literature are almost as good. The noble criticisms on Burns and Johnson must be familiar to every one. The critic's strictures on systems and politics we do not so much admire. His merely speculative inquiries do not amount to much. The critic has acuteness and force, but hardly equal subtlety and power of concentration. History, in the hands of Carlyle, is descriptive and illustrative, rather than purely narrative. He is much more of the critic of constitutions, measures and men, than the relater of events. He is picturesque and dramatic, but true history is epical and legendary. The (so called) history of the Revolution in France, is rather a gallery of portraits and scenes of civil war. It is wild and fitful, (like the blasts of winter howling over a desolate heath,) rather than a sustained elegy or a grand triumphal Ode to Freedom. It is, in a word, melo-dramatic. Compared with it, the classic historians are tame and insipid. The style is curt and *jerking*, and, like a careering horse, too often unseats the sober judgment of the historian.—Sartor Resartus is the master work of its author, (indeed, *such*, every clever writer can point to, some one superior thing which he could never surpass.) It is close, ingenious, profound, and earnest; full of a deep satirical humor that, like all true humor, conceals deep thought and feeling, striking scenes instinct with knowledge of life. It is, in fact, a philosophical picture of the inner life of a real man in the world; a magnificent piece of autobiography, satire, sentiment, and speculation. It contains the portrait of the true scholar, the genuine human being and not the mere pedant or outside man, whom it cuttingly exposes. It is brimful of admirable sense, the better for being good common sense, so much rarer than any other faculty. We feel warranted in calling this Carlyle's best work; the one genially meditated, most earnestly worked out; yet (we can't help discovering it) the work which first records that tortuous style of writing, which we cannot avoid thinking a vile form of affectation, itself one of the most disagreeable of the venial sins of authorship. When we compare the early and later styles of this same writer, the difference is more obvious. The life of Schiller is a model of pure English, while some of Carlyle's later works are horrible distortions of the language.

The cause of this great change is to us clear: some have conjectured it to result from confusion of ideas, the common apology for a dark style, but we believe it to arise from a perverse imitation of the worst parts of certain German authors. Carlyle is utterly destitute of genuine wit, though his admirers claim that for him, as well as partial genius. He sometimes discovers a streak of surly humor, as it were, such as Quin, the actor, was said to possess. Of light, pleasant raillery, he has not a particle. His jests are as awkward as the gambols of the elephant, in Milton. His wit—to copy an expression of his own, is a sort of small-beer faculty. Carlyle's favorite characters are rough, hardy Saxon men—somewhat in his own vein, as Knox, Luther, Johnson and Burns; and daring revolutionists preserving the parallel, as Napoleon, Danton, Mirabeau. Force of character and sincerity furnish his requisites for a hero. Carlyle paints with a bold hand—firm and free—uses strong colors without much grace or art, and with no elegance or taste. Still he has a certain peculiarity that is very striking. Among painters our critic would rank with Hans Holbein—the court painter of Henry VIII., and a friend of Erasmus. His descriptions have something of Salvator Rosa in them, as wild and savage. He is no Vandyke, no Sir Joshua Reynolds, no Sir Thomas Lawrence. He has no hand for depicting female grace; he paints *men, heroes.* Among artists of the last age, he would rank with Fuseli. Like him he succeeds in strong characters and tumultuous scenes.

XXVII.

LORD BOLINGBROKE.

THE reputation of Bolingbroke is now almost wholly a matter of tradition. The courted and caressed minion of fortune, the "all-accomplished St. John," the petted darling of fashion, the favorite son of genius, is, at the present day, a name and little else. The personal qualities of a brilliant manner and polished address, which, together with copiousness of language, both in writing and speaking, a certain elegance of air, and a superficial stock of showy erudition, conspired to render the name of Bolingbroke a talisman of magic power in his own day, have all now given place to an oblivion, rightly merited, by an absence of the chief virtues of the heart, and of all the really admirable qualities of the head—the only sure antidotes to mortality. We find in the history of Bolingbroke, a lesson to those who would elevate the character of a friend into that of a demigod; who judge too much from personal feeling, and make little allowance for the just, because utterly impartial, verdict of posterity.

If we gather our opinion of the genius of Bolingbroke from the reports of private friendship, we would place him on the pinnacle of fame; if we judge from his personal history, and from his own writings, we come to a quite opposite conclusion. The writers of his day seemed to have conspired to raise him to the heights of renown; but he had not the internal force to make good their endeavors. Resting on his own merits, he soon sank to his proper level of inferiority and general obscurity.

The praises bestowed on Bolingbroke fall little short of adulation. Pope's strain is always that of extravagant eulogium. Swift was not far behind in this respect. Later writers have kept up the ball. Bulwer, and the younger D'Israeli, in their early novels, painted him the hero of the boudoir and the saloon of fashion. The latest professed eulogy we have read of Bolingbroke, is from the pen of Lord Mahon, in his history—who coincides with the vulgar idea of a past school of criticism, in the opinion that Bolingbroke was, perhaps, the finest of English writers.

Writing chiefly either on political, and hence purely ephemeral topics, or on moral and religious, and hence permanent themes, Bolingbroke is to be judged as a pamphleteer, and as a philosopher. In the first character, he was eminently successful; his tenets were those of a strong partizan, and defended with animation and considerable force of declamation. Sometimes he rose into eloquence, but generally, his declamation was as cold and artificial as his reasoning was specious and shallow. Pitt, to be sure, used to say, the Letter to Sir William Wyndam was the most masterly composition in the English Language, but his wretched literary taste is well known. It suited his own style of political eloquence, being wordy, full and musical. The moral essays of Bolingbroke are equally worthless for the thought and the style. Some of his religious speculations were close on the verge of atheism; he adopted the French cant of freedom from prejudice, and denied the genuineness of certain parts of the Bible. His platonic aspirations have the appearance of utter insincerity; and his mouthing rants about patriotism and public good, can deceive only the most credulous of his readers. In a word, we look on Bolingbroke as a literary charlatan; and concur entirely with Blair—who, for once, forgot his formality and indifference, when he told his pupils, that for profit, no English writer could be read with so little advantage as Bolingbroke. His style, however meretricious, has the merit of copiousness and harmony.

In the best passages, we are sometimes reminded of Cowley and Sir William Temple, among his predecessors; and in the present day, we see a revival of the same power of amplification in a nobler spirit, in the works of Channing and Macaulay.

As an orator, Bolingbroke was rated very high by his contemporaries. His successors in public life (Pitt and Brougham,) have estimated him the very first of English orators. Lord Chesterfield thought him superior to the ancients. But, in his printed works, he is infinitely beneath Burke—who, singularly enough, commenced his career by an imitation of Bolingbroke—which proved superior to the original. We can imagine him, however, a very popular speaker. He had all the arts of oratory, and a fine person. He was quick, brilliant, energetic, fiery; his manners soft, elegant, refined; his scholarship, dazzling and deceptive. He was also, when necessary, untiring in business; and, perhaps, the best negotiator and diplomat among the English statesmen of his time.

The personal character of this "brilliant knave" was, in early life, grossly sensual;—he was a sort of Marquis of Waterford: only rivalling him in reckless licentiousness. He kept the most expensive mistress in the kingdom, and boasted of being able to drink more than any other man could bear. He once ran a race naked through Hyde Park. His lordship's ambition, when a collegian, and until the age of near thirty, was wholly of the puerile sort that distinguishes rich young men of fashion of the present day.

As he advanced towards maturity, he became the statesman and political leader. After the loss of power and influence, he turned philosopher. It may look like want of charity, but we confess we suspect it to be too true, that philosophy was the last resort of Bolingbroke, as patriotism has been said to be "the last resort of a scoundrel." And it is astonishing how men are allowed to conduct the affairs of the nation, whose private business is entirely neglected, and whose personal character is highly valued, at the very smallest premium.

Religion, Bolingbroke repelled with disdain, but rested firm in the consolations of philosophy. He died at an advanced age, and holding the same doctrines to the very last.

There must have been in the company and private character of this celebrated man, more than appears in his writings and public conduct, else how were the best men of his time so duped by his fascinating qualities. The stern sense of Swift, the acute satire of Pope, the comic subtlety of Gay, had pierced the hollow surface of pretence, and lashed the age; yet they united in one chorus of applause to the genius, the patriotism, the purity of Bolingbroke. It is a curious problem.

We cannot close this slight notice without paying a tribute of just compliment to the enterprising publishers. The work is printed with great neatness; the portrait admirably engraved. It is a cause of regret with us, that the subject matter, at this time, is not more worthy of the execution. How many far superior works lie mouldering in the rubbish of ancient libraries! St. John may be popular at the south. He inculcates a lax morality; and the style may suit the Virginia idea of eloquence—frothy and high-sounding. But here, in these middle states, and at the east, we know better what true eloquence and sound philosophy mean, and have living models of both.

The editor deserves some notice, but wholly by way of censure. In a pert, pragmatical preface, he speaks slightingly of the elegant compilation of Goldsmith, who has sifted the facts cleanly, and given the gist of the matter. It is a common criticism to speak of the indolence of Goldsmith, who, however, left a goodly number of volumes behind him, and wrote as no other man of his day could write. A similar vulgar error prevails with regard to Irving, (our Goldsmith,) who has written his shelf full of choice classics. With all his pretension, the editor has only contrived to make an unsightly piece of patchwork from Goldsmith, and some review articles. He employs the text of Goldsmith without remark, even after his scornful criticism; which reminds us of a similar spirit in the Wild Tartar, mentioned by Hudibras who—

When he spies
A man that's handsome, valiant, wise,
If he can kill him, thinks t' inherit
His wit, his beauty, and his spirit:
As if just so much he enjoy'd,
As in another is destroy'd.

XXVIII.

LITERATURE BY PROFESSIONAL MEN.

In this cursory sketch, we merely suggest the inquiry (which we shall not attempt to settle) of the comparative literary rank of the three learned professions: the genius exhibited in elegant letters, of professional men. And each may appear, from the statement of a partial advocate, to take the lead. The lawyer may claim to draw upon English literature alone, Shakspeare, who alone would outweigh all the clever authors among physicians, we can muster, by any diligence of research. The advocate may claim, too, Burke, the finest of political orators, and almost the first of English prose writers, putting out of view his later political principles; the long array of statesmen and able debaters and political essayists (one of the glories of England) are lawyers, almost to a man; and in literature, properly so styled, from the essays of Bacon to the Ion of Talfourd, we conceive no doubts can be raised, no question advanced, that they are not first among the first. Of the great dramatists, from Shakspeare down, excluding the professional poets and actors, which of the faculties compete with the Law? The fame of historical skill is pretty equally divided. The Bar boasting its More and Bacon and Clarendon and Hallam; and the Church its Fuller and Burnet and Lingard and Arnold. We recollect no classical history by a physician. In the field of fiction, or the page of the manners-painting novelist, the lawyers can point to their Fielding, the prose Homer of human nature, and the Ariosto of the North—Scott himself: the divines may boast of their Swift and Sterne, (though they are a little shy of both,) and the doctors have among them four capital humorous painters, Arbuthnot, and Goldsmith, and Smollett, and Moore. The divines bear away the palm in serious eloquence and in moral reasoning, as might be naturally expected: almost the single exception to this criticism occurs in Sir Thomas Browne. The minor forms of literature, from biography down, are better represented by briefless barristers than by well-beneficed divines or physicians in full practice. The poets are of every class and condition, though we think the best, in general, have followed literature alone. Neat, agreeable verses have been written by doctors, as by Garth, Armstrong, Grainger, Wolcot; and at home by Drake and Holmes, who, as genuine poets, rank above any of these; but the best poet among them, Goldsmith, was, essentially, an author by profession, as also were Akenside, and Smollett, and Darwin. Mere learning, as distinct from elegant literature, may at one period have been confined to the profession of physic: natural science, always the most popular species of knowledge, falls naturally within the scope of their studies, and certainly they have been great discoverers in natural philosophy: but in a higher philosophy, that of the government of men and the advancement of the race, the legal and political inquirer has greatly distanced these; whilst in the highest philosophy, that of the moral nature, aims, capacity, and sympaties of man, the individual, as contrasted with and distinct from man, the citizen, or political unit, the first class of divines, from Jeremy Taylor to our own Channing, deserve the highest place.

Lawyers have at all times done their full share in advancing the interests of society, and their memory should be preserved with reverence. The profession of the law has produced the greatest statesmen and most brilliant orators of modern times; some of the ablest divines have been originally lawyers, and have brought to the high topics of theology, an acute, logical head, as well as an ardent imagination and a pure heart. The greatest writers of the present century, for instance, from Sir Walter Scott down to a lively newspaper critic, as those of the London Examiner, and the best monthly and quarterly journals, have been lawyers. From the law has the world received the blessings of that profound and admirable philosophy, so conducive to public interest, and so well adapted to private happiness, which we read in the pages of Bacon, of Burke, and of Bentham. The sharpness and transparency of intellect that legal studies and legal practice afford, go far toward the general improvement of the faculties of observation and comparison. Hence, we find lawyers such masters of real life, and the best society (intellectually considered) of any place you may enter. In the country, the judge is the first man, and the principal advocate stands next highest. In the city, even, in this commercial mart, the profession of the law, as a profession, stands unquestionably the highest. At least six out of ten of our most distinguished public characters and persons of eminent private worth, have come out from the law. The most sagacious foreign critic of our government and its working, has most justly demonstrated the bar to be the bulwalk of our political liberties, the intelligent and fearless defender of our rights. Though law itself is unromantic enough in its study, let Eunomus and Lord Bolingbroke, Sir James Macintosh and Dr. Warren, say what they may to the contrary, yet it is very far from being a dull pursuit to a successful lawyer.

The most unexpected incidents and turns daily arise, the rarest characters are to be met with, the most open reference to the human heart is often made by the able lawyer, in a free and diversified practice. We are very far from thinking the legal life as it is, comparable to that of the true man of letters, as it might be; still, where there is much to praise, it is churlish to remain silent. Finally, as a class of men for general intelligence, clearness of mind, temperance of opinion, real force of character, polished amenity of manner, we can find no class of men superior to the best class of lawyers; the old senatorial band of judges and counsellors of long standing, or the new and fresher army of smart, young attorneys.

Having offered our humble tribute to the profession of the law, we should not omit to pay due respect to genius and virtue, as it is embodied in the Christian Church. As the noblest portion of that noble body, we shall glance merely at the general character of the standard old English divines, the Donnes, Halls, Taylors, Barrows, Souths, Mores, Earles, Fullers, Tillotsons, and Berkeleys. These great old masters form a choice collection in a select library of old English literature. It has been said, that a complete library could be formed from their works, and that, too, a most valuable one. For though divines, they were none the less wits, historians, scholars, poets, orators, and moralists. Unlike the French clergy, the ornaments of which have been, either mere declaimers, or else scholastic controversialists, the English divines wrote books of moral essays, satires, descriptions of characters, works on men and manners. They had wit and humor, as well as fancy and sentiment. They were not merely the spiritual guides, but also the popular writers of their day. As mere scholars, their acquisitions were wonderful: as thinkers, the richness of their matter is fully equivalent to its gorgeous setting. As men, where shall we look for a more primitive piety and holiness of character comparable to that of the heavenly George Herbert: what Christian, at once so simple and so learned, so wise and yet so humble as Hooker: whose devotional raptures (in our own day) equal the enthusiastic fancies of Crashaw: whose keen satire rivals that of Hall or Eachard: what later martyr to principle outshines the apostolic Latimer: whose golden eloquence casts the fancy and the imagination of Taylor or South into the shade? We should be glad to learn if ever there existed a more copious, exact and comprehensive reasoner than Barrow, or a finer model of the true Christian gentleman than Berkeley. Later metaphysicians have not yet obscured the fame of Clarke and Butler. We might run on with these glorious old names, and fill many a page.

With these tributes to the Law and Divinity, sincerely offered, and not introduced merely for the sake of a display of impartiality, we come at last to the Faculty of Medicine. And, in the outset, we may quote the opinion of Johnson, gained from a wide and intimate experience on his part of the skill and benevolence of physicians, the most eminent of whom, in his day, took pleasure in prolonging the life, and alleviating the poignant diseases under which this great man suffered, not only without fee or reward, but with a readiness, a patience, and an affectionate zeal that could not be remunerated by any merely pecuniary returns ; services to be commanded neither by the patronage of the titled, nor the applause of the famous. A strong feeling of personal attachment existed between Dr. Johnson and several of the first medical men of England in his time, and a mutual esteem honorable to both sides. In his case, too, the willingness to accept gratuitous services, discovered as much liberality of spirit, (for a man of such manly independence of character,) as the eager offer on their part to proffer them.

In Boswell's life, the commendations of the faculty occur in several places, but we have reference more particularly to a passage in the life of Sir Samual Garth, which reads as follows : "Whether what Temple says be true, the physicians have had more learning than the other faculties, I will not stay to inquire, but I believe, every man has found in physicians, just liberality and dignity of sentiment, very prompt effusion of beneficence and willingness to exert a lucrative art where there is no hope of lucre." Though we must readily assent to Johnson's own dictum in the matter, we are far from being governed to any great degree by the dictum of Temple, who has been shown to have been a very superficial scholar, and hence no safe critic. Besides, the period was not very distant from the age in which Temple lived, when the physician held not his present position, but ranked with the apothecary, or rather the two professions were more generally merged into one ; when the chirurgeon was generally the barber, and his operations few and simple. A similar analogy holds in regard to other offices ; the chancellor of Great Britain is now always a layman, but up to the time of Sir Thomas More, in the reign of Henry VIII., the office was invariably held by the primate, and the Court of Equity was considered the just province of ecclesiastical jurisdiction.

In point of erudition, we have little doubt that physicians formerly, and perhaps still, have surpassed lawyers, though we suspect not the clergy, who have an interminable professional literature of their own. But in regard to natural genius, with the exception of the choice instances we have collected, we are inclined to suspect the Faculty will not be able to sustain a fair parallel with the Bar or the Pulpit. This is, however, a point we are by no means solicitous to decide. Most physicians have too rare an opportunity of leisure to employ much of it in writing, and then we do not so naturally look to them as authors, as we desire to regard them as friends, companions, counsellors, acquaintance. We entertain for them rather a personal attachment, than an abstract literary admiration. We are touched by their kindness: excited to gratitude by their skill and successful endeavors, and rendered trusting by the confidential intercourse that so naturally springs up between doctor and patient.

It appears to us, therefore, no matter of wonder that the doctor should aim to excel in conversation more than in composition—and should seek professional rather than literary fame. To become skilful and discriminating in his art; agreeable and gentlemanly in his address; to perform well the character of a judicious yet kind friend, and entertain by all allowable arts the dull hours of the invalid: to act the part of the philanthropist and the good Samaritan; these surely are honors sufficient for the ambition of any reasonable human creature, and require the exercise of virtues that make men akin to the angels.

XXIX.

THE PROFESSION OF AN ACTOR.

THE life of an actor is a severe trial of humanity. His temptations are many; his fortitude, too often, ineffectual; his success precarious. If he be resolute, uncontaminated by the society of his associates, and a genuine artist besides, he is worthy not only of the praise of the moralist, but also deserving the admiration of the critic. The prejudice against the profession, like most prevailing prejudices, is founded on general truth; but it is frequently absurd and baseless. The dissolute lives of actors, even in the majority of cases, may be supposed to result at least as often from failure in their attempts to please, and ill treatment from the world, as from any other reasons. The very best men have sometimes been driven into vice, as well as seduced and insinuated into it. And how shall we dare to speak of the comparatively light vices of the actor without pity and tenderness, when we allow odious vices of the heart to go 'unwhipt of justice?' The sins of the flesh are visited in the flesh, and often end there. But the sins of the mind, the vices of the heart, are of a more incorrigible nature, are deeper dyed with guilt, the cancerous sores of the soul. There is this also to be considered —there are professional vices. Now, we would venture to declare, that there is no more dissipation, no more looseness of living among actors, than there is pettifogging among lawyers, or quackery among physicians.

We mean to write no apology for the actor; the worthy members of the profession need none, and as for the less deserving, or even the criminal, we deem it without our province to lay open the sores of the beggar, whose follies have induced them. It lies beyond our limits to lash the back already waled by the stripes of a cruel fortune. Ah! is not poverty, is not scorn, is not the solitude of their lives, is not the estrangement of the virtuous part of mankind from them, hard enough to bear without our adding to the mountain of abuse which has crushed many a human creature? Ye grave censors, who would crush the poor actor, thus overborne, are ye free from all weakness, not to say impurity? Do ye array yourselves in no borrowed vestments of virtue, to conceal therewith the detestable meanness, the intolerable corruption of your ignoble spirits? Can a line be drawn separating the righteous from the profane? Is one man perfectly good, and another perfectly bad? Are we not all nearer an equality? A man may, in his frenzy, or in a diabolical spirit, (little short of it,) commit murder—a crime neither you nor I, considerate reader, have committed—and yet he may have done much that we have left undone. May not the final account disclose an average of evil and goodness, much more closely balanced than we can now conceive of?

The actor, then, has not gained his just position. The statute gives him no better name than vagrant. It requires, however, but slight observation, and some acquaintance with the history of the stage, to discover that the art of acting is the most intellectual of all public amusements; is the profession of a gentleman, rightly considered; and is a walk of considerable dignity and usefulness. We are convinced of the truth of these positions—others may not be, and we must endeavor to make them good.

Let us only consider the qualifications necessary to form the excellent actor; thence we may learn his proper dignity. Both nature and art must unite in him to produce perfection, and nature both mental and physical, with a generous and peculiar education. An actor, with most people, is a mimic —a sort of speaking automaton, an intellectual parrot. He must be at least a good general scholar, and in his walk of tragedy or comedy, a master. He must possess a considerable knowledge of antiquity, without being a mere antiquarian. He must not lose himself in costume or attitudes, though a knowledge of the first and skill in the second are necessary to enable him to personate with effect and power the heroes of an early age. Coriolanus could have been supported only by Kemble, and Orestes by Talma. The actor must be a keen and close observer of real life, of the multitudinous characters that fill this earthly scene; he must, from self-study, have analyzed those flickering impulses that often turn a point of action ; to him must be familiar the wild havoc that passion, 'masterless passion,' makes, that forces us 'to like or loathe ;' he must be able to disentangle the endless shifts of meanness and avaricious cunning. The most striking points are to be gathered from literal observation. Most great actors have followed this rule. Kean went to see a notorious felon hung, in order to catch his dying expression of horror and despair; Garrick drew his idea of Lear, and that powerful expression he is said to have given it, from an actual occurrence. Acting is a matter of fact, as well as a matter of imagination and sentiment. Pure imagination must be sustained by literal reason. Acting is an art, and all art is experimental.

The actor includes also the critic,—neither can he play with any force or spirit without something of the poet. In some modern pieces the actor surpasses the dramatist, and creates the characters for him, from a very scanty outline. All the filling up is in his hands. What effect cannot manner lend, even to the loftiest conceptions ?

The actor is hence an intellectual artist, and, when truly excellent, a highly imaginative artist. That the actor should be a gentleman, a natural deduction would infer, from the intellectual nature of his pursuits, and from the education he must receive, or must give himself, to qualify him for the stage.

The education of the actor is a point to be briefly handled. We have in part spoken of this. The world and his own heart are his best and truest teachers. Dramatic literature is a rich department of our literature—perhaps the richest. He must be at home everywhere in it. Acting is an art. It is not study alone, nor experience, nor inspiration, nor the finest form and most expressive countenance, that form the great actor solely. All must concur and unite to produce that character. An artist, he must work by rule ; a man of genius, he must give himself freely to the impulses of his genius. Much must be done by the actor, for much is expected of him.

The actor is generally reputed to be born in the lower ranks of society, and yet he must play the fine gentleman, and the fine gentleman, too, of an age when a more courtly manner and elegant style was prevalent. This he must derive in part historically. In the instance of the finest actors ready access has been provided for them to the best circles. Garrick lived on terms of intimacy with Burke, Goldsmith and Johnson : Kemble was a frequent guest of royalty : Kean was the idol of Hazlitt and Byron : Matthews, the friend of Scott, Hunt, Hazlitt, and Lamb. Earlier yet, Burbage and Shakspeare were companions : at a later period, Booth and Betterton associated with Addison and Steele. These are a few of a thousand instances.

Though reality be the basis of acting, yet the actor should be richly invested with imagination ; for he must assume passions he never, perhaps, felt, or certainly never felt to such a degree of intensity, and sometimes must paint local manners of which no trace remains, and whichare to be gathered purely from tradition. Acting, then, is an imaginative art as well as experimental. As such it ranks just below the very highest of the fine arts.

True genius never yet starved on the stage ; give it display, and it must succeed. A man of genius may fail, but not a man of the right sort of genius. The author of Hamlet might be a very poor actor. The two lines ought to be kept apart. If vanity will carry a man on the stage, he must play what he can, not what he will. Shakspeare is said never to have risen above his Ghost—Booth assumed Hamlet at once. The theatrical talent is the most palpable and prompt of all other kinds of talent. Dramatic conception may be unaccompanied by physical power; failure must ensue. A dumb man might as well conceive himself fitted to sing well, because he had a fine ear. The able performer must unite force of sentiment with great mimetic powers.

There are born actors, natural players, whose destiny it appears to be to 'fret their hour on the stage.' That is their home. Such men are only natural on the stage—they are actors only when off: and those who are equally unaffected in both situations, might be rather more at home on the stage, since they can act with more license and freedom there; they there enjoy somewhat the privileges of the old court jesters. They may be supposed to act those characters the best which approach the nearest to their own. Hence they act out themselves more fully while acting an assumed part, than when they occupy their commonplace station in the real scene. Listless and dull at home, these children of impulse are only men in their own art; at least they can only do justice to their manly genius on the stage. Liston and Matthews, the two greatest comedians of the age, were said to be habitually taciturn, and sometimes morose at home. In Matthews this arose from disease, and in Liston, most probably, from want of the accustomed excitement. On the boards, all this disappeared.

The majority of candidates for theatrical fame, enter the profession only to show their entire incapacity for it. They have mistaken inclination for ability. In general, this is a weak ambition, a puerile fancy, a relic of boyish ardor. A large proportion who see their incapacity, and would leave the theatre, cannot return; some are fascinated by the glare and excitement; many want fortitude and confidence to repair to old or new avocations—to conclude an amicable treaty with lost friends. They are obliged by sheer necessity to remain. I can hardly picture to myself a more distressing trial, especially to a man of worth and sense, who, in a fit of delusion, embraced the drama as his profession, than a nightly exhibition of irreparable deficiencies; most unfortunate is that position—to be commiserated! More commonly, less is felt; the conceit of actors is proverbial and apparent. They are, as a body, not so easily daunted as we imagine; they can face a full audience with less apprehension than we conceive.

As to the morality and usefulness of his profession, we are apt to regard that point as long since settled; and we think, with the best critics and most liberal moralists, that a good play, well acted, presents a more impressive lesson than the best turned declamations against vice and in favor of virtue. Shakspeare's view of the drama includes the actor as the poet's representative; without whom the maxims of philosophy would be dead, and deprived of whose melting accents, the tender sentiments and generous eloquence of the heart would lose their effect and power.

That the true objects of the drama have been occasionally misconceived; that the acted conceptions of the poet have not always had their due influence; that defects have crept in, and now regarded (falsely regarded) as insuperable, are incidental evils, and by no means the original sin—by no means the design of the theatre.

XXX.

CHILDREN'S BOOKS.

THERE is a very large class of censorious critics, who plume themselves on their good sense, and here evince the most marked defect of it, who affect to speak of children's books as essentially trifling. They mistake *juvenile* books for *puerile* works: an egregious blunder. Robinson Crusoe is a juvenile, in the language of the trade; so is Peter Wilkins, so is Gulliver; yet are they so far from puerile, that to appreciate them fully, the fresh heart of childhood requires also the wise masculine understanding. The best child's books form notoriously the pleasant reading of all ages.

From the reason of this strange misconception, has arisen the idea of the ease with which such books could be composed, and the fact that the majority of the present race of writers for children have done all they could to stultify, enfeeble, and almost debase, the intellect and sentiment of the contemporary generation of children. They seem to think a child's book cannot be too childish; filling the blank pages with as empty prattle and insipid nothingness. Like the imitators of and cavillers at Wordsworth, they mistake folly for simplicity, and substitute inanity for innocence. They write alone to the stupid; a fault almost as culpable as writing over the heads of the majority, to reach the level of the brilliant and gifted. The cardinal rule should be, to write to the middling order of minds, the sensible and good-natured; those who have right feelings and natural impulses.

We say children's books are, of all kinds, the most popular—more copies are sold, even of the most indifferent productions of this class, than of any other class of books, except school books and religious works. Hence, there has been in this department of literature a great deal of mere manufacturing. Book-making has been most profitable, almost as much so as editing classics, from which source of profit many a dull pedant has reaped more substantial gains than the original author himself. From Goldsmith down to Hawthorne, (we take pleasure in writing these names in the same sentence,) tales for children, when executed as they, and Tieck and Grimm, and a few others, have composed them, have afforded the most agreeable kind of reading to all classses, ages, professions, and tempers. No man or woman, and certainly no child, with a pure heart, a healthy imagination, and a refined moral sense, can help loving a good fairy tale or romantic legend. Men of genius and practical writers, alone, then, can write proper books for children, which may also enlighten and charm their mothers and grandfathers. The best audience for the finest poet, would be the spirits of blessed children: and the true writer of genius, is the only fit author to write for a circle of little boys and girls.

Did we reflect but for a moment, it would appear sufficiently reasonable that none but the very best minds should be employed on works of this sort, since the effects of juvenile reading and first studies leave an indelible impression on the character. Some of the greatest men have confessed in after life, the effect upon their youthful minds, of books read in the early season of life, when the perceptions are quickest and the heart is fresh and joyful. Franklin thought the whole course of his career had been influenced by his perusal of Defoe's Essay on Projects, during his boyhood. The child Cowley devoured Spenser at an age when the music of the stanza alone attracted him. Byron's boyish readings of folios of Turkish History gave a strong oriental bias to his poetic genius. And a hundred similar instances might be readily enumerated, if the point were not sufficiently clear. Childish associations tend much towards coloring the maturer temper. Pleasant family connexions sweeten the mind, as it were, for life; whereas, an unhappy childhood will leave a gloom and distrust in the disposition that can scarcely be eradicated. The companions of our infancy and youth; the sports in which we joined with them; the places of our birth and the scenes where the most important early episodes of our lives occurred; all engrave themselves on the memory and character. With no less force do we remember or are we affected by our first readings. It may serve to change a man's whole course of life, whether he read Cook's voyages, or the Life of Colonel Jack, when a boy. Assuredly, whatever he read, became part of himself, and might form either the intelligent navigator or the reckless adventurer. The reading of books of piratical adventures, has made villains out of otherwise tame dullards. Since, then, our first books are so important in their effect for good or evil, we think too diligent a regard cannot be manifested for a delicate choice in the selection of volumes that should compose the child's library.

Most tale-writers are altogether too didactic; so eager to impress truths and facts, that they cannot avoid direct teaching, by which they lose all the advantages they expect to gain, since a tale is not a lecture. If it teaches, as it certainly ought, it should do so incidentally. It should not make its advances too palpably, so as to frighten the child into the belief of its learning a task, instead of unconsciously imbibing pure truth, "in fairy fiction dressed." The writer should address the heart and the imagination, leaving the reason to work out her convictions on the basis of their pleasing illusions, as a cynic might term the most real of all things. Children learn by loving; they are informed when they are interested; they delight to be taught what entertains their fancy and captivates their attention in the teaching. You must acquire a hold on their affections, when you may wholly command their devotion." "Here the heart may give an useful lesson to the head: the child and the sage meet on an equal footing.

A prominent fault in some books of this class is, the instilling prematurely of merely worldly knowledge; by which, in this particular connection, we mean to imply, a knowledge of evil rather than of good. With many, a knowledge of the world implies an acquaintance with trick and craft, with vice and sin. But, though, to discriminate properly good and evil, not only in the abstract, but more especially in practical life, requires a knowledge of opposites, in the man, yet it is worse than useless in the child, to be taught to go out of his way, gratuitously, to learn evil. Soon enough comes a knowledge and that science, of which it has been said, "the children of this world are wiser in their generation, than the children of light," but after all, much of this boasted wordly shrewdness is worth little enough. It serves as a defensive weapon to withstand the artifices of cunning, and the impostures of wicked men. It is a shield in the Battle of Life. But it has negative properties only; it does not advance the learner a step in the search after truth. It affords little aid to the poor wanderer in the wilds of error lost. Children, of all human beings, need it least, as they are under protection, can obtain advice, and appeal to superior strength, as well as superior wisdom.

The notion of popularizing difficult propositions, and explaining in an easy way what is inherently difficult of comprehension, has been proved unwise by fair trial. It is necessary to stimulate curiosity and encourage labor. There is no royal road to learning, to quote a trite maxim; none the less true for being trite. Some difficulties must be encountered, if only to harden the mind and strengthen the character. By facilitating acquisition, the mind becomes effeminated, instead of advancing, and is unfitted to contend with difficulties.

By mere dint of memory we master some things that we cannot at first even understand, but which, the oftener they are recalled, the plainer they seem, since the perception generally views the idea in a different manner every time it takes any notice of it, and in this way many subborn facts are treasured up, and many complicated problems are at last resolved.

A very ordinary but most pernicious fault of all teaching is to rate all minds alike; give lessons of the same length and in the same sciences, to all children of the same age or size; a Procustes method of gauging the abilities and tastes of children. After a very early age, each child requires an individual treatment suited to none else. Yet this is seldom attended to.

Thus much for the more striking faults of the majority of the new child's books; we must, to obtain the best mental food for children, go back to the books and authors of the last century, and even earlier. Very few of the living writers in this department are to be found really worthy of perusal.

In a final paragraph we would insist upon the necessity of a rich, pure, and varied literature for children; not only from the vast importance of captivating the imagination and warming the heart at the most impressible season of life, by generous principles of action, and refined sentiments of duty, but also that the youthful associations may form the basis of the best character, and bring the purest joy in after years. It is fame enough for any author to be loved by children, generation after generation, long after he himself has left the scene. Nor can he be considered an useless writer, who has done something towards forming a single worthy character. The greatest writers are the world's best benefactors, friends, teachers, lovers, companions, and fellow-citizens.

At an epoch when cheap literature is so popular, and reprints of good old books so common, why, amid all the collections, we have not a cheap Library for children, not mere Fairy Tales, (there is one such collection,) nor useful tracts, nor sets of travels and biographies, but a careful selection of good books in all the departments. An enterprising publisher who would get out such a series, in a neat portable form, would deserve the praise of a real benefactor to the young, and fill his pockets at the same time.

Every man looks back to his childhood, as to the Paradisaical period of his life, his Eden before he was driven into the world by sin. Ought we not to try and make it so much happier and wiser that the period may be indefinitely prolonged, and the purity and innocence of childhood carried as far as possible into coming years? The best man preserves the heart and the imagination of a child, through age and experience to the very Gates of Death. For a child, too, that dies young, we should strive to fill its whole life with Love, Religion, and Beauty. This is the true office of Genius tempered by affection, the work of an Angel, and to be rewarded as such. It is great "the applause of listening senates to command," and to become endenizened Poet or Philosopher, the world over: but it is, if not so glorious a national fame, still a more delightful private honor, to live on the lips of admiring childhood, and to possess a place in those cherubic hearts that know no metaphysical distinction between delight and love.

XXXI.

A RAINY DAY WITH THE POETS.

A CHOICE catena of fine passages and poems might be compiled under this caption. We will suggest a few of the most prominent that we can recall.

In the old ballad literature, there is that rare old song, of which Shakspeare has preserved a line:

> "And the rain, it raineth every day."

The locality of this poem must have been somewhere in the West of Scotland, or in Wales. In the Highlands of the former country, a remarkably moist district, a country lad was asked by a stout gentleman (probably Irving's) if it *always* rained there. "Na, na," returned Sawney; "sometimes it *snaws*."

Motherwell, the delicate Scottish poet and modern ballad writer, has left a fine ballad, full of the old spirit of romance, the burthen, "Heigho, the wind and rain!" appropriately to be said or sung, on a dark, gloomy evening in November.

Of a wild winter's night, the rain beating against the window, the wind howling down the chimney, and soughing through the key-hole—then is emphatically the season for reading Lear, and to appreciate "the pelting of the pitiless storm" on "the white, discrowned head" of the noble old king, on the wide-stretching, houseless heath.

Shenstone used to say, that of a rainy day he loved to read over the letters of his friends—often a sad employment. He is himself a rainy-day author, calling up, in his most elaborate poem of "The Schoolmistress," visions of innocence and infancy; and in his prose miscellanies, evincing a nicety of judgment that marks the man of reflection ; but above all, for his inimitable lines written at an inn at Henley, the delight of Dr. Johnson and of Leigh Hunt, and indeed of all wise and social spirits who have ever read them.

Hunt himself has a gossipping paper on a rainy day, in one of the numbers of the *Indicator*, how to pass it pleasantly —by no means one of his best essays. In the first half of it he is merely lively and somewhat commonplace, but as he gets into the literature of the subject he is more at home and proportionably entertaining. He quotes admiringly capital lines from Swift's "Description of a City Shower, or Town Eclogue," that first appeared in the *Tatler*, and on which Steele wrote a generous encomium, with fine passages from Green's "Spleen," that delightful though little-known poem. He might have added lines from Gay's Trivia, on walking the streets in rainy weather ; and he might have retold, as he could have done to the life, Charles Matthews's "leetle" anecdote of the old Scotch woman.

A fine American anthology might be collected of rainy-day verses, from Brainard to Hoyt.

Brainard's are homely but domestic rhymes. Longfellow's "Rainy Day" has a fine moral, (he is essentially didactic, in a true sense, as well as tasteful and harmonious) and is a most musical poem, imbued with the mingled tones of sadness and hopeful anticipation. This fine writer's "Rain in the City" is beautifully written, and as picturesque a description as Swift's, though wholly unlike it ; as unlike as a street view by a Flemish painter is different from a piece of city elegance by Watteau. It is as artistically executed as Poe could have made it. Emerson's poem we shall quote. It enforce's the scholar's duty ; after the quaint fashion of the seventeenth century, it has a taking title :

SUUM CUIQUE.

"The rain has spoiled the farmer's day;
Shall sorrow put my books away?
Thereby are two days lost.
Nature shall mind her own affairs;
I will attend my proper cares,
In rain, or sun, or frost."

This is right stoical philosophy all can not practise. Ralph Hoyt's "Rain" is as perfect a picture as his "Snow;" the two most delicate cabinet-pieces of rural art we know of. The "Shower" is a pearl pendant from the ear of Venus. Hawthorne's picture of a shower, in "Sights from a Church-steeple," is the best *prose* shower we can remember; at least, not surpassed by Irving's "Rainy Day at an Inn."

The last characteristic piece of writing on this subject we can refer to, is Read's poetical picture, entitled

A MORNING, BUT NO SUN.

"The morning comes, but brings no sun;
The sky with storm is overrun;
And here I sit in my room alone,
And feel, as I hear the tempest moan,
Like one who hath lost the last and best,
The dearest dweller from his breast!
For every pleasant sight and sound,
The sorrows of the sky have drowned;
The bell within the neighboring tower
Falls blurred and distant through the shower;
Look where I will, hear what I may,
All, all the world seems far away!
The dreary shutters creak and swing,
The windy willows sway and fling
A double portion of the rain
Over the weeping window-pane.

But I, with gusty sorrow swayed,
Sit hidden here, like one afraid,
And would not on another throw
One drop of all this weight of woe!"

A fine sympathetic melancholy doubtless inspired the lines, which find an echo in the heart of every reader of taste and feeling.

Something germane to this topic is that of the influence of the weather. Some pretend an exemption from all "skyey influences," while others suffer a complete martyrdom to clouds, storm, and rain. It is, doubtless, a matter of constitution and temperament. A sensitive being will be exhilarated or depressed by causes completely trivial to the robust or unimaginative. A man may by fortitude breast his sufferings and brave the storm, but he must have little discrimination if he perceive no difference between the genial heat of a fine day in June or the cordial cold of a clear December morning; if a dusty day, a rainy day in spring or fall, a bitter cold day, are equally agreeable or indifferent to him. How can he appreciate good who sees no distinction between it and the bad?

So feel not the true poets or men of poetical temperament. Crabbe made verses best in a snow-storm; inspiration descended upon him with the falling flakes of snow. Jean Paul could not invent with his usual facility if the sky was leaden; it transmuted his golden thoughts to the same metal. Burns found his impulse of composition strongest in winter and amid external desolation. Milton fancied his genius was in its fullest force in spring and autumn. Numberless instances might be added.

Mr. Tuckerman has penned a very pleasing paper on this subject in his "Rambles and Reveries," and, if we are not mistaken, lately included it in the *Optimist.*

XXXII.

TEA-TABLE TALK.

Most raillery is mere impertinence in disguise; sarcasm, rudeness; and humor, buffoonery.

A fool thinks a man of sense, who looks grave at his stupid jests, incapable of pleasantry or of understanding ridicule; not suspecting that one may not choose to take what is offered to him in the guise of a joke, any more than he would be willing to accept counterfeit coin for legal currency.

There is a good deal of coarse familiarity in what passes for modern friendship.

Annuals are, of all books, the most ephemeral.

Standard authors, to be read for pleasure, (implying intimate knowledge,) should be read without note or comment.

The Baptist sect in England have produced at least two very great men, John Bunyan and Robert Hall: the former a poet of the first class, though he wrote in homely prose, a man of true and high genius; the latter a scholar and orator of brilliant talents.

Tennyson's blank verse is Milton's effeminated; Antinoüs in the part of Hercules. The idea of the Princess appears to have been originally suggested by a paper in the Tatler.

A fool is wise in one sense—*non-sense.*

The breast is properly called the *chest,* since it contains the richest of man's treasures—the heart—locked up in it.

The Moravian Society, like that of the Shakers, flourishes more naturally and luxuriantly in country places. In the city of New York there never has been more than one congregation of that sect. To see them at home, one must visit Bethlehem or Nazareth, in Pennsylvania.

Bishops are said to be of divine institution, but Archbishops are confessedly of human creation, an after-thought of the ecclesiastical polity; and yet Canterbury and York would swallow up a score of the poorer sees, (as those of the colonies, for instance,) and in worldly dignities rank much higher.

How they who hold the doctrine of innate, utter depravity, can by any means account for the pleasure every unsophisticated heart receives from the company of pure, innocent children, we are very much puzzled to account. The love of a fond mother must appear to them more senseless than the dotage of feeble age. These little creatures are angels in truth, as well as in fancy, for the Divine Master has declared of them, that "of *such* is the kingdom of heaven." They have genuine faith and truth, and are much nearer heaven than the best of us.

The presence of a sweet young chlld is a more cogent argument against the dogma of universal and utter innate depravity, than all the controversial discussion in the world.

No poor-laws can altogether eradicate poverty; no charitable provision suppress the cause of pauperism.

All of the great old English writers give excellent counsel on all subjects, *travel*, among the rest; but Bacon and Fuller, amidst much good advice, press a particular point, not always adverted to. Bacon: "As for the acquaintance which is to be sought in travel, that which is most of all profitable is acquaintance with *the secretaries and employed men of ambassadors;* for so, in travelling in one country, he shall suck the experience of many." Fuller enjoins: "Contrive correspondence with some choice foreign friend after thy return; as some *professor or secretary*, who virtually is the whole university or state."

DISPARITY OF AGE IN MARRIAGE.

Mahomet's first wife, Kadyah, was at least forty, when he, at the age of tweny-five, married her. Shakspeare's Ann Hathaway was seven years his senior. Dr. Johnson's wife was literally almost double his age. The wife of Lord Herbert, of Cherbury, six or seven years older than her lord. Sir Thomas More's wife was also seven years older than her husband. Howard, the philanthropist, at the age of twenty-five, married a first wife, who was then fifty-two. Mrs. Rowe, the authoress, was fifteen years older than Mr. Rowe. Rahel, the German De Staël, was about as much older. The Countess D'Ossoli (Miss Fuller,) was nearly ten years her husband's senior. Jenny Lind, too, is said to be eight or ten years older than Herr Goldschmidt.

COMPLIMENTS.

The two most elegant prose compliments we recollect to have ever read, are recorded by Lord Herbert, of Cherbury, the celebrated philosopher, as made by himself in his entertaining Autobiography. At Venice he heard a beautiful nun sing, to whom he declared, after a ravishing musical performance, that "She needed neither to change voice nor face to become an angel." In Paris he met a distinguished French Marshal, who was quite deaf, and begged him to excuse his infirmity. The chivalric philosopher answered, that it was "for him (the hero) to speak, and for others to hear: that he was to command, and they to execute his orders!"

DISTINGUISHED FOREIGN VISITORS TO THE UNITED STATES.

William IV., then Prince and Midshipman, saw Nelson for the first time (Captain of the Albermarle,) lying in the Narrows, off Staten Island. The same jovial sailor king is said to have entertained a party of British officers at an old stone house, still standing at Ravenswood, L. I., a mile below Hell Gate, on the East River.

Louis Phillippe was in the United States in 1796, a traveller, a schoolmaster, and an exile.

Louis Napoleon was a denizen of New York, and one of the Metropolitan lions about 1836–37.

MISCELLANEOUS THOUGHTS.

Collections of poetry made by poets are generally indifferent. Taste is not always the concomitant of genius and fancy, and even when exhibited in the works of the poet himself, he often seems to want it when selecting from the works of others. The collections of Southey and Campbell have as much inferior as really admirable matter. Southey has included much lumbering verse in his English Parnassus; and Campbell's anthology contains at least as large a proportion of mediocre and meagre verse as of really fine poetry. Our two finest American poets have edited two selections truly inferior to most of their own productions.

A FEW NOMINAL PARADOXES.

Maids of Honor, who have little of the article to boast of; Keepers of the Royal Conscience, without any of their own;

Irreverend Reverends; Irreligious Religionists; City Pastorals; Patriot Kings; Honest Thieves, and Incorruptible Politicians.

THEATRICAL PORTRAITS.

Cibber's Apology for his own life, a most entertaining piece of autobiography, contains the first prose gallery of theatrical portraits in the English language. Contemporary notices in the Tatler, Spectator, and Guardian; and later critical sketches and allusions, chiefly incidental, as of Garrick, in Tom Jones; of Quin, in Humphrey Clincker; the masterly portrait of Garrick, in Retaliation; notices of Clive, in Gray's Letters; long before, of Nell Gwynne, in Grammont's Memoirs; and of Garrick and Siddons, in Boswell and Cumberland's Autobiography, contribute to keep up the succession of original sources for a history of the stage, to the period of the publication of Churchill's Rosciad.

The Rosciad forms a poetical pendant to Cibber. It is a gallery of miniatures in verse, as his sketches are in prose. Exquisitely finished, terse and pointed, they undoubtedly are, but no less prejudiced and satirical. Churchill was, as a celebrated critic has written, "a fine, rough, manly satirist." The first and third of these epithets only can, with truth, be applied to a just critic. Effect, however, not justice, was the object of these witty strictures and lively caricatures.

For a long period, theatrical biography, as well as criticism, fell into dull hands. Galt's Lives is the best general work of this class; but the crude Scotchman wanted geniality, to appreciate with cordiality the heroes of the sock and buskin.

Boaden's name is a synonyme for dullness. Our worthy Dunlap, too, was literal and tedious. Even men of genius, and poets, of late years, have failed in dramatic biography—Campbell's Life of Mrs. Siddons and Barry Cornwall's Life of Kean are acknowledged failures.

A new generation of theatrical critics sprang up in the magazines and journals in London, some thirty years since, of whom Hazlitt, Lamb and Leigh Hunt are the brilliant leaders, whose ablest disciple is Foster, of the London Examiner.

Here, at home, we have had good criticism, in the Old Bachelor, in his description of Cooper's Macbeth, and Dana's exquisite *critique* on Kean's acting.

XXXIII.

PHILOSOPHICAL CHIT-CHAT.

THE study of even inexplicable problems is by no means altogether useless, if they effect the sharpening of the critical faculties. The reasoning employed is generally inconclusive; the evidence is apt to be unsatisfactory or insufficient; yet the powers of the mind are braced by the exercise of ingenuity, of patient thought, of careful analysis. Mental activity-the habit of cautious investigation, self-knowledge, and candor, ought to result from these pursuits.

It is well to ascertain the fruits of human inquiry, to know the unknowable, to speak after the German fashion, or as Locke has happily stated this position: "When we know our own strength, we shall the better know what to undertake with hopes of success; and when we shall have well surveyed the powers of our own minds, and made some estimate what we may expect from them, we shall not be inclined either to sit still and not set our thoughts on work at all, in despair of knowing anything, or, on the other side, question and disclaim all knowledge, because some things are not to be understood. *It is of great use to the sailor to know the length of his line, though he cannot with it fathom all the depths of the ocean.*"

On some of the most important of these topics, (considered as *speculative dogmas,*) the proper state of mind appears to be that of philosophic doubt. Indifference promotes clearness; a clear thinker can distinctly express his doubts; liberal views beget a tolerant temper in others, and imply the possession of it in the theorist.

Beattie, himself a writer on these subjects and a Professor of Moral Philosophy, expressly admits, "All the practical, and most of the speculative parts of moral science have been frequently and fully explained by the ablest authors." In any thirty or forty volumes of ethical discussion, you will find here a new term, there a novel illustration; for the most part, a constant recurrence to admitted principles and facts, varied in their applications to life and conduct to be sure, but essentially the same.

Two or three of the ablest works of this class, with an accurate and succinct historical survey of the doctrines and characters of the leading philosophers, will be of more real service to the honest student than a small library read and collated after the old fashions. Most of these works, as Bacon advises, may be merely "tasted," (read in part or hastily,) others *by deputy*, (in reviews, commentaries, critical dictionaries,) and a very few thoroughly studied—the master minds, as infrequent here as in every department.

Of the great mass of ethical and metaphysical writers, the style is extremely poor, mean, bald, and tedious. They seek to be so distinct, and are so copious, as to become tiresome, and that too, in the discussion of conceded truths. They reverse the self-censure of Horace on his concise obscurity, and overwhelm a few commonplace ideas in a *copia verborum*. But this waste of the syllogism is as great an error, as a matter of taste, as the most verbose declamation. Diffuse logic is even worse than diffuse rhetoric, as well as inimical to the very spirit of reasoning. Rhetoric admits copiousness; logic is close; beauty is strength here, as well the essence of wisdom as of wit.

After the piles of controversial tracts, sermons, and philosophical treatises on the subjects of liberty, freedom of the will, moral necessity, &c., the sum of the matter, it appears, may be thus briefly stated. Moral necessity appears to be a fair logical inference from the premises, but freedom is safest to assume as a ground of practice; as a question, it is still open to the metaphysicians.

Philosophical necessity, practical freedom—to reconcile History and Providence, freedom of the will and the foreknowledge of Omniscience, (wholly a mystery,)—is logically impossible.

Systems are invariably one-sided and exclusive, exhibiting in general but a partial view of any question, and upon which an immoderate emphasis is laid. Truth lies between the extremes of opposite theories. Thus, men are both self-lovers and benevolent, selfishness and disinterestedness being both of them original instincts. It is untrue to predicate of either of these principles, that they alone govern society. The dignity of human nature is to be cherished, while we must confess that imperfection is germane to the constitution of man. We should endeavor to preserve what is good in human nature, endeavoring at the same time to elevate and purify it.

Extreme characters are unfair illustrations of any doctrine, as much so as any extravagant doctrine is of sound philosophy itself. A mere politician is no proper specimen of human nature, any more than a mere talking philanthropist.

In a letter of Archbishop Herring, (the only Archbishop we can at present remember, who was at the same time a pleasant and elegant prose writer,) to his friend Mr. Dunscombe, occurs the following admirable sentiment, and the justest criticism on the rational school of morality, *i. e.*, that which based the foundations of morality on reason, and at the head of which stood Dr. Samuel Clarke: "The reasonableness of virtue is its true foundation, and the Creator has formed our minds to such a quick perception of it, that it is in almost every occurrence of human life self-evident; but then I am for taking in every possible help to strengthen and support virtue, beauty, moral sense, affection, and even interest; and it seems to me as if the Creator had adapted various arguments to secure the practice of it to the various tempers of men, and the different solicitations which they meet with. And virtue thus secured and guarded may perhaps not unfitly be compared to those buildings of a Gothic taste, which, though they have a good foundation, are furnished, nevertheless, (against all accidents,) with many outward supports or buttresses, but so contrived and adjusted by the architect, that they do not detract from, but even add to, the beauty and grandeur of the building."

The philosophical claims and literary character of Lord Shaftesbury, so impartially stated in the analytical review of Sir James Mackintosh, have been pretty closely scrutinized by former critics: both poets, Beattie and Gray. In Forbes' Life of Beattie we read this criticism: "Plato was one of the first who introduced the fashion of giving us fine words instead of good sense; *in this, as in his other faults, he has been successfully imitated by Lord Shaftesbury.*". Gray writes with equal severity: "You say you cannot conceive how Lord Shaftesbury came to be a philosopher in vogue. I will tell you: first, he was a lord; secondly, he was as vain as any of his readers; thirdly, men are very prone to believe what they do not understand; fourthly, they will not believe any thing at all, provided they are under no obligation to believe it; fifthly, they love to take a new road, even when that road leads nowhere; sixthly, he was reckoned a fine writer, and seemed always to mean more than he said. Would you have any more reasons? An interval of above forty years has pretty well destroyed the charm. A dead Lord ranks with commoners; vanity is no longer interested in the matter, for a new road has become an old one."

If after such men we may presume to add our opinion, it is perfectly in harmony with theirs. The works of Lord Shaftsbury appear to us a repertory of ethical topics, in which too many points and questions are comprehended under single heads, by no means sufficiently distinct and separate, full of commonplace, dressed up affectedly in stale metaphors and the cast-off imagery of the Platonists. He is absurdly verbose and magniloquent. His egotism is awkward, his circumlocutions clumsy, his pleasantry pompous. His style is in general heavy and languid, the style of a nobleman turned metaphisician. He is truly a philosophical *petit maître*, infected with the vilest pedantry and the French taste in criticism current in his day.

Gray's character of Aristotle appears to us even more just and better written than his portrait of Shaftesbury. As we have given Beattie's opinion of Plato, we may subjoin the following: "For my part, I read Aristotle, his poetics, politics, and morals, *though I do not well know which is which.* In the first place, he is the hardest author, by far, I ever meddled with. Then he has a *dry conciseness that makes one imagine one is perusing a table of contents rather than a book; it tastes for all the world like chopped hay, or rather like chopped logic;* for he has a violent affection to that art, being in some sense his own invention; so that he often loses himself in little trifling distinctions and verbal niceties; and, what is worse, leaves you to extricate him as well as you can. Thirdly, he has suffered vastly from the transcribers, as all authors of great brevity necessarily must. Fourthly, and lastly, he has abundance of fine uncommon things, which make him well worth the pains he gives one."

We know Aristotle wholly from translation, to be sure, and hence cannot judge of him as of an English author; but we believe all of Gray's *critique*, save the last clause, which must overrate him. He is crabbed and unreadable to a wonderful degree, analytical to excess, harsh to austerity and baldness. As a mere writer, though he may be, at times, profoundly suggestive, yet the matter of his works may be far better studied in modern authors, who are greater masters of form. As a moralist and metaphysician, much of him may be in Hobbes and Locke, yet they are far more able in developing the thought. In rhetoric and æsthetical criticism a score of writers, Greek, Roman, English, and German, may be mentioned vastly superior. In the philosophy of politics, France, England, and the United States have produced disciples that have transcended their master's skill; and in natural history, France, Germany, England, and America, during the last fifty years have accumulated a mass of scientific information, probably far beyond all the resources of antiquity in the same department.

Speaking of the *medium of translation*, we offer the dictum of high authority on this subject—Dugald Stewart: "A very imperfect one, undoubtedly, where a judgment is to be passed on compositions addressed to the powers of imagination and taste; yet fully sufficient to enable us to form an estimate of works which treat of science and philosophy. On such subjects it may be safely concluded, that whatever is unfit to stand the test of a literal version, is not worth the trouble of being studied in the original."

In a single tract of Hobbes, of some ninety duodecimo pages, occur some of the most suggestive passages in modern philosophical treatises. We find here the original of many famous theories and systems, the authors of which avoid, as far as possible, any mention of Hobbes, unless to abuse him, so obnoxious is his name, and so much has his reputation suffered at the hands not of critics only, but of theological and political partisans. This tract was a favorite with Addison, and is highly praised by Dugald Stewart and Mackintosh; contains the very marrow of Hobbes' philosophy, as Hazlitt has clearly shown in his admirable Essay on the Writings of Hobbes. The life of Hobbes has been written by the antiquarian Aubrey. The English Aristotle was, at one time, secretary to Lord Bacon, and the philosophical idol of Cowley, who has penned a noble ode to his memory. Locke owes an immense debt to him; but so fickle is Fame, the latter philosopher is regarded as at the head of English metaphysicians, while the earlier, his master, and an original thinker, as well as a masterly writer, is classed with atheists, paradoxical sophists, and sensualist worldlings. Errors, and grievous ones, are to be found in Hobbes, and of which we shall attempt no defence; still there is much truth, penetration into human motives and characters, force of style, independence and manliness in his Treatise of Human Nature—a body of philosophy in itself. At present we intend merely noting some remarkable coincidences of thought and expression between the elder writer and the others, generally his successors, though in some instances almost contemporaries.

"The consequences of our actions," says Hobbes, "are our counsellors by alternate succession in the mind."

In a noble, serious poem by Beaumont and Fletcher, the brother dramatists, we read:

> "Our acts our angels are, or good or ill,
> The constant shadows that walk by us still."

"In dreams," Hobbes finely suggests, "*our thoughts appear like the stars between the flying clouds.*" Locke, in

Book II. Chap. X. of his Essay, has hit upon a similar illustration. Speaking of the facility with which in most minds ideas fade in the memory, he concludes: "In all these cases, ideas in the mind quickly fade, and often vanish quite out of the understanding, leaving no more footsteps or remaining characters of themselves than *shadows do flying over fields of corn.*"

Hobbes has anticipated Gall and Spurzheim, where he writes, Chap. XI. of the Treatise, "The Brain, the common organ of all the senses." Truly, the new thoughts come out of the old books, or as Dan Chaucer has declared:

> " Out of the olde fieldes, as men saithe,
> Cometh all this newe corne, fro yere to yere;
> And out of the olde bookes, in good faithe,
> Cometh all this newe science that men lere."

Rochefoucault's definition of Pity is almost identical with that given by Hobbes, who styles it, "Imagination, or fiction of future calamity to ourselves, proceeding from the sense of another man's calamity."

After making, as we thought, quite a discovery, we found Hazlitt had, long before, pointed out the whole thing. So most of the new revelations of modern criticism are merely "new found old inventions," according to Butler. Chap. II. is an Essay on Idealism, a Berkleian speculation. Now, Hobbes died in 1679, Berkeley was born in 1684, and it is fair to infer the later philosopher *borrowed* from his predecessor. The sum of the doctrine is contained in the tenth and last paragraph: "And from hence, also, it followeth, that *whatsoever accidents or qualities our senses make us think there be in the world, they be not there, but are seeming apparitions only;* the things that are really in the world without us, are those *motives* by which these seemings are caused. And this is the great *deception of sense*, which also is to be *by sense corrected:* for, as sense telleth me when I see directly, *that the color seemeth to be in the object;* so, also, sense telleth me when I see by reflection, that color is not in the object."

We will conclude this discursive paper by quoting a common saying, that has passed into a proverb: "The worth of a thing is what it 'll bring," neatly framed into one of the most telling couplets of Hudibras. In Hobbes, we find it thus expressed: "So much worth is every thing, as a man will give for all it can do."

XXXIV.

A WELSH RARE-BIT FOR ST. DAVID'S DAY.*

St. George he was for England, St. Dennis was for France,
St. James for Spain, who by his fame the Gospel did advance;
St. Anthony for Italy, Andrew for Scots ne'er fails,
Patrick, too, stands for Ireland; St. David was for Wales.

As we are not speakers, nor lecturers, nor clergymen, but mere *litterateurs*, we don't know how we can more appropriately honor the natal day of the patron Saint of our ancestors, than by a *petit morceau* of literary tribute to the glories of the Welsh race. We shall not attempt to enter into an historical or antiquarian discussion of the origin of the Cymry, of the early establishment of the Cymric Church, or the story of English invasions and Cambrian struggles for independence.

* March 1, 1854.

The French historians Michelet and Thierry, have penetrated the Welsh character, and vividly narrated the history of the race. In episodical passages, they have done more than the regular histories of Wales have accomplished.

The Welsh character, brave, generous, choleric, patriotic and hospitable; proud of family and race, tenacious of particulars, logical and enthusiastic; the music and poetry of the bards, the learning of their theologians and lawyers, and their philologists, are universally admitted. We present a pot pourri of research, under the following captions: "Shakspeare's Welshman," the Language and Literature of the Cymry, and the Worthies of Wales.

SHAKSPEARE'S WELSHMAN.

Schlegel, the celebrated German critic, calls Owen Glendower, in Henry IV., "a well-meaning, honorable, but pedantic Welshman." Campbell, the poet, writes with generous justice, in the preface to his edition of Shakspeare, "Owen Glendower is a noble, wild picture of the heroic Welsh character; brave, vain, imaginative and impetuous. He was the William Wallace of Wales, and his vanity and superstition may be forgiven, for he troubled the English till they believed him, and taught him to believe himself, a conjurer." A sensible and patriotic Welsh biographer of the hero declares, that "Shakspeare seems to have embodied, in his portrait of Glendower, all that was romantic or marvellous in the traditional account of his life and character." A critic on Shakspeare, more bold, acute and brilliant than either, if not than all three of the foregoing—Hazlitt—has done full poetic justice to Owen Glendower, Fluellen, and Sir Hugh

Evans:—"Owen Glendower is a masterly character. It is as bold and original as it is intelligible and thoroughly natural. Fluellen, the Welshman, is the most entertaining character in the piece (Henry V.). He is good-natured, brave, choleric and pedantic. His parallel between Alexander and Henry of Monmouth, and his desire to have some disputations with Captain Macmorris, on the discipline of Roman wars, in the heat of battle, are never to be forgotten. His treatment of Pistol is as good as Pistol's treatment of his French prisoners. The Welsh parson, Sir Hugh Evans, (a title which in those days was given to the clergy) is an excellent character in all respects. He is as respectable as he is laughable. He has very good discretions and very odd humors. The duel scene with Caius gives him an opportunity to show his choler and his tremblings of mind, his valor and his melancholy, in an irresistible manner. In the dialogue which, at his mother's request, he held with his pupil, William Page, to show his progress in learning, it is hard to say whether the simplicity of the master or scholar is greatest. (Vide Hazlitt's characters of Shakspeare's plays.)

THE LANGUAGE AND LITERATURE OF THE CYMRY.

"The language of the British Bards," concludes Sharon Turner, "must have been substantially the same with the language of the Britons who withstood the valor of Cæsar, and of course must present us with a venerable image of perhaps the earliest language that appeared in Europe. No other nation but the Hebrew can show such a body of ethical and intellectual thought, and of versified composition of the same antiquity. In the twelfth century, there were writings of old British Bards extant, which were *then* called *ancient.*" —See Vindication of Ancient British Poems.

Amid the noble array of Bards, four names appear to stand out with brilliant prominence. Taliesin "radiant front," Aneurin, Llywarch Hen, who is said to have lived 150 years, and lost twenty-four sons in battle, and David ap Guillym.

Among the annalists, Asser, the friend and Historian of Alfred, Giradus Cambrensis, Gildas.

Howel Dha has gained the appellation of the "Welsh Justinian," Pelagius, one of the greatest of theological leaders —chief of the Morgans. Other great names we must reserve for a very imperfect miscellaneous list of Welsh worthies, most of whom flourished within the last three centuries. Numerous laudable attempts have been made to collect and preserve the relics of early bards, by enthusiastic and diligent antiquarian commentators. Stephens, in his Literature of the Cymry, has pointed out the treasuries of poetry and learning. Even a lady, Lady Charlotte Guest, has translated the Maginobion, a storehouse of natural legendary romance; and such able scholars as Dr. Owen Pugh and others have elaborated the lexicography of the language.

The fame of Welsh poetry rests very materially, so far as the English reader is concerned, on the admirable paraphrases of Gray, whose taste, enthusiasm and lyrical genius, shone with genuine splendor in his spirited versions—(we suspect superior to the original in execution, if not in the primary conception)—of the Triumphs of Owen (Gwynnedd) and the Death of Hoel, from the Gododin. The magnificent ode, "The Bard," is composed in the true Cambrian spirit, and worthy ef the noblest of his name. The tradition, by the way on which this fine poem is founded, has been ably controverted by Stephens and Parry, who have made out an ingenious case against the probability of the event. Of David ap Gwillym, we might quote the eulogistic criticism of Borrow, in Lavengro, if we had the book by us. In effect, he places him in company with the dozen capital cosmopolitan poets, and translated him with ardor. Was it Mrs. Murray who refused to publish these fine versions, as they must have been, if they any way resembled the translations of Danish ballads, by the same author, whose poetical talent is far beyond that of the only English translator of ap Gwyllym, we have encountered ?

WORTHIES OF WALES.

In the following list of the worthies of Wales, which is avowedly far from complete, we have brought together all the most distinguished names we could at brief notice collect, and without any regard to chronological order or gleaning. First, from Fuller's Worthies, we must enumerate three Sovereigns of England, born in Wales, Edward II., Henry V. and VII. Under the caption Princes, the noble old wit says, "I confess there were many of this Principality, but I crave leave to be excused from giving a list of their nativities. They are so ancient I know not where to begin, and so many I know not where to end." Yet, of a noble line, four at least should not be omitted—Arthur, "mirror of manhood ;" Owain Gwynned, the hero of Gray's noble poem ; Llewelyn ap Gruffydd, the last of Welsh descent that bore sway in the Principality, and Owen Glendower.

Caractacus, "that valiant British General, who for nine years resisted here the Romans' puissance."

Hugh Johnes, Bishop Llandaff, the first Welshman elected Bishop of Wales for 800 years.

Sir John Rhese, "noble by his lineage, but more by his learning."

Madoc, the hero of Southey's epic (?)—the traditional Welsh Columbus of the 12th century.

Sir Rhys ap Thomas, "never more than a Knight, yet little less than a Prince."

Merlin, the famous necromancer of the legends, probably an able chemist and man of science.

Devereux, Earl of Essex, the favorite of Queen Elizabeth, and rival of Leicester for her favor.

Bishop Parry, whose name is borne by many celebrated men.

Bishop Morgan, the first translator of the Bible into Welsh.

Vaughan, the Silurist, author of a few charming poems, from which Campbell did not disdain to borrow.

Archbishop Williams, whose life was written by Hackett.

The celebrated Herbert family, including Lord Herbert of Cherbury, the chivalric Knight and subtle metaphysician; George Herbert, the poet of the English Church; and in the present century Dean Herbert, and his son, William Henry Herbert, the popular writer.

James Howel, the earliest English letter writer, and one of the best.

Sir Hugh Middleton, who introduced the new river into London, the ancestor of the South Carolina family of the same name.

Powel, the historian.

Dr. Price, the political pamphleteer, ethical writer, economst and divine, of revolutionary fame.

Pennant, the antiquary and tourist.

Picton, the brilliant soldier, who has a grand-nephew, his namesake, in this city.

Inigo Jones is supposed to have been a Welshman. The father of Sir William was a native of Wales—an eminent mathematician. Jones, of Hafod, the celebrated book collector, proprietor and improver of a princely establishment, destroyed by fire, translator of Froissart and Monstrelet.

Wilson, the landscape painter, some of whose finest views were taken in Wales.

Gibson, the sculptor.

Owen, a great Welsh cognomen, borne by the Princes and by modern celebrities, *e. g.*, the famous divine of Cromwell's day, the portrait painter, the socialist politician, father and son.

Dyer, the descriptive poet, whose Grongar Hill is a Welsh scene, a lineal descendant of Shakspeare on the mother's side.

Baxter, the Calvinist. Jurists, one famous, Kenyon; one infamous, Jeffries.

There are pleasing literary associations connected with Wales. Jeremy Taylor's "Golden Grove" was written at Lord Carberry's seat, so called. Steele died at the house of his second wife, in Wales. Milton's "Comus" was performed at Ludlow Castle, and one of his wives, Mary Powel, must have been Welsh or of Cambrian descent. An enthusiastic Welsh antiquary of our acquaintance argues, from certain evidence in his possession, that the scenes of Gray's Elegy must have been in Wales. Among the Welsh characters of fiction out of Shakspeare, we do not recollect one more characteristic than "Mr. Morgan, the wild apothecary, (or rather naval surgeon or sea-going Doctor of Dickens,) whom

Thackeray remarks in his criticism of Smollett, 'is as pleasant as Doctor Caius'"—a high compliment, to compare any other man's characters with Shakspeare's.

We will conclude this desultory lucubration by a sketch of the patron Saint of Wales. The apochryphal writers make him one hundred and forty-one years old when he died, therein agreeing with the age of the Patriarch Jacob. The most probable accounts represent him to have been between 80 and 90, deducing his pedigree from the Virgin Mary, of whom it makes him the eighteenth lineal descendant. His character, drawn by Giraldus, represents him "a mirror and a pattern to all, instructing both by word and example, excellent in his preaching, but still more so in his works. He was a doctrine to all, a guide to the religious, a life to the poor, a support to orphans, a protection to widows, a father to the fatherless, a rule to monks and a model to teachers, becoming all to all, that he might gain all to God."

APPENDIX.

XXXV.

LITERARY EGOTISM.

It appears to me that a writer may be permitted publicly to decompose the state of his mind, and to make observations on his own character, for the benefit of other men, rather than to leave his body by will to a professor of anatomy.—ZIMMERMAN.

WE all love a frank, engaging temper. We are won by an open demeanor, which debars any thought of cunning or reserve. To say that a person is affable, is one of the greatest praises that can be bestowed on his manner or conversation. Is it not strange, then, that most of us are so horribly shocked at anything like an expression of individual opinion or feeling in a writer? Yet is this one of the commonest criticisms you shall hear passed on an author of original genius, who evinces in his writings any marks of a communicative disposition. 'Tis from a deep-rooted self-love; we hate to hear a man talking of himself—arising from the feeling of our own deficiency in having done nothing about which we can talk ourselves.

The introduction of personal character into literary composition, is an original feature in modern literature. Casual allusions to themselves and their works are, to be sure, not infrequent in Horace and Cicero; but nothing of that free and undisguised self-anatomy which we find in the works of such men as Montaigne, Rousseau, and Hazlitt.

The imitators of the ancients shrunk from any such confession as humiliating and undignified, with a sickly tastefulness more congenial to the schoolgirl than to the healthy intellect of a man.

The great charm of this marked personality lies in the intimate connexion growing up between the author and reader. The latter is placed upon the footing of a friend, and treated with all the confidence attributed to that noble relation.

Commonplace people turn up their noses and sneer at any exhibition of this sort in print, while in their conversation and daily intercourse with the world, they offend in the same way (if it be an offence), with this great difference, that instead of revealing noble natures, they discover nothing but the workings of mean, captious, shrivelled souls. The truth is, they dare not be confidential, else they would be hooted at; as their whole course of life is one prolonged tissue of little thoughts and petty actions. In one sense, indeed, they are the greatest of all egotists, for they rate themselves too highly to risk any confession whatever.

Egotism is often (almost always) found in company with vanity, rarely with pride. It renders a man's writings more valuable and sought after, after his death than while he is living. In the latter case there is palpable knowledge of him obtained through the coarse medium of personal communication; in the former, the hazy clouds which hang over his past existence seem to spiritualize whatever is material and unattractive. Besides we read his works with more interest than while he was living, and we could see him by taking a turn in the street. In the creatures of his brain we perceive a finer essence and a more distinct individuality than we could gather from any intimacy. They afford, in addition to their intrinsic merit, an historical record of himself. They present to us his peculiarities of mind and person, his original bias and prejudices, and his acquired habits. This species of personal authorship is as delightful as a fine piece of biography, with the advantage of its coming from the writer himself. Others may judge more fairly of his writings, but he certainly knows better the secrets engraved upon "the red-leaved tablets of the heart." He pours these out with a liberal profuseness worthy of his magnificent spirit, for they are his riches and pure ore to us. If a man in any other situation in life speaks with confidence of himself, and dwells with satisfaction on his performances, we forgive his openness and acquit him of the affectation of modesty. We place reliance on him who relies boldly on himself. In the case of a writer, the tables are completely turned. The world looks with a jealous eye upon his fame and genius. They seek to depress him in every possible way. They patronize or neglect him to show their power. He is at their mercy. He appeals to them. They alone can save and honor him. They are at once judge, jury, and advocate. They must plead in his behalf, consult together respecting his merits, and decide accordingly. It is in their hands to acquit or condemn. In other characters, as, for instance, in that of a professional man, they speedily acknowledge mediocre talents, and raise them to an undue elevation. He may obtain office or enrich himself with the spoils of party. If he turn to trade, he is welcomed with open arms, and a shower of gold is rained upon him. But let him turn author, and no epithet is deemed sufficiently degrading for him. He is then a vacillating, shiftless fellow—an idler—a mere vagabond. Thus must he submit to be esteemed by those who cannot confer the glory he seeks, while he has the ready and hearty approbation of those who can. Zeal and a partial interest in the literary character, have diverted us a little from the topic with which we set out. To return; all great and original thinkers must be, at least in some measure, egotists. Solitude and reflection, let them be ever so busy, leave them much leisure to look into their own minds. Every action of their lives, the habits into which they have become indurated, their present feelings—all refer to some peculiar circumstances fixed in their memory by the iron chain of association. They are creatures of sentiment as well as of intellect. Every idea in their minds is influenced by every pulsation of their hearts. They feel acutely as well as think profoundly. Their hearts do not ask leave of their heads to feel. The one may give the other a useful lesson. Hence they hoard up as a precious relic every token of their past pleasures or sufferings, and at the moment of writing are impressed as sensibly as when they first felt those emotions. They are the only true chronologists of feeling. Their memory is retentive of impulses as well as of ideas.

The personal history of many distinguished authors is full of instances to this effect; and of none, perhaps, more so than the late William Hazlitt. It was this coloring of mind and character which pervaded his masterly criticisms and profound metaphysical disquisitions. It breaks out in a dramatic criticism, or bursts full upon the reader in the discussion of some subject far abstracted from the remarks to which it may give rise. His love, his faith in man, his airy hopes, the characters of his friends, his mental weaknesses, the brilliant points of his genius, pass in review before us, and melt in the thin air of his gorgeous rhapsody.

In many writers the passages oftenest turned to are full of this self-confession, and constitute the best portion of their works. Though incidentally most delightful, yet it is dangerous for a writer to make this the staple of his composition. In fact, it can never be done with success, unless by a master; otherwise it will fall to the ground, a baseless fabric, unsupported by the groundwork of past performances.

It is an error to suppose egotism consists in speaking well of ourselves only. It lays in frequent mention of ourselves, whether with approbation or not. Besides, it may be discovered in different ways;—a marked style, a certain manner of treating a subject, and a particular vein of speculation, render a work as individual as the constant use of the personal pronoun. The most subtle form of egotism is, to make a third person speak your own sentiments, painting him after your own character. The novel and the drama are the true provinces for the exercise of this talent. These methods have been employed by most writers of eminence. Shakspeare alone has been pronounced an exception; for, in the multifarous characters which stud his pages as stars the firmament, there is none which can be fastened upon him who painted them all.

Egotism assumes a different aspect in different characters. In the man of the world, it is gay and cheerful; in the contemplative scholar, more abstract and refined. In the poet, it is lofty and elevated; in the metaphysician, complex and subtle. The best specimens of agreeable egotism may be found in our periodical essayists. The finest sample of profound egotism, in the poetical speculatist and sincere self-student, is Rousseau. Epic poets are inclined to egotism, as Milton: dramatic authors less frequently, though Ben Jonson was an instance to the contrary.

To sum up the question in few words, Is it not as reasonable for a man to dissect his own mind as to leave it to some one to mangle for him? Is he not surer of hitting near the truth, and bringing out traits undiscoverable by others, who draws from individual experience and feeling, instead of transferring this task to a stranger?

should he fall into the hands of a friend, one who loved him dearly or hated him most cordially, he would inevitably be overpraised or underrated as affection or envy swayed the balance. He is certain of being dealt with unjustly by an enemy in many particulars. He has no alternative then but to sit as critic upon himself, and be his own historian. When he dies, he will then leave the world a copy done by the surest and truest hand.

XXXVI.

ON WALKING THE STREETS.

The streets present to our eyes a moving panorama. Fancy can hardly suggest spectacles more incongruous than the objects with which they are filled. To look around one from the corner of a street for a quarter of an hour, is fully equal to beholding a raree show or a dramatic performance. Everything is alive: nothing remains stationary, save here and there a small knot collected around a mob orator, who stands in the midst, on a hogshead; or a few loiterers cheapening some apples or pears, at the tables of the fruit-women; or a circle round a drunken man, who has fallen against the pavement; or a person in a fit; or a crazy woman; or an Irish fight; or a child that has lost its way; or a rogue that has found his—to the temple of justice. Even in these collections there are many still moving off, whose places are filled up by others, and so on till all are dispersed. One may live in a large city all his life, and yet see a new set of faces every day. There are some which he repeatedly meets, and after a while recognises as old acquaintances, yet the majority are still changing.

Let us look out and see what we can of the passing scene. Yonder is a long procession of butchers, who are paying a sort of posthumous respect or funeral obsequies to the dead cattle, drawn and quartered, which they are gallanting along in solemn order. From out of that tall mansion, across the way, issues a long array of mourners. It is a funeral—one of those reliefs to the gaieties of life, without which the picture would be too light and gaudy. It throws, like the shadows in Rembrandt's pictures, a seasonable darkness and gravity over the otherwise gay and frivolous scene.

The sound of the drum and "spirit-stirring fife" announces a company of soldiers, all prankt in gay and martial attire, affording infinite delight to children and the rabble who troop after and before them in a spirit of emulation—aye! and to wiser folks, too —shop-keepers and chambermaids, whose heads are seen peeping through the blinds and staring out of the open windows. A whoop and cry suddenly breaks on the ear, and "look out for the mad dog" resounds from a hundred mouths. The mad dog, apparently out of spite, bites the dogs in his way, and finally, either beaten or stoned to death, gives up the ghost in a neighboring gutter.

A volume might easily be filled with a series of street pictures. We must omit many; but stop, however, to solicit a little attention to a very interesting portion of the *dramatis personæ:* we mean beggars—not purely those by profession, (though even they have a claim upon us as representatives of an ancient nomadic race, to which they have become bound by custom,) but they who are incidentally such, as widows who cannot obtain employment or support, orphans, the infirm, the aged, emigrants deluded from their homes, and the remaining sad catalogue.

A little may afford great relief—the withholding it may drive to starvation and crime. Relieve every one and each of these: remember the promise made to him "that giveth to the poor."

The gait of different classes of individuals is worthy of observation. It has been said that no two persons walk alike. To observe thus is to consider too curiously; certain it is, however, there are marked differences in the carriage of different persons. The tailor is known by his stoop and bandy legs; the jockey by his feeble and tottering step; the sailor by his roll and swagger; the beau by his solemn pace, as if stepping to the dead march; the man of business by his quick shuffle and nervous anxiety; the fine lady by her affected step, as if disdaining the earth she trod upon; the milliner by her coquettish airs; the gouty old gentleman, hobbling and cursing at every step, and the fat market woman, who waddles along with a huge basket on her arm.

No one can avoid speculating on the faces and appearances of those he meets with in the streets. The whole mass of persons form a picture of almost infinite detail, and inexhaustible fund of amusement. The janty air of the man of fashion, the formal manner of the spruce apprentice, the stolid look of an over-fed alderman, are all characteristic.

To walk perfectly at ease, and enjoy the full current of reflection, without any one to jostle or interrupt you, tread the pavement of some mighty thoroughfare at the silent hour of midnight, with the moon wheeling in her course over your head, the whole city wrapped in slumber, and a death-like stillness pervading all things. This delicious quiet is superior to any day-scene, save a fine Sunday morning in a beautiful part of the country: a neat village, for instance, embosomed among lofty hills, whose sides are covered with forest trees, and whose tops project their bare and rugged summits high into the sky—a small church—the great wheel of the mill standing still—the cattle lolling in the noontide heat—the clear lake without a ripple—the gardens of the villagers, sending forth showers of perfume from their beds of flowers—the air calm as the breathing of a sleeping child, save when it is vexed by the drone of a bee, or the distant low of cattle. This is a scene for the landscape painter of the rarest skill and most poetic feeling.

XXXVII.

THE HOUSEWIFE:

A CHARACTER.

The housewife must be a middle-aged woman, and of a bustling disposition. In house-cleaning, a peculiar part of her vocation, she rises even to a pitch of enthusiasm. This is no wise diminished by the pailsful of cold water that she constantly lavishes in scrubbing and washing the woodwork. She must have Dutch blood in her veins, stimulated by her American birth and education, and crossed with English method and prudence. Her forte is dusting, for which she employs more old handkerchiefs and rags than would furnish out a picturesque army of beggars. She has a mat before every door, and allows none but guests and strangers to come in by the street steps. The family enter by the basement. She says she never cleans, but keeps clean. She will not suffer a crumb on the carpet nor a drop of tea on the table. A stain on the table-cloth is as bad as a stain upon her reputation. Her conscience is absolutely harrowing on these points. I once trod on a door-sill in her entry which had been newly painted, and this offence was not obliterated from her memory until long after it had vanished from the floor under a fresh coat of paint—nay, I have little doubt she remembers it still to my disadvantage.

She generally lives in the poorest room of the house, under the disinterested plea of saving her fine furniture for company. When she has friends to tea she is very fidgety about having the chairs removed out of their places. In the midst of the parlor stands a table covered with elegantly bound books and fine engravings, which it is treason to touch or open. She has a keen eye for finger-prints on doors near the handles, and traces of one's feet on a newly-washed stoop. She is a great admirer of Mrs. Glasse, and keeps a large book full of receipts and directions. She is a capital fancy cook and confectioner, and can make a blanc-mange or jelly equal to a professed artist. A fine stirring housekeeper she esteems the perfection of her sex. Her carpets are covered with baize, and her lamps and glasses with paper, to keep off the flies. She is particularly careful about fires and candles, and goes about the last thing at night, to see that all in the house are put out. The servants often grumble at this inspection. It is a maxim with her, that not one person in a hundred can carry a candle straight. When her friends bring children to the house she is in an agony lest they break the jars or throw balls through the windows. To speak the truth, she is otherwise very kind to them, stuffing their pockets with dough nuts and krullers worthy of her Dutch grandmother.

On Sundays she stays at home, and sends the servants to church. In her person she is invariably neat and tidy, unlike that boastful woman who told her one day, "My dear Kitty, I'm the only thing

..a my house that is not as clean as wax," to which she made answer, in a dignified manner, "I think, Mrs. A., you ought rather to reverse your attention, if it is impossible both should be clean." She loves to keep old family and personal relics, old linen, fashionable dresses when she was a belle (forty years back,) old china, glasses, silver mugs, curious coins, painted tumblers, and such like closet antiquities. She exhibits her affection in keeping locks of hair and pulled teeth of her relatives and acquaintance. If she is musical, she keeps a collection of old music, where the latest is one of Burns' fine songs. Her piano is crazy from age, and out of tune; her harp has two or three strings broken, and her flageolet is cracked like her natural voice. She has her hair dyed, and wears a set of false teeth. Her natural vanity not allowing her to wear spectacles, she complains of being fashionably near-sighted. Otherwise she preserves her looks very well, and is quite a fine-looking woman.

Her talk is almost entirely with ladies of her own stamp, about servants, dresses, dishes, children and furniture. She often asks Mrs. Siddons' question of the linen-draper, though in a more familiar tone, "Will it wash?" She prefers, nevertheless, taking a hand at piquet or backgammon, to spending the evening in conversation. I should not be surprised if at this very moment she was innocently delighted at having made a hit—I am sure I hope I have, in my portrait of her.

XXXVIII.

READING AND STUDY.

Of all the trades to which that multifarious animal, man, can turn himself, I am now disposed to look upon intense study as the idlest, the most unsatisfying and the most unprofitable.—*Beattie, Let.* 33, *to Capt. Mercer.*

The main distinction between reading and study is, that the latter is generally regarded as synonymous with labor and attention, while the former is understood rather as a relaxation from business or professional cares, than as a source of elegant gratification. Now we think, despite of the slurs cast upon that liberal minded and truly intelligent class of readers commonly called "general readers," there is no body of men to whom an author of genius and elegance can more appropriately address himself. The term "general reader" is in very low esteem with those scientific or professional pedants who, confined in their studies merely to professional topics, have not comprehension of mind or elegance of taste enough to relish anything beyond their accustomed round. The mind of one of these excluded from general information by devotion to one science, something resembles the lady in the Italian tale, who, wishing to hide herself in sport from her lover, took refuge in a chest, the lock of which shutting on the outside, it became a living tomb. Thus these narrow minded cavilers at versatility, embalming themselves in their favorite subjects, become intellectually dead, as regards the external world and familiar things.

There is nothing so delightful (not to mention its advantages) as desultory reading. It is detached from all system and scholastic restraint. The mind is "studious of change:" it hates regularity *always*. There are times and occasions when method is au essential virtue; in our recreations, however, it is a complete damper—it chills enthusiasm and disperses the fine thoughts of genius. Besides, in the present state of society, we must be encyclopædical in our acquirements; it will not answer for a man to be deep (as it is styled, which after all means dull and prosy) on a *single* subject. He must have much and varied knowledge of many things. The mere any thing, now-a-days, is entirely out of place. Even a poet must be in some measure a man of the world. How, we would ask these learned philosophers, would it look in a company of some dozen persons, if every man had a distinct profes ion, art or trade, and knew nothing else? The poet and the merchant, the lawyer and the orator and the dominie, the painter and the chemist, would be entirely at loggerheads. Let a man follow a grand object if he will, and aim at perfection in it; but let him not reject other and perhaps more excellent acquirements. This is perhaps the strongest argument to be brought against the classics, for they, of all other studies, demand a minute attention and thorough surrender of time and talent. Hence we rarely see a pure classical scholar at all acquainted with the various literature of the moderns—with the literature of his own country—least of all, with the literature and wisdom of the old masters in our early tongue.

Theologians are a fair instance of the effect of one pursuit. They are (to speak of them as a class) the dullest of mortals, knowing nothing, or next to nothing, of literature, art, life and character. These men are the moles of literature, always grubbing their way amid dark, unprofitable and stupefying studies.

Lawyers are very different from these, young ones especially. Perhaps there is no one profession which embraces so much talent, clearness and taste in elegant matters, with gentlemanly feeling, as the Law. Much leisure, with their natural inclination, leads them to these pursuits; but wearisome plodders, who can climb up the high road to Learning's temple with slow and heavy step, having neither the wings of the poet, nor the lightness of the prose writer, nor the energy of the orator, are the bane and pest of letters.

> "Study is like heaven's glorious sun,
> That will not be deep searched by saucy looks;
> Small have continual plodders ever won,
> Save bare authority from others' books,"

is the opinion of the greatest master of character, as well as the profoundest philosopher and the finest poet that ever lived. Scholars, however, have in general a higher opinion of one who can defend a moral commonplace by his quotations, than of him who brings out from "the coinage of his brain" sentences, equally fine, of home manufacture.

"I seek," says one with equal frankness and wisdom, "in the reading of books, only to please myself by an irreproachable diversion; or if I study, it is for no other science than what treats of the knowledge of myself, and instructs me how to live and die well." A most admirable remark indeed! in this world, where so many and so great subjects draw off our attention from the study of the most important subjects—our own minds and hearts. This "half good fellow, half gossip," goes on to say, "I do not bite my nails about the difficulties I meet with in my reading; after a charge or two. I give them over. Should I insist upon them, I should both lose myself and time; for I have an impatient understanding that must be satisfied at first." If this confession be not good advice, we know not what is. In reading, if we cannot, "after a charge or two," master the author's meaning—provided we be capable of so doing—we may rest assured it is not worth our while. The purest writers are the most perspicuous, and when a great man declares himself obscurely we may take it for granted that he is in a fog himself. What Montaigne styles his "impatient understanding," is a keenness of perception and quickness of judgment which can master the most intricate subject with little trouble.

The great advantage of miscellaneous and desultory reading is, that it prevents the mind from becoming cramped by any particular set of notions, or chained down to one topic. It evinces the same influence as the wisest philosophy, and breathes a similar spirit.

This is a total freedom from dogmatism which may run into scepticism, but which is more likely to produce that equable state of mind and of opinion which is the heaven of the scholar. Let us not forget that this state of mind must not be applied to matters of business or of determinate action, but for the man of letters and the author, it presents a picture on which he could gaze for ever with delight, dreaming away his existence like the elegant and luxurious Gray, who thought it the height of happiness "to lie on a sofa and read *new novels*." We agree most heartily with him in all this, save the last, and for which we would substitute old poets.

XXXIX.

ON THE VALUE OF METAPHYSICAL STUDIES.

The true estimate of metaphysics, considered apart from its applications to ethics, logic, or criticism, has scarcely, we think, been rightly considered. Mere speculatists have on the one hand elevated this science to an undue height; while on the other, men of business and of the world have been too apt to regard it as a pursuit of little or no utility. The latter have been disgusted by subtleties to which their intellects may not have been always equal, and by refinements of the understanding, in unravelling which they could discern no real profit. The bare generalities thrown out indiscriminately by mere metaphysicians in every company (and most frequently in companies where they could never be appreciated) have tended towards creating a general dislike to them, and in this way, the study which of all others deserves the highest attention of the true philosopher, has been cast into contempt by the unadvised conduct of its professors.

The philosophy of mind lies at the base of all knowledge. It has for its object the ascertaining the faculties of the mind, their nature and force, in what degree and to what extent they may be cultivated, how error may be eradicated and truth instilled, in what the first principles of all truth consist, and what the functions of the soul may be. Besides these, it investigates the traits of character and motives to action, the feeling of beauty and the perception of every species of excellence. It affords some of the best arguments in defence of the Christian religion, and furnishes a clue to the noblest sentiments of virtue.

The greatest benefit, however, accruing to the metaphysician is the insight into his own mind and feelings, whereby he obtains the greatest of all treasures self-knowledge. It is this will guide him in the fit direction of his powers, expose his deficiencies, exhibit his individuality and manifest the bent of his disposition and character.

Another, is the acuteness and perspicuity imparted to the perceptive faculty by frequent exercise. And this prevails not only in metaphysical subjects, but also in all the affairs of life, and in reasonings on all other questions.

It further begets a love of philosophizing on all subjects, enlarges the liberality of our views, and widens our comprehension.

It colors every topic, and throws a new light upon what was before dark and confused.

The logical faculty—that great index of the soul—is also vastly improved by these studies ; it is rendered subtler, and sharper, and readier. The employment of analysis developes powers of which we were hardly conscious, and compresses scattered facts and opinions into eternal and immutable truths. And here is seen the superiority of metaphysical over mathematical studies, as an exercise of the reason. The objects of the former are of far greater impo.-tance, and this alone is sufficient to prove our position; the latter having reference to lines, and figures, and numbers, while the former is employed in investigating the furniture of the noblest production God ever made—that of the human mind. The effect of mathematics is to make the mind hard, rigid and stubborn, pliable to no demonstration but that which is purely scientific and exact. The effect of metaphysics, on the contrary, is to open and expand all our powers of speculation and argument. In regard to many topics it admits of testimony less fallible than that of the senses or of mathematical demonstratton. It recognises ideas hanging sometimes on a mere thread of conjecture, and is cautious not to break it, since they may reveal truths the exactest science could never discover.

The pursuit of metaphysics exclusively for a long time must needs be hurtful to the understanding: but, in connection with language, criticism, or ethics, its practical bearing is of the highest value.

All great poets are of necessity metaphysicians, for they feel acutely and reflect deeply on their own nature and the natures of their fellow-men—on the springs of action as evinced in the characters of those around them—on their own ideas of supreme goodness and perfect purity, and on the forms and shape of intellectual as well as physical beauty.

After a regular course, then, of purely methaphysical writers, it is both delightful and useful to read the great poets, as their true masters and best expounders.

XL.

MALE SCOLDS.

The species of eloquence most cultivated and general, is the objurgatory. When everything else fails, this is ever ready and in good favour. It is common to confine this talent to the softer sex; but such a view is too restricted, and by no means fair: yet, the Common Law supposed it to be their peculiar property—the common scold, "*communis rixatrix*," was in every instance of the feminine gender—so much the more disagreeable and unfitting does it appear in man. It is as if he should borrow the woman's dress as well as the woman's prerogative.

A male scold is one of the most hateful creatures in social intercourse. He undertakes to lecture every person he come across, without respect to age, talents, or station. He speaks in threats and censures. Having conceived the idea that carping is acute criticism, he expresses dissatisfaction at everything. He fumes all day long like a little household shrew. He is continually the Æolus of some domestic tempest. When he does not speak out, he endeavors to put one down by a frown or a sneer. He is the cur of conversation, ever snarling. He laughs at no jests, and calls pathos drivelling. He is without any sentiment whatever. He is (if of a literary turn) a critic of the severe order, and delights in controversy; indeed, he has no idea of composition except as a medium of attack and defence. This kind of writing alone, he thinks, brings a man out. He is consequently a vast admirer of Cobbett, and places Junius at the head of English prose. He thinks to be regarded only by being bearish, and piques himself on the intractability of his humours. He loves to hear it said of him, "Mr. —— is a very particular man, and you must study his whims if you would get into his good graces." His spleen is his better genius. He is quite in his element in finding faults, but inadequate to any sincere eulogy. He cannot for the very life of him turn a compliment pleasantly. If he can gain attention by his rudeness he is content. He wishes to be esteemed very nice and fastidious, and prides himself on an exquisite taste. Wisdom and the habit of unvarying censure are the same in his vocabulary. He reproves a gay countenance with becoming severity. The humorous man he calls "a good fellow, but rather weak." He forgets the fine old stave—

"The wisdom that would make us grave,
  Is but an empty thing;
What more than mirth would mortals have?
  A cheerful man's a king,"—

or cannot appreciate the truth of it. Relaxation he esteems highly unbecoming and undignified. He lays vast stress on that hollow mask of wisdom (so imposing in the eyes of the vulgar) animal dignity. As the world stands, perhaps, one must occasionally give in to this system of behavior. A wise man among fools must sometimes assume their deportment.

He act s the part of Bruin* to his wife, and is the perpetual torment of her existence. He comes in to his dinner, tastes and pishes at everything. He turns up his nose at the best prepared dishes, and exclaims, "his partialities are never consulted." He is a very tyrant over his whole household. His children, from dreading, get to hating, and end by despising him. He lectures them all round for the slightest breach of the laws of etiquette. Thsee are more sacred in his eyes than the Ten Commandments or the Laws of the Twelve Tables. He is a Sir Anthony Absolute to his sons, and always speaks to them in the imperative mood. He takes his servants to task before company, to impress them with an idea of his authority. He will never hear an answer or an excuse. He is the highest tribunal, from which there is no appeal. In criticising an author, he is sure to fasten on the minutest defects, and is blind to true excellence. He lights on the most impure parts, like the carrion crow, He admires Gifford hugely, who was a man after his own heart. When not employed in reproof, he is then a dumb dog that can only snap and show his teeth.

It is a boast of his, that he always speaks out his mind plainly on every occasion—he means in the way of dispraise—and arrogates it to himself as a great merit. This is a most silly device, and the sure mark of a coward. He fears such an imputation, and thinks an exhibition of spleen will exonerate him from it. He is skilful in a warfare of words, but sinks with dread under the fear of blows. He acts on the principle of frightening people by face-making and calling hard names. But this method won't work with every one. Thersites is his favorite Homeric character, and his great aim is to rival him in foul-mouthed eloquence,

To take pleasure in giving pain—to court opportunities for censure, and hunt for occasions of giving unasked advice, are certain evidences of a contemptible spirit. To perform these offices in the proper manner, is, of itself, a matter of rare tact and considerable

* Mayor of Garratt.

nicety. One apology, only, can be offered for such people, which is, that having been disappointed themselves in their plans of life, they take revenge by endeavoring to make people dissatisfied with themselves and each other—fostering bad feeling, to have companions in misfortune. Sometimes this habit is the offspring of an irritable temperament—more frequently of long indulgence and custom.

I wonder that neither Addison nor Steele ever delineated a character of this description. It lay entirely within their province of observation, and they must have known persons of this sort. Artificial life they knew thoroughly: the male coquette, the beau and his co-mates, the pretty fellow, the rake, &c., all came under their vigilant observation. The male scold only seems to have escaped it. Perhaps they fell into the general notion of appropriating the title of scold to their sister woman alone; or they may have considered a man exercising the same talent to be an orator of the higher class, ranking with the Satirist and the Censor.

XLI.

THE SEXTON.

A CHARACTER.

THE Sexton should be a man of staid and solemn aspect, not over-gay, but rather given to melancholy and gloom. Shakspeare exhibits him in Hamlet, a merry wag; but this is a freak of his great genius. Steele hit nearer the mark, when he represented his undertaker, (who is often a sexton,) lecturing his hired mutes on the propriety of their behavior at funerals. Lamb calls him "bedmaker to the dead." Perhaps he might be as fitly named "an earthly upholsterer."

He should be a serene man, except when bustling about the rooms before the funeral procession is ready to move—otherwise sparing of his words, and meditative—neat in his dress and decorous in manner. He ought to be fond of serious reading, chiefly of divines. He has ample opportunity for criticising every variety of contemporary preaching. He is fond of church music, revelling in the chime of bells, and has an especially fine ear for the saddest music in the world' *i. e*., the fall of the dust on the coffin. His thoughts should be dark and murky, like the black air of a vault. His frequent descent into such places gives him rheumatic pains, which, martyr-like, he endures as *professional* evils. He is attached to fine linen, and loves nothing better than a handsome suit of grave clothes. He has an old-fashioned partiality for the rod, and gives the younger portion of the congregation sundry intimations of his skill in applying it. He is also peculiarly great in a frown or awful nod. He takes a stranger up the aisle with all the formality of a Presbyterian deacon. Nothing pleases him more, however, than to stop him, to speak in his ear during his perambulations around the church. On a public occasion, he sits (Janitor) at the church door stately enough, refusing admittanee to all not possessed of tickets. This is some week-day festival or celebration. A slight douceur will, however, procure your admittance through the densest mass. He has the highest opinion of the Pastor and the Vestry. The Wardens are his Castor and Pollux, and the Choir his angelic host. He is Death's valet or gentleman of the bed-chamber—chamberlain and master of the wardrobe.—A necessary man, and if you treat him well, grateful.

XLII.

THE LINGUIST.

——— he that is but able to express
No sense at all in various languages,
Will pass for learneder than he that's known
To speak the strongest reason in his own.—BUTLER.

A CHARACTER.

THE Linguist is a creature *all tongue*, without "a garnish of brains;" or rather, he has the *gift of the tongues*. He could have set them all right at Babel, had he been living at the time of the Great Confusion. Charles V. proved himself no very sagacious critic, when he said, "He that could speak five languages was five times a man." Suppose he could say nothing of consequence in any one dialect;—even allowing, however, his sense to be weighty, is it improved by passing through the strainers of five different national idioms? Is it not at least probable *that* alone would have perverted the original meaning? The greatest thinker that ever lived could think in one language only; for if he pretended to speculate in another, it must have been as a mere translator of his first thoughts. These always are formed in the mother tongue. But this is irrelevant. In point of fact, our linguist regards language, the symbol of thought, as equally important with, or perhaps more important than, the thought itself. A long and intimate acquaintance with literary history and the arts of composition, inclines one to rate *expression* and style a great deal too highly. Indeed, some have gone so far as to say that style alone preserved an author. One who is for ever turning over lexicons, grammars, vocabularies, tables of roots, &c., &c., cannot fail to form a very extravagant estimate of philological studies. Such a person becomes, from long habit and intolerable prejudice, cramped and confined in all his ideas, and is gradually transformed into a perfect Polyglot. He might be bound "in congenial calf," a terror to all similar offenders. His ideas are arrayed in tables of contents, and his writings are indexes. His highest literary attempts are notes, emendations, scholia, glosses. He corrects misspellings and errors in punctuation. By his blundering, he often spoils a fine passage. Fitz Osborne's satirical hit on "tweedledum and tweedledee" is very fair and in point. To edit a classic tops the bent of his ambition. He is, besides, a powerful writer of prefaces and introductions. In regard to profit, he clears more from a spelling-book than the first poet of the age for his finest work. The editors of Horace alone have fattened where their great original starved. He will spend hours in searching for a preposition, or chasing an adverb through successive editions, and yet censure the modern Nimrod. He professes no charity for poetical reveries. He takes more delight in the muddy crudites of Lycophron than in the clear beauties of the silver Virgil. The more trivial and obscure an ancient author is, the more he reveres him. He might sometimes write even better himself in the same strain; especially if his idol be crabbed and musty. His taste is most depraved. I knew one before whom was placed a Persian grammar and a volume of Irving, who studied the former with undisguised pleasure, but threw aside the latter as a mere child's book. The senseless classifications and absurd theories of affiliation of languages, and all such pedantic trumpery, were forsooth of greater mark than refined satire, picturesque description, a rich vein of masculine humor, and the utmost grace of style. I suppose he would have preferred Warburton or Parr to the glorious Shakspeare. He had rather read, as some literary glutton honestly confessed, a criticism on Homer, than Homer himself. His contempt of the moderns is so great, he can only converse with the ancients. His appetite for the latter is voracious, and by no means fastidious; for the former, his stomach is very squeamish. He can, like certain epicures, relish only what is past eating in the opinion of everybody else. His style of discourse is described by Butler with admirable effect:

> "A Babylonish dialect,
> Which learned pedants most affect;
> 'Twas English, cut on Greek and Latin,
> As fustian heretofore on satin," &c.

His plainest English is most execrable Latin. He teaches his little daughter Latin, and has his sons "well seen" in Greek and Hebrew. Perhaps he forgets where Hebrew roots grow, and in what soil they flourish best.

The head of a Polyglot may be compared to a pawnbroker's shop, where you may find every variety of dress, but tarnished, and in a state of dilapidation. He knows the exterior sign of every language, but has never penetrated the interior signification of any one. He apes the manners of the ancients, as a footman his master's air. The dinner of the ancients is a capital satire on this propensity. He cannot ask for a glass of cold water, without introducing the "*fontes Bandusiæ*," or the Pierian Spring; nor help a friend to bread at table without a pun on Pan.

He has his pet letters—vowels and consonants, and will sometimes array them in mimic battle against each other. To some he is indifferent, to others he bears a grudge;—rainy-day letters and holiday favorites. In his opinion, *a b* and *c* are worth their weight in gold; while *x y* and *z* are comparatively worthless and inefficient.

He is, in the most liberal acceptation, a *man of letters.* While we speak thus of the mere philologist, we would by no means intend to underrate the benefit derived from the study of other languages beside our mother tongue. Indeed, we can never hope to appreciate its beauties precisely, without a comparative reference to the languages of other nations and countries. The only evil arises from constantly dwelling upon mere signs, without gaining the substance. After a certain period of life, we must look more to things and less to words. It is then, an undue attention to the study of languages is censurable in the extreme.

Languages are highly useful to the commercial, and interesting to literary men. Many tongues are not only unnecessary, but even hurtful to the mind. Could a man of elegant taste be improved by the acquisition of Chaldee or Turkish? The learned professions require learned men; and, to a certain extent, repulsive studies are proper to be followed. Languages are the keys of learning; they serve to open its stores and unlock its treasures; they serve to embalm ideas, and render images and sentiments eternal. All this they can do; still they are but the willing servitors of thought, and must not presume a rivalry. Independent of sense and meaning, they are more worthless than tinkling cymbals. Joined to sense and meaning, they can shadow forth the finest essence of intellect and mysteriously unveil the immortal glories of the soul.

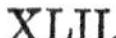

XLII.

THE ITALIAN OPERA. *

"I wonder how 'tis possible that the opera, with all its exquisite music and almost regal magnificience, should yet so successfully tire me."—*La Bruyere.*

THE Opera is the last refinement of Musical Science. It has carried the most delightful of the Arts to an unnatural pitch of perfection. It has destroyed (in all those who cultivate it) a taste for

* 1838-39.

the pure, simple and unobtrusive beauties of Music, "while, heavenly maid, she [yet] was young," and introduced a love for exhibitions of mere skill and ingenuity. The enjoyment of the Ballad, the artless strain of former days; the hearty relish of the fine old songs of England and Scotland; the noble music of our venerated ecclesiastical mother; the sweet hymn (the pious embodiment of devotional melody)—all, all are gone, and in their place we have the warbling plaint, the long-drawn sigh, the up-trilled treble, the deep grunting bass, the falsetto, the cantata, the bravura, the scena, the solo, the duett, the quartette, the chorus, and heaven knows what, of madness in Music and harshness in Harmony.

Among a people of strong sense and keen discernment, the Opera can never become a permanent national amusement. The cases of England and our own country prove this sufficiently. In Italy and similar countries where the mind is enervated by climate and luxurious indolence, mere sounds take precedence of sense. In the former, however, the melody must be an echo of the sentiment, deep-seated, and struggling for expression.

What is the Opera? Why, a sort of middle estate between the Melo-drama and the Concert. It resembles nothing in nature—'tis neither Comedy, nor Tragedy, nor Farce. Each of these have their counterpart in "this living, breathing world." The Opera is a sort of composite of the three, and of the most indifferent parts of the three. It has none of the light elegance of the first, nor the sublime energy of the second, nor the broad humor of the third. The Italians seem utterly deficient in wit and humor, unless of the grotesque sort, as well as in a severe sublimity and daring flights. To this last remark their great poets are undoubtedly exceptions—but we were speaking of their Opera. Their comic attempts descend into and seldom rise above fantastic buffoonery, and their flights of imagination are mere melo-dramatic bombast. And then their presumption—only to think of Othello being converted into an Opera!

The mere music of these Operas is frequently very fine—but what is the dramatic interest? What is represented on the stage should have a dramatic interest, else why bring it on the stage at all? If singing alone or mimicking, a room will answer as well or better. The very object of the stage is "room to bustle in." If there is no action, or very little, no room for display is wanted. There is but little action in the Opera—no character, with any traits of consequence no dialogue. What, then, is there? Notes, bars of music, the gamut, vocal sounds. The unnatural recitative, neither speaking nor singing—the dwelling upon the slightest things with an emphasis as earnest as on the greatest—the complete sameness of manner, varied only by a vicious extravagance of gesture and expression, and the interminable choruses, deprive the Opera of all interest, in our eyes.

To relish the best Operas, neither understanding nor heart is at all necessary, for neither are addressed. What pathos there is in some is totally lost in an eager desire for display. To give the singer a chance, the incidents must be stopped and the story stand still—a drag is to be put upon the wheels of the Car of Melody. An aria is more important than an action; and bravery is less effective than a bravura. Dramatic illusion there is none, or, if any, of the most improbable kind. We have devils in hell, as in Der Freischutz; or we see the Oriental Brahma ascending to heaven, in the Bayadere; or the dead are raised to view in their shrouds and coffins, in Robert the Devil. The characters are without variety. Heroes, lovers, tyrants, dancing girls, peasants, princes, form the whole dramatis personæ, and "ex uno disce omnes"—all alike. There is no discrimination—no shading.

We are willing to confess ourselves lovers of every species of music—even of operatic music in moderation; but at the same time we interpose that to sit for three or four hours to hear a set of fellows (generally poor actors) squalling, screeching, grunting, grumbling, groaning, hissing, hooting and playing all manner of tricks with their voices, is one of the most vexatious things in the world. To hear that beautiful art so bedeviled and reviled by its professors is enough to make one sick of music for ever. What can be more delicious than a charming song of Burns', expressive of love and the tenderest gallantry? Amor triumphans is here sung in a right masterly strain; but love in an Italian Opera is generally a hot-house flower, which dies on exposure to the air. What patriotic effusions kindle generous fire quicker than the pieces of that class by the same author? Among the Italians, this public virtue exists but in name. Music, soft, artful and effeminate like theirs, flourishes only in despotic governments. The free air of Liberty alone can inspire such strains as "Scots wha ha' wi' Wallace bled," and "Ye

Mariners of England." America should for this reason be the land of the patriotic lyre. We have had few spirit-stirring tones so far, but the full force of the instrument will one day be wakened by some master hand.

In a word, we do not wonder at the "bad success" of the Italian Opera here, since the defects which strike us as insuperable to its advancement, are inherent in its very nature. Let us, then, "chaunt then old heroic ditty o'er;" let us have the gay song, the soothing hymn; but for the Opera, let us have none of it. May Burns, Percy, Moore Heber, and a host of sweet lyrists, be cherished. Of Rossini, Bellini, Cimaroza, &c. &c., we would hear their overtures, grand and stirring as they are—their barcaroles, soft as the breathing of Dorian flutes —their dashing bravuras, singly or a few together—but from a long Opera, comic or tragic, recited or sung, heaven defend us! We must except from this censure the finest Italian Operas which have been well translated, and as sung by fine English vocalists, and also the late admirable Opera by Mr. Rooke; and further, the few English productions which go under that name—as the Beggar's Opera, Love in a Village, the Duenna, and a few others. These are just the thing. The dialogue in them is neat, spirited, and witty, and there is enough of character and action for a light comedy. Give us, then, a good comic English Opera, or else give us an Opera containing juster sentiment, sweeter songs, finer hits at character, and a manlier style of writing, than Love in a Village, if ye can—else we want none of your Italian Music, ye "fanaticos per la musica"!

XLIII.

THE MODERN POLITICIAN.

A CHARACTER.

THE modern politician is a very scurvy sort of fellow. He is the old-fashioned statesman in his lowest estate, an image of fallen greatness, shorn of his beams. The sun of his glory is set, and his path is illumined only by the flickering light of intrigue and cunning.

It is a noted saying of the great Lexicographer, that "Patriotism is the last resort of a scoundrel." This is true in the present sense of the phrase, for is not patriotism, now, a mere mask, a name? It is very far from true, however, in the correct meaning of the term. In the real view of things, politics is a science of great dignity, worth and usefulness, and requiring, in the practical part of it, the most consummate tact and nicety. It requires great knowledge, both of facts and opinions; of persons, their characters and manners and motives; a comprehensive judgment, firm principles, unswerving integrity, a lofty tone of thought and action, far-reaching views, keen penetration. To make the character complete, the accomplishments of the polite gentleman, the resources of the hard student, and the eloquence of the practised orator, should be united. Nor are all these worth anything to the possessor, if he do not superadd to them the qualities of a manly character: honesty, moral courage, humanity, justice. No trimmer, no party man; but a stiff-necked patriot of the times of Cromwell and our own Revolution.

This character has gone quite out of fashion. It is sneered at, at present, as out of date, and behind the spirit of the age. It is certainly ill-suited to the current state of things, being too unbending, strict and rigorous to find favor with the complaisant, fawning myrmidons of popular power. It wants the urbane spirit of the courteous demagogue, the supple policy of the hireling courtier.

The modern politician is a man without independence of opinion, or freedom of will. He is a practical fatalist, a philosophical necessitarian—obliged to act, think, and speak exactly in the spirit, according to the views, and in the very phraseology, of his party. He is, politically, an infant after the age of twenty-one years, never attaining to maturity of judgment in the eyes of party. If he once presumes to set up the keel of the political vessel, in ever so slightly a different course, he is turned off forever as a mutinous sailor. He must follow in the wake of the party, or he founders on the rocks of opinion.

Is he a speaker? Then you may know just what he will say on any given occasion. Is he none? Then you may, instead, recognise his hurrah in a crowd; may see him holding banners, or escorting great men; a complete servant of the sovereign people. If a working-member of the body politic, you may find his chief duties to consist in counting votes, handing out tickets, marching to and fro, during an election; or at other times, dining in public with great men, "the roses and fair expectancies of the state," *rising suns*, toasting absent personages of official dignity and real meanness, and making himself drunk in the operation.

Nor is the modern politician bound only to govern his own conduct according to the directions of his party; but also he is bound boldly to defend their every plan, system, and design. Thus he is not only a time-server himself, but a wretched sophist in palliating the time-serving of others. He lives but in the popular breath, and his very existence hangs on the irregular pulsations of the mob. So miserable a slave is he, who gives himself up to other men's uses, and deprives himself of the free agency of a Patriot and a Man!

XLIV.

THE FAMILIAR PHILOSOPHY.

NOTWITHSTANDING the numerous divisions of philosphy, there yet remains one, simpler than any yet suggested. It is two-fold, and separates the whole into the abstract and the familiar. The one has been wire-drawn in the discussions of metaphysicians, while the other, though current in every age, is little talked of, still less defended by the writings of its adherents. A class of men, however, more numerous than the ancient philosophers or their modern successors, have made it their rule and standard of action. It consists mainly in cheating life of its ills, by cherishing the illusions of fancy until they ripen almost into realities—mingling gay colors with the melancholy aspects of Fortune, and bearing with a cheerful face and gay heart the rude jogs and mischances a traveller must meet with on the journey of life. It takes another form when it looks on self-love, and cultivates its own interests amid the selfishness of the world. It then calls into exercise a talent which, although not of the loftiest character, is still the most useful; the clear and quick perception, united to sound sense, which we commonly term shrewdness. There is no faculty so readily appreciated as this, when exercised in penetrating the actions and characters of mankind. It is of admirable use in the business concerns of life, but not at all fitted for higher duties. A union of shrewdness and of pathetic power is the mark of a truly great genius; for in this case what would otherwise degenerate into mere cunning, when occupied on themes of deep interest and elevated by an entirely opposite and nobler quality, rises in the scale of intellectual excellence, and the specious rogue becomes a Burke or a Shakspeare.

The majority of authors who have secured for themselves a niche in the Temple of Fame have been masters of the Familiar Philosophy, and in this have evinced the greatest practical wisdom. For, building their works on principles and characters which always exist, they have laid a base, broad and tenable in the feelings and passions of mankind. The abstract philosophers appear to have obtained no more than a purely ephemeral reputation, from the caprice or ignorance of their own age; but have been unable to maintain an equal renown from more equitable posterity.

That the philosophy of men of the world is faulty in reference to a future state, we cannot deny. But that the children of this world are wiser in their generation than the children of light, is expressly declared in holy writ. Their philosophy is wholly for this life, and looks not beyond it. For this purpose, what system better answers its intended aim? The more elevated philosophy allows for the imperfections of human nature. The worldly, or *science du monde*, proceeds on the principle, that man, in the limits it prescribes, may become perfect. It is complete of itself, and for the present, but utterly deficient in any great views of another state of being.

A very great advantage possessed by the Familiar Philosophy over its scholastic rival, consists in its total freedom from all bickering and controversy—a vile fault in the latter. The confusion of tongues which arose at Babel has not yet ceased, nor will it ever cease till the universal clamor be merged in the archangel's trumpet. A clatter, as from assembled thousands, rises on my ear, as I reflect on the wranglings of polemics and the disputes of the schoolmen. Theological knights-errant and metaphysical disputants are the genuine descendants of the latter loquacious multitude. The theological, cut off as they are by their profession from many innocent pleasures, make amends for these deprivations "by envy, hatred, and all uncharitableness." Into these do their controversies at last descend. They backbite each other in a style which, in the pulpit, and on a far higher authority, is deprecated with the greatest earnestness. They follow with zeal the maxim of Hudibras, to

"Compound for sins they are inclined to,
By damning those they have no mind to."

They add to the sum of their transgressions by continual slander. Their guilt, like the sorites argument, is accumulative. A specimen of this class is by no means so rare as a true friend or an honest man. To this the philosophy gained from a knowledge of the world and of human nature opposes a love for mutual kindness founded on mutual dependence and a dislike to argument merely for its own sake—its maxims being the fruit of observation and experience, and not reached by artificial deductions or false, strained reflections. In fine, it is a philosophy, which, revealing the natural corruption, as well as the innate goodness (not quite extinct) of the human heart, improves every opportunity of bringing the latter into the service of the public and private good, and palliates the former by considerations of human frailty.

XLV.

THE OLD ENGLISH COMEDY:

A STRICTURE ON WYCHERLY AND HIS BRETHREN.

The sanction of two very admirable writers of the present century has given a station to the comedies of Wycherly and his brother dramatists, Vanburgh, Congreve, Cibber, and Farquhar, very far, as we conceive, above their real merit. Both of these critics, Hazlitt and Lamb, gifted with the most delicate perception of genius of every order, and possessing intellects through which ran, like a vein of gold amid the sands of Pactolus, a subtle spirit, indiscernible by the coarse vision of a vulgar mind—in one point, at least—the dramatists they idolized. This resemblance lay in their love of conceits, of ingenious sallies, and of the niceties of colloquial discourse, of which these old comedies are full. Similarity of taste has betrayed these writers from the truth into an exaggerated opinion of authors, by no means deficient, in their own peculiar view, but quite wanting in those numerous excellencies with which they fancy rather than the judgment of their partial readers invested them. We will set out with the nature of genuine, unadulterated comedy, then apply the test to these productions, declare in what they are truly excellent, and point out the objections they must incur.

Comedy we apprehend to be the vehicle for polished and caustic satire of the follies and vices of mankind in general. Judicious sentiments on morality and duty must be occasionally introduced, not only to prevent the too frequent warfare of wit, but also to infuse a warm and ennobling feeling, better, far better, than the cold philosophy of stoicism. Instead of observing these ends, these comic poets seem to agree with Hazlitt that "to read a good comedy is to keep the best company in the world, where the best things are said and the most amusing happen." These are certainly among the chief requisites; but it is a confined view of the subject to limit its characters, dialogues and incidents to a single class of society. In these plays, the fine gentlemen, the fine lady, and the cuckold, usurp the whole *dramatis personæ*—the others being undistinguished by any personal or individual character whatever. Alas for the "infinite and unstaled variety" of Shakspeare! Hazlitt can decry the true comic muse, and prefer the Confederacy to the Merry Wives of Windsor!

Another quality we look for in comedy is a faithful and exact copy of "the manners living as they rise." In reading these plays, however, we would suppose the world to be composed only of courtiers and gallants, of ladies and their little coteries; that the rest of the nation lived on indifferently, while these feasted upon the sweets of Love: that a continual banquet was served up by Venus and her train, while the Muse, mistress of melody, breathed forth notes of gladness for them to dance and sing. But, there are utterly wanting any beings on whom the hand of nature has stamped a freshness like the rich bloom on the cheek of childhood, or the pure beauty of a flower enameled with the dew of the morning. They are equally destitute of moral sentiment, the expression of generous sympathy or true compassion.

The wit, though, of these comedies? I fear even that has been greatly misstated. The wit of Congreve has become the standard of jesting repartee. It bristles in his comedy as bayonets in a modern army. Brilliancy, lightness and ease are its chief characteristics; but it is cold, malicious, icy—unfriendly to a high estimate of the best part of human nature. In his pictures of high life, he was a consummate master, but there is not in all his works a single character worthy of our love and admiration. All are ready, quick, sharp and witty talkers; even in this, highly artificial; while the grossness of their language is unpardonable, since the most licentious thoughts and freest allusions may be enveloped in polished and delicate expressions. Their satire delights in disclosing vices—not in lashing them. Thus they gloat over the description of an intrigue merely as a luscious picture for the imagination!

The general aim and tendency of this comedy is faulty. It is to render man ridiculous; not so much from a laudable desire to represent folly in its meanest forms of degradation and selfishness, to expose foppishness or depress unfounded pretensions, as to indulge in a heartless jeer at everything worthy of respect among men. Virtue is laughed at as a prudish thing, out of date; and conduct pursued on the principles of honor and integrity is thought proper only for priests and placemen out of office. We do not desire that the stage should occupy the place of the pulpit; we only wish to express that a comedy, however gay and lively, should illustrate some universally true and sound maxim. This is not to be thrown into the faces of the audience at every turn, but it is to stamp the play with the air and character of a philosophical lesson.

Charles Lamb endeavors, in one of his delightful essays, by very ingenious sophistry, to prove that what we disapprove of in these comedies are sins purely ideal, and affirms that, when we visit the theatre, it is to escape from the reality of life out of doors, and enjoy the magical scene raised for his pleasure by imagination and art—a scene which has no counterpart in reality, but the perfection of which consists in its thorough ideality. This is but a fine vagary of a man of genius. The true charm of the drama undoubtedly lies in the very reverse of this. We go to see life as it is. The prince of dramatists is most conclusive, in his inimitable summary of the stage—"Whose end, both at the first and now, was and is, to hold, as 'twere, the mirror up to nature; to show virtue her own features, scorn her own image, and the very age and body of the time his form and pressure." Such was Shakspeare's Comedy; such was not that of our later writers. The dramatic authors who have followed him deserted nature for art: they have left us brilliant conversations, but an entire lack of character, feeling and sentiment—of all that tends to instruct the understanding or purify the taste—to soften the heart or engage the affections of the soul.

XLVI.

THE OLD SONGS AND BALLADS.

"Old songs, the precious music of the heart."—WORDSWORTH.

"They were old-fashioned poetry, but choicely good—*I think much better than the strong lines that are now in fashion, in this critical age.*"—ISAAC WALTON.

THE great contrast between the inspired rapture of the muse in the morning of her charms, and the productions of her ladyship in these later days, must be very apparent to every student of "the gay science." In the early age she was sincere, honest, direct, simple; now she is coquettish, artful, and made up of borrowed beauties. Then she was

"in her prime,
Free from rage and free from crime;"

but she has committed many a petit larceny since, and sometimes an offence which might almost be considered capital. She has made herself quite conspicuous among felons. She is stript and whipt like a common baggage, and her followers are turned out of doors to starve. To leave allegory for plain speaking, the characteristics of modern poetry are excitement and passion, and passion of the least noble character; and rich fancy. The latter appears to have been the product of men of a rare contemplative genius; the former, of men of an artificial fancy and of exaggerated passion. There is nature (at least) in the one, but a sheer want of it in the other. If it be concluded that to be violent, rapid and startling is to be natural then we are mistaken. But we apprehend such features of character, and such a description of incidents, are comparatively infrequent and episodical. The main current of life is not for ever turbid and foaming. Mountain torrents may be found thus, but the noiseless river, the silver lake, the crystal brook are not. There is a greater calm spread over the face of nature, however man may strive to mar its beauty by turbulence and crime. As it is with physical, so is it with man's moral nature—the one being but the shadowing forth of the other. The feelings of youth bud with the green tree, and the withered marrow of age is best depicted by the bare branches and decaying sap of the old oak. Besides, the poetry of sentiment must be allowed superior to the poetry of passion. In itself, sentiment is purer and nobler than passion. Passion is selfish, sensual, fierce, savage, gross, earthy, compared with sentiment. When passion is refined by sentiment, elevated and spiritualized by intellect; when it borrows the mantle of affection, and not the fires of hell, then it is omnipotent and grand—though poets who paint passion, generally, however, represent its dark and terrible traits, or its loathsome features. As the old poets seldom picture such scenes, they arrive (it appears to us) nearer to the beau ideal of poesy than their modern successors.

The old song and ballad writers come closer to our idea of primitive poets than any other class. They carry us back to the first glimmerings of poesy, and their melody is fresh with innocence and purity. They bear all the marks of antiquity, older than the Homeric poems, and coeval with the Cylic bards vastly older in appearance than they really are, from their form, language and metre. They are remnants of the Gothic spirit, and like all the remnants of those times, more ancient than a far earlier period. The Gothic architecture has a more venerable and antique air than the Grecian; and so it is with poetry.

These old songs may be divided into two heads, the amatory and the convivial. They are all gay catches, though, in the first the sentiment is dashed with a certain tender softness, inexpressibly charming; and the second, like all other pieces in the same way, are light, gay, cheerful.

This good fellow whose portrait Denham has drawn with great spirit, was (with them) the king of men. Cheerfulness was their philosophy, and the art of life its great practical aim. A merry wag was their sage, and a laugh worth all the homilies of all the grave teachers of morality.

In the old collections, you find no such songs as Dibdin's, no pieces purely patriotic, and no high-toned moral odes. There were, however, sweet singers of the temple—Herbert, Farrar, Quarles, Walton—who raised many a lofty note to heaven, unheeded perhaps by men, but caught up by the choir of angels; and strewn among old treatises, as "Walton's Angler," but more especially in the elder dramatists, are exquisite snatches of song, which can hardly be classed in any one formal division. Love ditties, dirges, gems of pastoral scenery, enchanting pictures of beauty, sonnets, sparkle like gems in their rich volumes.

No species of composition is harder to dissect or analyze than song writing. It cannot be analyzed from its unity and simplicity. A perfect song should be a complete development of a single sentiment or idea, without episode or digression. It should be a burst of music, a gush of feeling, easy, artless, unlabored. It can no more be criticised than a sunbeam, or the sparkling of jewels, or the fall of a cascade. It may be called sweet, beautiful, natural, gay, tender, or melancholy, no more; the epithet embraces a criticism.

The old ballads, or rather the best of them, are equally fine. They are heroic, pathetic and humorous, descriptive of the broad, open hospitality of the olden time, or imbued with the spirit of manly sports or rustic revels, presenting a perfect picture of the manners and spirit of the age. They are full to overflowing of an honest sentiment and a liberal courtesy, revealing the substantial character of our forefathers, with their noblest traits. They are simple without any circumlocution, and explicit without any unnecessary diffuseness. They speak out the truth, and make no boggling. Common things are told with indifference, and noble deeds and thoughts are not boastful nor eloquent. They are without any garnish of rhetoric. The heroic ballad relates the deeds of heroes and the turmoil of battle. The din of arms is heard, the clashing of shields, the shouts of the horsemen, the braying of the trumpets—then we see the vast, irregular old castles and fortifications, fosses and drawbridges, banners streaming from the turrets and from every tower, and the whole air filled with martial music.

In the more social and familiar scene, we are warned by the uprightness of intention, the steadfastness of faith, and chariness of honor, the generosity of affection, and the universal spirit of humanity.

Where love is the theme, either successful, firm in constancy and ardent, or in distress from false lover, these early masters of the tender passion are pre-eminently faithful. They depict it in all its artless purity and confiding faith. The single ballad of Childe Waters is a leaf out of the great book of human nature. Whoever can read it, without feeling his eyes fill with tears, must, indeed, be a worldling, a genuine earth-worm. Compared with the modern drawing-room rhymers, the fashionable lyrists of the day, they are vastly truer, and certainly more poetical. It is in fact an argument against the latter, that they are sung by jeweled throats, since the very essence of love is solitariness. It is too sacred to be indulged in crowds. The clear vein of sentiment and romantic beauty is not turned into eddies by glittering similes and strained rhapsody, but such as the modern favorite might envy with despair. To attempt to rival his elder brother in the glorious art, were as presumptuous as for the most skilful musician to endeavor at equalling the involuntary strains of the nightingale. "Percy's Reliques" alone may be opposed to all the lyric poetry since the time of Burns. He was the last who inherited the genuine spirit and the poetic heart of the old minstrels. Scott's "Young Lochinvar" is the best since, and "The Brave Old Oak," and "The Sea," in different lines are very fine specimens.

Scott was a great lover of the old ballads, and his taste for them formed a part of his noble nature. There was no trickery in his attachment to them. He had an unshaken relish for them, inasmuch as they evolved much of his own character. The battle-scenes, in particular, must have been a source of great delight to him, inasmuch, as he has caught their spirit very exactly, in thedescription of tournaments.

Among our own writers, Irving's fine taste has in no respect appeared to such advantage, as in his admiration of the same rich stores of poetry and romance.

The taste of the age is coming round by degrees. The old dramatists and prose-writers are beginning to be more generally known, though they, always, (except during one period) have obtained the admiration of the few. May we not hope, that the old English ballad and the song may revive in its primitive sweetness; that tales of blood and terror may be superseded by that more genuine picture of nature, in which simplicity and innocence are the finest features? Oh! that the day may come, when the voice of the muse may be heard as artlessly captivating, as

> " the shepherd's pipe upon the mountains,
> When all his flock 's at feed before him."

XLVII.

SUGGESTIONS FOR THE REFLECTIVE.

What can be more distressing than to be drawn into acts of deception by the force of circumstances—to be obliged to conceal the Truth?

The true philosophic character is composed of a love of truth, scepticism, benevolence of heart, firmness of purpose, mental courage, and a constant inclination to ascend to first principles.

There are incidents occurring in the life of a man of true sentiment too sacred to be drawn, with levity, from the deep recesses of his own heart.

The man of the greatest abilities and of the most versatile talents must be excused for many defects and numerous slips in conduct.

There are redeeming traits in the characters of nations, as well as of men. "The web of life is of a mingled yarn."

Our dearest companions are our best friends. Why should it not be so? For he who participates in our most secret sympathies should of right mingle in our gayest pleasures. The pleasantest companion is a man of great experience, and consequently of great liberality of sentiment, with a talent for conversation, and a sweet demeanor.

Compliments are elegant refinements upon truth.

Which is better—to praise a man to his face and slander him as his back is turned—or to speak roughly to him personally, but eulogize him as soon as he is out of hearing?

A clear and distinguishing judgment, joined to an infirm and unstable will, makes a philosopher in speculation a fool in practice.

The nicest tact of a man of address is shown in his manner of saluting persons of different rank.

Marriage is a contract where Judgment must be equally Advocate and Judge, in connection with Love, who generally gains the cause, without the aid of any other counsel.

Every thinking man has sensations of mental pleasure and of mental pain, which are entirely inexplicable. And yet, this very insufficiency, if possible, enhances his joy and embitters his anguish.

Does not every one experience a state of feeling on a fine morning in Autumn, very different from what he is aware of on a glorious day in Spring, an evening sunset in Summer, or a gloomy night in the depth of Winter?

Most men regard a merry Christian as an anomaly; surely a sad one presents no very encouraging spectacle.

The lawyer thinks the noblest *principle* is involved where the *principal* sum at stake is largest.

The three professions have had their satirists—the only checks on them. Without satire, the world would run mad.

We can never think of poets as old men. Everything connected with them is imbued with the charm of immortal youth and perpetual spring.

Some whose individual perceptions are very quick, are slow in apprehending the ideas of others. They can invent and find much easier than they can follow and penetrate. Such make better leaders than followers: they can address a large body with far greater effect than they can take part in a debate. Perhaps this is the reason why great orators are generally such bad talkers.

Sectarianism we have known carried so far that persons of the same rank in society would never interchange civilities, because they happened to belong to different communions. What sort of a meeting might one imagine between a Quaker and an Episcopalian, a Baptist and a Catholic, a Jew and a New-Jerusalemite—in heaven? On earth, they can hardly sit in the same room together!

The most original and refined wit can be relished only by a very few. The grosser mind is more popular. A delicate wit requires fine judgment to appreciate it. A wit needs to have his audience *packed.*

Extremes are bad things, (it is generally allowed,) and those placed in them are the worst judges in the world of *relative* merit. Thus the solid man thinks the gay companion a mere trifler; while the latter esteems the former a very dull fellow. Imaginative persons cannot endure *judicious* people, nor can the man of method be captivated by flights of fancy.

Truth is like medicine: we can take neither without something sweet to remove its unpleasant taste.

Grave men see no difference between a buffoon and a man of genuine wit. They laugh with similar relish at absurd antics or delicate repartees.

Maxims contain the pure essence of truth.

Rules are the result of experience.

Melancholy passes for sulkiness, merriment for frivolity, honesty for rudeness, and courtesy for cunning; self-denial for ostentation, decision for obstinacy; pity is called weakness, while justice is called severity. The world is governed by names.

Want of sympathy, and deficiency in the power of expression, contribute to render a highly sensitive being wretched.

The traveller wonders why all the world is not travelling.

It is a singular thing to remark how differently a man is affected by the same passions and sentiments at different periods.

The most eccentric man is often the most reasonable—following nature.

What are called paradoxes are frequently old truths in a new dress or disguise.

The malice of our enemies often conduces to our benefit and to their harm.

With the great mass of mankind, delicacy and refinement in wit, humor, sentiment and criticism constitute affectation. Quaint fancies and brilliant conceits pass under the same name.

The blackest man is a white person painted to resemble a negro: so the fairest saint, when he plays the hypocrite, (no uncommon thing,) makes the vilest sinner in the world.

We gain the respect of mankind by expressing their vices. We are rewarded with their contempt by dwelling on their good qualities. Swift is feared, hated and admired; Mackenzie is liked, pitied and despised.

Satire is the most useful of all forms of writing. Sentiment is literally wasted upon nineteen readers out of twenty.

We must expect to make enemies if we will tell the truth: therefore we cease.

XLVIII.

THOUGHTS ON THE INTELLECTUAL CHARACTER AND WRITINGS OF EDWARD LYTTON BULWER.*

No contemporary writer surpasses Mr. Bulwer, either in pretension or popularity. The admirable successor of Smollet and Fielding, Mr. Dickens, equals him in the last respect, but is, withal, a very modest man—for an author. The first named gentleman is the most successful of literary imposters, having palmed off more absurdity and nonsense on the public than any other writer of the present day. Possessing one quality alone in perfection, he has obtained from a skilful exercise of it, the credit of possessing all others. Were we weak enough to be deluded by the baits he holds out in his prefaces, we should have considered him the most original of writers, as well as the profoundest of philosophers. He speaks of analyzing certain passions and painting characters, as if no one had

* 1838-9.

ever succeeded before in similar attempts. He will show how faulty other writers have been, to infer his own superiority—building his own reputation on the ruins and fragments of other writers, like those modern architects who would erect edifices of stone from the defaced statues of antiquity.

As a writer of fiction, Mr. Bulwer has attempted much: let us see what he has really accomplished. In what has he succeeded, or in what failed? His failures, in our estimate, predominate so greatly, that we will begin with them.

His chief *characters* are, lovers, students, fine gentlemen, men of the world, and public personages. The first are anything but true and sincere; they are, rather, elegant libertines. His students—intended, as we supposed, as representatives of their author under different phases—are good critics enough, and shrewd observers, but feverish in their aspirations, and misanthropic. His fine gentlemen and men of the world, are well drawn; this is his forte, and he executes it *con amore.* He is strongest in delineating heartlessness and worldly folly. Of late, since he has been elevated into public life, he has conceived a great passion for describing public men. An intense egotism pervades all his characters. He draws from himself, we suspect, for most of his material; and from the singleness of his own character, there results a great sameness in all his works. His egotism, too, is not of the frank, relying nature of the great old writers, but it is an uneasy composition of artificial modesty and irritable vanity. All of the *dramatis personæ* are cut after the same pattern, and made from the same block; each one of a class resembles all the others of the same class. Their sentiments are provided for the occasion—second-hand, not of spontaneous growth; they set awkwardly on them.

His *philosophy* is borrowed from the French; his head is filled with maxims drawn from the moralists of that nation, and from Latin writers. He is a great admirer of Helvetius—a sensualist, a glittering, paradoxical sophist. He is a Frenchman in disguise, with nothing of the Englishman about him; without the brilliancy of the former, and certainly, destitute of the solidity of the latter. His intellect is of an intermediate quality between the two. He affects the metaphysical critic and speculatist; but is a most shallow theorist in morals, though nice in discriminating artificial characters, and their governing motives. His morality is most dangerous in its tendency, and licentious to the core. He is thought very philosophical by those who study metaphysics in works of fiction—the last resort of "divine philosophy."

In point of *style*, he is mechanical, elaborate, strained, and tedious. There is no easy current or plain groundwork; everything is perked into the reader's face. He writes as one who reads everything in an emphatic tone. All his sentences out to be printed in capitals, for he tries to be startling in every phrase. He has no repose—no calm—no dignity. He has striking observations, but seems to care little about their truth. His style is partly French, partly German, and slightly English. In his epigrammatic passages, which are his best, he is French; in his rhapsodies, where he drops down plump into the region of bombast, he is German; and in his prefaces, where he aims at elegant criticism, he is a writer of most slovenly English. His familiarity is labored and heavy, his trifling ridiculous and silly. To trifle with elegance is a nice art, and Mr. Bulwer cannot acquire it; the more eagerly he pursues it, the worse he writes. He is utterly deficient in humor; and the semblance of wit he has is a certain smartness, the effect of style. He has none of Irving's fine description and nice skill in the conduct of his narratives. He is a great admirer of Tom Jones; why not study that perfect narrative?—perfect, at least, as a work of art. His story is inharmonious in the management of incident, and abrupt. He has no power of fusion in his mind, and cannot melt down his materials into a continuous whole. Everything stands out by itself—the incidents being the essence of commonplace. His high personages are inflated talkers, his low characters retailers of ribaldry and vulgarity. His essays at eloquence are lamentable instances of sheer rhapsody. What, then, has he? Why, these practical qualities, which carry everything before them. He knows the public taste well; just what it will take—how much it will bear. He has calculated all the chances of imposition, and is familiar with the art of making the most of the very meanest materials. He has tact, and great industry; a very clever compiler of romances. He is a perfect master of all the tricks of authorship and all the devices of book-making. He wants nature and genius, but he has ability and perseverance. No one can deny his general scholarship and critical acumen; but then he has a Frenchman's taste, being easily caught by glitter. The high opinions he entertains of Young, and writers of his description, discovers the tone of his taste very plainly.

He is the painter of the fasionable world and of artificial life. He rules supreme in the dress-circle and the salon. He is a master of badinage and railery. Into the world of nature he has never found entrance; to natural passion, which, "masterless, sways us to the mood of what she likes or loathes," he is an utter stranger. Whenever he assumes enthusiasm—for it never has the appearance of rising out of the subject—he writes with a bastard heat, as different from genuine enthusiasm, as gold leaf is different from pure gold, or as fire painted on the canvas, is different from the real element. He wants the lofty dignity of the greatest intellects, but frets and fumes on every occasion, into something like declamation. In fine, he is a skilful literary manufacturer, but will rank with the Capulets twenty years hence. If he lives that length of time, he will outlive his own reputation; and may cry out, if wise, with good-natured Master Betty, in the decline of life, "Oh, Memory, Memory!" &c.

XLV.

TABLE TALK.

THE SCOTCH SCHOOL.

The Scotch are a prudent, and cautious, and logical people. They are prone to inquire into the reason, search out the cause, and deduce the effect, of everything. They are close reasoners rather than deep thinkers. They examine much better than they speculate. Philosophical invention they have none, whether in theory, argument, or illustration. They abhor paradox, but take refuge in commonplace. More attached to fact than opinion, they are oftener governed by statistics than by se timents. They are better acquainted with figures of arithmetic than figures of rhetoric. Hence their philospphy is the best index of their national character. Hence they are better logicians than metaphysicians. They are slow and wary in their abstract speculations, as well as in everything else. They forever err on the right side. They keep to the windward of Fortune. She blows them none but propitious gales. They take Burns's verses for their motto—

> " For know,
> That prudent, cautious, self-control,
> Is Wisdom's root.

They are sensible writers on philosophy. Faithful compilers, but no more. They have no originality: Reid being the only one who offers the show of it even, and he certainly deserves the praise of a sober, patient, sincere inquirer after truth. They are (as a class) men of but moderate powers, and popular in their style and manner. They have none of the acuteness of Berkley, nor his grace of style—none of the compact sense of Hobbes—none of the vast capacity of Bacon.

The principle of the common sense philosophy is widely at variance with all lofty speculation. Common sense is an admirable quality for everyday people in everyday matters. It is an excellent and sure instinct for the conduct of affairs in common life, but it is entirely unfitted for higher themes. Neither religion nor poetry (which appeal to the highest faculties of our nature, faith, and imagination) appeal to this. They are above it, as faith is above reason.

The nature of common sense may be derived from its very name. Nothing can be more characteristic. It is the faculty so universally possessed as to be styled *common* in consequence. It cannot, therefore, be of a very superior nature, rarity being more commonly the badge of genuine merit. Whatever is pre-eminently excellent is, in general, uncommonly scarce. Else, why are Goodness, Virtue, Wisdom, Genius, Strength, Beauty, so highly esteemed? For subjects of a spiritual and internal nature, it is by no means an efficient guage. It cannot fathom the depths of the mighty ocean of philosophy, (on which so many frail barks have been sunk forever,) nor scale the lofty heights of speculative inquiry. It has no sufficient measure for such questions. A fly might as well attempt to take the altitude of Mount Blanc. It deals with the world of matter only. It wants faith to remove mountains of metaphysical difficulty.

A great defect in the common sense system, is in its conceited and pragmatical tone. It professes to account for everything in the simplest manner. Now, *this* is impossible. Such a boast is most presumptuous and silly. It discovers the real weakness of their philosophy. Where everything is plain and apparent, there can be no speculation;—where there is no speculation, there can be no abstract inquiry;—what is obvious, needs no search. But what is philosophy but a search after truth? Besides, the higher philosophy requires faith in its principles, even though they be not perfectly clear. *This* philosophy aims at proving whatever is incomprehensible is false? That is its grand maxim. It sneers at enthusiasm, at visions, at ghosts. The whole spiritual world is destroyed. The finer essence of the soul is denied. Matter and tangibility are its darling points. The maintainers of this system are, in fact, infidels. They are not atheists nor skeptics, avowedly; still, they are practically such, inasmuch as they cry down all genius, all imagination, all creative invention, all high-raised fervour, (the gift of God.) *They* are, forsooth, above all such credulity, Incredulity, however, is but a negative virtue. They are materialists, whatever they may call themselves. They must touch, and weigh, and handle substance and matter. What they cannot manage in this manner, they spurn and condemn. They have no insight into the dark obscurities of inquiry, nor do they rise to high themes. They look along the dull plain of the commonest realities. They dogmatize on the tritest texts—

> "They say an undisputed thing,
> In such a solemn way."

This is *the* grand end of their system—admitting nothing as true and certain, which has not been demonstrated "*ad nauseam*"—they ring everlasting changes on the self-same tunes. This is the very opposite of the German school of transcendentalism. These two are the very antipodes of the philosophic world—Aristotle and Plato, modernized. Plato was only a Greek Kant, somewhat his superior (it must be confessed,) and greater (inasmuch as his original and master :) and Kant is but a reviver of Plato, though without a tythe of his gorgeous imagination, and utterly deficient in that beauty of style, for which Plato was so famous. Both were mystics; both seekers after the right, the true, the good, the beautiful. The Scotch are rather, from the constitution of their minds, followers of Aristotle. Not that they really copy him, but they have the same hard, careful sense; the same love of scientific formality; the same endeavors after simplicity and precision, which distinguish his writings and philosophic teaching. The former are infinitely clearer and more readable, which is little praise: for Aristotle is the most unreadable of writers.

SOME QUERIES REGARDING NATURAL AFFECTION.

——— " the near in blood,
The nearer bloody."—SHAKSPEARE.

——— " It is by experience to be discerned, that this natural affection, to which we give so great authority, has but a very weak and shallow root."—MONTAIGNE.

May not what we call natural affection be anything more than the result of a habit of close intercourse?

Would two brothers (separated from their earliest childhood) who met in afterlife, recognize each other by the force of blood? Dr. Franklin's case in regard to his mother, who is commonly supposed to cherish much more affection than any other relation, is rather against it.

Who hate each other most bitterly, relatives or strangers?

With which, of the two, have we most disputes and trouble?

What is the state of feeling between fathers and sons, when the latter become men?

Who perk more advice into our faces, insult us more ignobly, or assist us least, when we most need aid?

And yet—towards whom does our blood warm quickest? To a stranger?

Whom would we soonest help?

Is there not a *family interest*?

Is resemblance in features, form, voice, smile, frown, gait, and general manner nothing? Are tastes and feelings in common, nothing? Are strongly marked hereditary traits, nothing? Are not *family quarrels*, even, bonds of attachment? Are not *family secrets* powerful chains of connexion?

Here are both sides of this delicate question—one will incline to or decide in favor of either of them, rather from his feelings than judgment. Having been happily or unfortunately situated, will determine his opinion. This is one of those subjects which reasoning only confuses, and to understand which (as far as it can be understood) we must draw upon our personal experience.

PRINCIPLE AND FEELING.

Principle may be likened to a stone table of the law; but feeling may be best compared to the warm, beating heart and its genuine impulses. In many cases, our hearts are far better casuists than our heads; and on all the grand points of truth, honesty, right and virtue, they admit of no comparison. *Out of the heart come all the issues of life.* A tender heart and a weak head are often confounded as synonymous. But by whom? By the hard, calculating worldling, the keen, selfish politician, the grasping, avaricious idolator of mammon.

We frequently hear it said that principle should be our only guide, and that we should give no heed to (if not utterly root out) the impulses of our hearts. But is there not something above principle? Act beatified spirits from that alone? Not rather from an impulse of divine love, a joy intuitive and celestial? And so with man. The love of virtue is, surely, a nobler incentive than the fear of punishment. Principle implies the latter, a reward being its object. Who are they, we would ask, so severe on principle, so virtuous by rule? Why, the powerful, the mighty, the rich, the greatest hypocrites. These can afford to be destitute of bowels of compassion. Besides, it is much easier to wear a severe look and a mortified expression, than to act the part of a philanthropist and the good Samaritan. Selfish men act on principle, *i. e.*, on a selfish principle. That is a profitable course.

All men of principle, who declare themselves as acting without feeling, act merely from a verbal proposition. As, thus, one acts from habit, according to prescribed maxims. He acts from precept, but what is a precept but a lifeless proposition? Example and feeling give it a soul; action alone can inspire a life into it. Yet further, his principles may be false, untrue, illogical. He may have been, as is often the case, browbeaten by the reasonings of more sophistical heads. His principles, then, are directly hurtful. They possess a character by no means nugatory. Ignorance, then, is his only true plea.

Nor should many acting from right principle claim any vast praise therefor, since they have no desire to act otherwise. Their goodness and rectitude is no further praiseworthy, than the chastity of a woman of cold constitution, or the honesty of a rich fool. Their virtues are entirely of a negative character.

Let us examine, however, the internal nature of these two opposite incentives to goodness.

Principles are habits of opinion and rules of conduct. We may think or speculate upon them, as intellectual problems. The germs of virtue are the noble impulses of the heart. There is a fine mixture of these two, which may arise in this way. These delicate "impulses of soul and sense," may become fixed by custom and result in perfect laws. This is rare, since most men of principle seek no basis of moral action in the heart. Impulse is heaven-born; pure, at first, though it may become tarnished and corrupt. This must be felt, not proved; being one of those intuitive truths of which we are perfectly well aware, though we cannot prove it to demonstration. Our noblest virtues are only noble instincts. This is not meant to deny man's responsibility, for his duty is clear. But instincts were planted by a master-hand.

It is a great error in our divines, generally, to insist so impressively on the corrupt nature of man, to the exclusion of any eulogium of the magnificent fragments of divinity still extant in the choicest specimens of human nature. Man is fallen, but not crushed. He can yet exhibit a faded brilliancy of powers once resplendent. And, therefore, might not encouragement and exhortation avail more than censure; and glory be made more effective than dishonor?

Benevolence is scouted by the disciplinarians, as infirmity of moral purpose. Correction is still enjoined as a duty—as if to punish some were enough, without pity and without aid, to others who deserve no punishment; besides, even the worst deserve compassion, and all deserve to be treated as men. No degradation is sufficient to extinguish the spark of divinity within us. Man, in every state and in the lowest condition, is still man. These "unco guid" would make this world a prison, and stifle the free air of liberty, till we were choked into an insensibility to oppression and wrong.

It must be confessed from this, that, with a great part of the soul of man, ethics is but slightly conversant. He who despises human weaknesses, can have little fellowship with human virtues, since the most endearing of the latter are separated by very thin partitions from the former. The true philosophic character enjoins severity on his own conduct, and a liberal charity towards that of others. A man of principle may act very correctly in regard to himself, but he may act very inhumanly towards others. He may not raise a fallen brother, nor lead a truant fellow-creature back whence he has strayed. He thinks he performs all his duty, if he abstains from any open violations of it; but as for doing what he thinks he is not bound to do, there he ceases to act. Voluntary kindness, spontaneous charity, are not in his catalogue of virtues. Oh! he that knows frail humanity, will confess that the occasions are not few, when a generous impulse is worth an army of principles.

Logical men are men of principle; poets, invariably men of feeling. The reason is plain: the first act from their heads, the last from their hearts.

Still, though virtue, truth and goodness are essences, immutable and eternal, innate and never-dying, few will so sufficiently cultivate and manifest them, as to demonstrate their real existence, independent of modes of thinking and general custom.

Virtue is not mere expediency; goodness, a habit; nor truth, conventional belief. Merit is certain, moral excellence is real; and yet, our best deeds, our finest thoughts, our purest feelings, our highest aspirations are involuntary.

We follow the bent of our natural temperament in spite of ourselves. This will unravel many moral paradoxes, otherwise inexplicable. Our intellects have little power over our tempers and hearts. To act well, we must feel honestly,—a true heart makes a true man; but a mere prater of maxims is an impertinent fool.

"These moral writers," shrewdly observes one, in a pleasant comedy of Steele's, "never practise virtue till after death." Before, they have enough to do to talk about it.

FINIS.

WM. C. BRYANT & CO., PRINTERS, COR. OF NASSAU AND LIBERTY STREETS, NEW YORK.

www.ingramcontent.com/pod-product-compliance
Lightning Source LLC
LaVergne TN
LVHW010230110826
845151LV00004B/1252

* 9 7 8 1 4 2 5 5 2 5 3 5 4 *